Staying Red:
why I remain a socialist

NORMAN HARDING

Index Books
London

Published 2005 by Index Books
16 Electric Avenue, Brixton, London SW9 8JX

Cover photo: Mikko Eley

A C.I.P. catalogue record for this book is available
from the British Library

ISBN 1-871518-25-3

Dedication

This book is dedicated to all those throughout the world who are struggling for socialism, and to all those who are fighting against oppression. We need a society where social relations will mean that adequate food, clean water, clothing, and shelter will be available for all. A society where wealth (for example, oil) will not just benefit the rulers of these areas, but benefit all. A society with no national rulers using military might and superiority to invade any part of the world to steal its resources — as is happening now, in 2004, in Iraq.

Long gone are the days when a community was simply all the people living in an area, based on a local industry. Globalisation of capital and ownership means that the world is our community. The old slogan 'Workers of the World Unite' has never been more urgent and necessary.

Acknowledgements

I thank all my comrades and friends of the late Socialist Labour League and Workers Revolutionary Party for their support and encouragement over the five years writing this book.

Every attempt has been made to contact all those mentioned. If anyone has not been contacted, please accept my apologies.

Special thanks to Clare Cowen and Bridget Leach for their unstinting hard work, devotion and care taken with the finer points that were needed to arrive at the finished product, and to Brian Eley for designing the cover. Thanks and appreciation to Cathy Brown at the Micklefield BT Cyberstation for help and advice. Thanks to Paul Jennings (Australia) and the many others who helped.

Thanks to John Davies, Cliff Slaughter and Stephen Drury, who have constantly been available whenever I needed their special skills or just needed a chat.

Many thanks to my wife Pauline: without her support I might never have been able to start, never mind finish, this book. Thanks to our family who have always shown an interest in the book's progress and some pride in the fact that we will have it on the bookshelves.

CONTENTS

WHAT THIS BOOK MEANS TO ME

I was born into a working-class family. As a class we are encouraged by the ruling class to think that our role is to do as we are told. To be brought up by our parents to the point of speech and the ability to walk. Then to be educated to just the level required to do the type of work that society needs us for. To expect nothing more than to sell our labour power, for as little as possible, so that the next generation has little choice but to carry on with the process. I wrote this book to show that my life was an integral part of the development and evolution of our species and of the social relations in society.

The ruling class created the conditions so that any decisions workers made could be kept under control as much as possible. We get up in the morning, go to work, and earn just enough to keep life and limb together, to enable us to go to work the following morning. And even this low standard of living had to be fought for by previous generations of workers.

But a point comes for many workers and intellectuals when they start to ask questions and to learn about the class-ridden society we live in. They break with the theory that class division is a normal way of 'progress', that war and unemployment are natural developments, 'human nature'. They take a conscious decision that the social structure has to be changed and replaced by communism (that of Marx, not Stalin) or social democracy, and that the historical role of the working class is to do just this.

I feel very proud that I am one of the millions who took that decision to fight against capitalism and the global domination it was historically heading for. I am proud to have taken individual responsibility to work for the bringing down of capitalism.

My book outlines the development of my life and the kind of individual that I became: compassionate, understanding that the oppressed of the world are part of my community, but never taking my eye off the real enemy, capitalism and its supporters.

I began to write this personal history not to record every detail of my life, but to explain my involvement in politics. The early part of the book covers the periods that influenced my future political activity. I then trace the politics that allowed me to spend 31 years (1954 to 1985) in intense activity, building what I believed was the party that would free the British working class and also play a leading role in liberating the oppressed of the world. Grand aims: feeding instead of fighting; building instead of bombing; a society that would use knowledge for progress and not as a means to oppress and make profit for a few.

Then in 1985, that struggle for a revolutionary party changed. The organisation that I had been involved in building had to be smashed, and our long-time leader Gerry Healy expelled from the Workers Revolutionary Party along with his supporters, on 19 October 1985.

To this day the reasons for Healy's expulsion have not been understood by many people. After twenty years some comrades still hanker after the old ways of the Healy WRP. They find solace in words and slogans that keep them in glorious isolation and sectarian solitude. Words from past situations. But the world has changed and is still changing. If millions take action against oppression and then find that they have to take on world capitalism, do we participate with them only if they agree with our slogans of the past?

The principles described by the word communism are being struggled for in many parts of the world, including the ex-Soviet Union, yet because of what happened in the former Eastern Bloc, communism is a dirty word to millions of people. Should we continue using words that make us feel pure and virtuous, enabling us to go into the working class as prophets with all the answers?

And if they do not listen then that's their problem? The alternative is to do it the hard way: to find ways and means of joining the working class in the looming struggles, to help build stepping stones for the development of the mass movement against capitalism.

The break-up of the former Eastern Bloc (all countries run by what we called Stalinism) changed the political map of the world. We Trotskyists can say that our analysis of the Soviet Union has – in large part at least – been borne out. There are to be no centuries of immovable Stalinism. But the very existence of our Trotskyist party was based on the exposure of Stalinism. The two pillars that held our party up were Trotskyism and Stalinism: we were Trotskyists, but our existence was based on a fight against Stalinism. Then when Stalinism collapsed Trotskyism had to question its purpose. Everything was changing, everything had to be re-examined – but not in order to destroy our past. (Sometimes comrades think that to re-examine has something to do with capitulation to bourgeois pressures.) In this context Marxism has to be used as a method of developing our work in the new situation.

It is absolutely essential that we do not continue with the old methods, using the same old slogans, raising the same old banners and trying to build the same type of organisation, albeit without the 'bad bits' that we began to destroy in 1985.

But I won't go into this in great detail here. It will be hard for readers who did not live through these battles to grasp all the political problems we were wrestling with. I want readers to understand the reasons I spent my life as I did. I hated (and still hate) what capitalism does to people. I came to the conclusion that it needed overthrowing and replacing with socialism. But there was already something in the Soviet Union and elsewhere which claimed to be socialism – and this thing was a terrible dictatorship. So less of my life was actually spent in fighting *for* socialism than fighting *against* this thing – Stalinism – which was trying to usurp its name.

Mum, Dad and me (above).

With my baby brother Keith

1

THE HARDINGS

I was singing *Lazy Bones* sitting on the top step of our home in Shakespeare Street using one of the wheels of my little metal tricycle as the steering wheel of my imaginary car. From the top step Mum and I would wave to the old people who were in St James's Hospital, Beckett Street, housed in what had been the old workhouse and is now Thackray's Medical Museum. Dad came home from work, pushed past me on the steps, and smiled when he heard me singing 'the Lazy Song', the song I would ask for whenever he was playing the piano.

'You can bring him in now.' That was the voice of 'Aunt Maggie', our neighbour. The date was 27 June 1933. My father came into my bedroom, picked me up out of my bed and carried me into Mum and Dad's bedroom and pointed to my brother Keith, who was lying in a drawer taken from the sideboard that was acting as a makeshift crib. I was four years and two days old.

I was born on 25 June 1929. Dad was an engineer in the 1920s and early 1930s, not knowing if there was to be a day's work when he set off in a morning. He was then made unemployed, in the early 1930s. Later he managed to get a casual job on the railway, following in the footsteps of his father. My Grandad had brought his wife Ruth and two sons, Herbert and Noble, to Leeds from Northumberland at the turn of the century. My Dad and Uncle Noble also became railway workers.

My grandfather, Noble Harding, had married Ruth Allison Johnstone in the 1890s.They had three children. The first-born died as a baby. Two sons followed: the older was my father, Herbert Johnstone Benjamin (Bert), and the younger, Noble. Bert married Emma King in 1926 and had two sons, Keith and me. Noble married late in life and did not have any family.

Before I move on to my maternal grandparents I have to relate the story told to me by my Dad's uncle, Ben Johnstone. The male members of the Johnstone family made annual summer trips to Canada to find work. Two would take up residence while the others went off in different directions. After a few months they would meet up at base, have a share-out and return home to the North East of England. Apparently they earned the title of the 'Battling Geordies'.

Then came the time when the family decided that young Ben was old enough to go with them. The story that he told to me was a fascinating one. When they landed in Canada two of them set up a base house and young Ben was one of those who went off to find work. The first chance of a job appeared when he came across some men laying pipes in the road. He asked for the foreman and asked him for a job. 'Can you fight?' was the reply. Like my Dad, he was five foot four in his stockinged feet and slightly built, but to keep with the tradition of the Battling Geordies, he said yes. Uncle Ben said it was more of a rough-and-tumble than a fight, and he got the job. He was able to stay at the base house until the job was finished, but the time came when he had to leave the area to find other work.

One of the jobs that he was able to get was in a lumber camp and this turned out to be very character building. Great Uncle Ben told me his exploits in Canada after we had been discussing the pros and cons of the politics of Nye Bevan and the left wing paper *Tribune*. 'You have never seen a trade union organiser like the ones on the lumber camps,' he told me. The hardest men on camp would be the union organisers, whom he described as tree trunks with arms and legs.

I had a great deal of respect for my Great Uncle Ben, and that respect grew when he told me that he had joined the IWW (Industrial Workers of the World). At the time when he was talking to me he was no longer anywhere near the IWW politically, but he

Family tots up nearly two centuries on rails

WHEN East Leeds railwayman Keith Harding hung up his signal technician's cap for the last time, it brought to a total of about 190 years the Harding family's service to the trains.

Not only has Keith spent 46 years with what became British Rail, but his wife, father, mother, uncle and grandfather have also made their livings on the railways.

Keith, who will be 61 in June, began work in 1948 as a signal lad months before nationalisation — when the network was called London North East Railways — and finished at the time of the new privatisation.

But the Harding family story begins around the turn of the century when grandfather Noble Harding moved from his home town of Byker, near Newcastle, to take a position at Marsh Lane goods yard in Leeds.

Noble retired in 1936 but his son Herbert (known as Bert) was by then established in his own railway career, begun in 1921 after a short spell in engineering.

During his 44 years' service Bert worked at a variety of locations including Cross Gates and Headingley before retiring from Wellington Street goods yard.

And it really comes as no surprise to know that Keith's uncle — another Noble — also put in 46 years' service, retiring from Wellington Street.

By Mike McCormack

Said Keith, of Torre Road, Burmantofts: "If my brother Norman had not failed his eye sight test during a medical he, too, would have remained with BR."

He recalls a time in the 1940s when his mother Emma was working at the now-defunct Penda's Way station and opened up the waiting room to shelter rain-drenched revellers on VE Day. If anyone has photographs of this station or the VE Day party Keith would be glad to hear from them on ☎ 351413.

Since those days the major single in the railways for Keith has been the disappearance of steam, with engines becoming diesels and diesels turning to electric.

As a signalman he is also conscious of the way signal equipment changed from being mechancially- to electrically-operated and how the emphasis has moved from goods traffic to passenger transport.

The Hardings love travelling by train for pleasure also, and in his retirement Keith plans to do plenty more. Wife Joyce will have to wait a while, however — she is not due to retire from her job as a Travel Centre assistant at Leeds City station until 1999.

▷ Keith shows a picture of himself at work as a young man and one of his mother in rail uniform (W7501/2).

Working on the railways: Keith keeps up the tradition, as reported in the Leeds Skyrack Express, *1 April 1994*

maintained some pride about his membership which he kept throughout the various jobs in Canada. But this was to be his last trip; the following year they were refused entry because they did not have jobs to go to.

On arriving home Ben got himself a job in a butcher's shop. One day while still a teenager he went to work with his best suit under his butcher's coat. At lunchtime he went to meet his girl friend Elizabeth (my great aunt Lizzie). They got married and sent a friend home to tell his and her parents. The marriage lasted well after their diamond wedding. I don't know when they came to live in Leeds but they lived in Horsforth from at least the middle of the 1930s and were affectionately known as the unofficial Lord Mayor and Lady Mayoress of Horsforth.

My paternal grandparents, Grandad and Grandma Harding, kept a pub in Carlisle but when my Dad was still a young boy they left so that Grandad could take a job on the railway in Leeds. The only address that I can remember them living at was 27 East Park Mount, near East End Park, off Pontefract Lane, off York Road. When Grandad retired he was the first tenant of a railway bungalow, 10 Sussex Avenue, close to Horsforth Railway Station.

I was told that either my Grandad's or my Grandma's brother, after hearing about the 1903 earthquake in San Francisco, decided that, being a plasterer, there ought to be a lot of work for him there – so off he went, never to be heard of again. I wonder what became of him?

Unfortunately I never met my maternal grandparents Mathew

King and Edith King (née-Turnpenny). They had three children: Ada, John and Emma. Ada King married William Dixon and had two children, Lilian (Lily) and Alan. John King married Jessie Gough. They had two children, Iris and Beryl. Emma King married H.B.J. (Bert) Harding and had two children, Keith and me.

Photographs of Grandad King show him as a tall upright man in a dark suit with pocket watch and chain on his waistcoat, complete with bowler hat and moustache. He was a moulder at Catton's iron foundry He was union leader there and became secretary of the Leeds moulders' union. Judging by the stories told me by Mum and Aunt Ada he held some very strong working-class principles.

Mum and her older sister Ada worked at the same mill. They used to go to work with the big pockets in their aprons bulging with ready prepared bobbins. The kindly mill owners used to allow the women and girls to take the bobbins home with them for preparation – work they didn't have to pay them for. The two girls would walk down Pontefract Lane about two miles, then take a penny tram ride to the bottom of Cherwell Hill and walk up the hill to the mill in Morley to be ready to start work at six o'clock.

At the time when Mum was a two-loom weaver the workers in the weaving shed were asking for an increase per yard on worsteds. The management had refused to meet this request. She discussed the situation with her father. 'Well Emma,' he said, 'you will have to stop shop.' 'How can I do that?' 'Kick belt off pulley,' he told her. Mum went to work the following day and got the girls to again put in the request and put a deadline time for the answer. The time arrived and there was no reply from the management. From Mum's description I have the picture of Emma King walking down the weaving shed in her long black dress and white apron with head held high and her hair, usually half way down her back, tucked away. After kicking off the belt she walked back to her looms. How long it took I don't know, but the end result was they won their increase.

Years later when making one of my infrequent trips to Leeds to visit Mum in a sheltered housing complex, I went into her flat to find that she had a visitor. It was a new resident in the complex and they had not seen each other since working at the mill. Through talking to this lady I found out that Mum became known in the Leeds weaving sheds as the girl who stopped the looms. I bet Grandad King was proud of her. I certainly am.

For tens of thousands of families the 1930s were very difficult. We were more fortunate than many others because Dad, who was a talented pianist, was able to supplement the family income. He did this by playing as resident pianist in pubs and as an accompanying pianist on the club circuit in Leeds. He sang too, but purely as an amateur.

My grandfather brought a piano to Leeds from Carlisle, where Dad had his very first lessons. It was given to him when he and Mum married. My earliest memory of hearing him sing in public was when he was principal tenor at the Leeds Town Hall when a number of Leeds choirs came together for Handel's *Messiah*. I remember him standing up to sing the opening tenor solo *Comfort Ye My People*. But I think his proudest moment was when he was given the opportunity to sing with the Huddersfield Choral Society. This was in the days of such singers as Frank Titterton, Walter Widdop and Elsie Suddaby. They were a great Yorkshire front row.

Music was his great love. In his early teens he played at the silent movies and as a 'song plugger' in Hartley's music store in Vicar Lane, Leeds. As a song plugger you had to be prepared to play any sheet music thrown at you and this helped to develop his skills as a sight reader.

At one very difficult period, when Mum and Dad were experiencing an acute shortage of money during the first couple of years of their marriage, they applied for help from the equivalent of today's social security. A representative of that department made a visit to the house. The interview did not take long – as soon as the piano was seen Mum and Dad were told that there was no chance of any financial help whilst ever they owned a piano. I don't know what was said but if Dad did not say anything, Mum would have asked the Social Security man to 'please leave the house', or something that could be translated to mean that. Mum was more forthright than Dad.

A very pleasant memory of Shakespeare Street is coming home from Beckett Street School on baking day and turning the corner to be met with the wonderful aroma of newly baked oven cakes resting on the top step of the houses in the street, and with a hole in the middle to let the 'divil art'. You walked home that little bit faster so that you could get a wedge of oven cake. Those who have experienced this will by now be drooling over the thought of a wedge of freshly baked oven cake, the butter and strawberry jam oozing out of the corner of your mouth. A quick wipe with the back of your hand cuts off the escape of the jam, then a lick at the back of your hand. End of bite one, now for bite two.

In 1935 we moved to 4 Accommodation Road. My Aunt Ada and Uncle Will were leaving their little general shop to go and live in Rookwood Avenue, off York Road, near to the Halton Dial. Mum was to take over the shop. That same week Dad became a permanent worker on the railway, which was better than being a casual employee, never knowing if you would have work when you arrived in a morning. The shop was situated on the corner of Accommodation Road and Broadfoot Street. On the other corner of Broadfoot Street was the Cosy Picture House and the Miners' Institute, where the Independent Labour Party held many of their meetings. When the Jarrow marchers passed through Leeds they stayed at the Miners' Institute and my Uncle Bill used to take my young cousin Lily Dixon there to hear speakers such as Helen Wilkinson. At the top of Broadfoot Street we had the slaughterhouse and the backyard entrance to the Stag public house.

The slaughterhouse meant that pigs were herded up Broadfoot Street, cowboy style. The sound of hooves on the cobbles was just another sound of the area. It was not uncommon for a frightened animal to escape and run amok with us kids running after them, no doubt making matters worse. The cattle were slaughtered across York Road, close to Shannon Street.

The local East Leeds Swimming Club, based at the York Road Baths, was a centre of activity for the community. I used go to these baths three or four times a week plus the club night and the family get together on a Sunday morning. In Leeds, as in many other cities, there were several of these local swimming baths and each one had a swimming team and many a water polo team. Each month there would be a swimming gala held in one of these baths

Doris Storey (back, left) before the Berlin Olympic Games 1936, with Dad and Yorkshire swimmers Lily Dixon, Marie, and Jacqueline de Sadeleer

with the host team providing the prizes. The supporters of each club would follow the team to each gala. One of the teams to beat was East Leeds. In the early and mid 1930s we had a cracking team with many talented swimmers. My two cousins Lily and Alan Dixon both became Yorkshire champions. The club also produced an Olympic swimmer in the shape of Doris Storey (who later became Doris Quarmby). Doris in her early days of club swimming had become a very close friend of my cousin, Lily Dixon, and of the Dixon family. In spite of the difficulty of training in a 25-yard-long pool and working at Montague Burton's as a sewing machinist she battled and clawed her way into the 1936 Olympic Games in Berlin to represent Britain in the 200 metres breaststroke final.

Just before she left for the Olympics Doris came to the shop to show us her uniform. Mum could not resist trying it on. Doris became the British, European, and Empire champion as well as the world-record holder of the 200-metres breaststroke, winning two gold medals in the 1938 British Empire Games in Sydney, and becoming a local hero in the process.

The second world war was fast approaching but like most families we just carried on not really knowing what was happening. Our family parties were as lively as ever. Boxing night was always a happy event, with the carpet rolled up and as much furniture moved out as possible. Dad on the piano, and let the dancing commence! Lancers, Gay Gordons, waltzes, two-step – the lot. A game of darts being played in a corner with the throwers trying not to pin someone's ear to the board as one of the dancers came dangerously near to the line of fire. This would go on into the early hours with us kids falling asleep in some corner or other. Then came the walk home where we shared our carpet space for those who had too far to walk – there was not a car between us. I know there is a tendency to idealise the 'good old days', but it was a great atmosphere to be brought up in.

Nearly opposite the shop was a pub called the Spinners Arms and on the other side of York Road opposite Accommodation Road was the Hope Inn – it is still there. Closing time on a Saturday night could be very entertaining. On one occasion I was awakened by a lot of noise. I came down the stairs into the main room. This served as a sitting room, kitchen and living room and as a bath room when us kids was bathed in a zinc bath placed on the clip rug in front of the fire. When finished, the zinc bath was hung up, behind the cellar door. I went through into the shop area and noticed a policeman's cape laid just inside the door (I wondered if it belonged to Rocking Horse, a much respected and feared policeman in our area.) Mum was standing in front of the front window of the shop wielding a broom and letting everyone know that if they came too close to the window she would have to clobber them.

On a Sunday morning men would gather on the street corners throwing coins in the air playing heads or tails. We youngsters would keep a look out and if a cop came in sight we would shout 'Cops!', they would scatter and we would collect the coins left on the ground. It wasn't unknown for there to be a false alarm now and then.

There were some jobs that have long disappeared. There was the lamplighter, for example. I remember when lamplighters were made redundant when a timing device was introduced for automatic lighting. We used to kick the lampposts to make them light, or turn off. There was the 'knocker up' lady, who for a penny or two would wake you up by knocking on your bedroom window with her long, padded pole. She'd shout the time until someone responded. This continued into the war, until alarm clocks became available to everyone, not just those involved in essential war work. Following an air raid or anti-aircraft gunfire I used to search the streets and spare ground for shrapnel. This became a hobby, as did aircraft recognition. There were loads of characters. Mum always had a pack of five Woodbines and a book of matches for 'Woodbine Lizzie' (known throughout Leeds) and the same for the tingerlary man (barrel-organ player).

From a very early age I was brought up on music of the likes of Gershwin, Berlin, Porter, and all the wonderful music of the 1920s and 1930s. Dad was a particular fan of Fats Waller and the singer Elisabeth Welch. I had the pleasure of meeting Elisabeth Welch in the late 1970s. The first time was when she did a concert for the Young Socialists. She was in her 80s but still had the gift. Maybe she had on occasions to rely on her wonderful sense of timing rather than to try and hit too high a note, but she held that young audience in the palm of her hands. What a lady. After the show Kika Markham arranged for me to meet her in her dressing room. We talked about Dad being a great admirer of her and the period when she became famous. I told of Dad's collection of music that had in it the professional copy of *Stormy Weather*. She agreed that if I got the copy to London we could meet for her to autograph it and to have a chat. Unfortunately Mum had given every single copy he had away. This included all the music that he had been given by older musicians when he was playing at the latter end of silent movies as a boy. I later discovered that it would have been worth a small fortune. I never did tell Mum. In spite of this setback Elisabeth Welch agreed to meet me socially for her to tell me about the old times.

It was very exciting listening to her talk about all those wonderful composers and artists who were only names and pictures on the front of sheet music, to me. In those early years I had not even been to the picture house (cinema). I still have a copy of a video that Elisabeth gave me, *Keeping Love Alive.*

Songs and music of the shows of that period became so familiar that if Dad skipped over any part of shall we say *Land of Smiles* or *Show Boat* I would let him know. If I was going to bed before he finished playing he had to play certain songs – and he dared not miss any. My parents always said that I could recognise music before I could talk.

We were now attending York Road School. It was here that I was given special permission to go swimming with the school, although I was still in the infants. I remember Dad picking me up from school to take me to see Malcolm Campbell's car 'Bluebird' that was on show in Lewis's store on the Headrow.

It was at York Road School that a teacher spotted that I was developing a speech problem and I was given special attention by Mrs Jackson, a speech therapist. I was under her care until I left school at fourteen years of age. I had a regular session once a week, along with other children from various schools. This lady was a keen supporter of the methods used in the USA by Helen Keller's teacher. Helen Keller was deaf and blind from being a very young infant, yet she was taught to speak. She became a writer and spoke out against injustice at many a public meeting. I will leave to you to work out just what a gigantic achievement that was. Our teacher always reminded us that you do not stammer when you sing, and insisted on breathing exercises and letting your words come out on a gentle exhale.

At 11.00 hours on 3 September 1939 war was declared and York Road School was closed down to become a centre for air-raid wardens and for the street fire-fighting committees, as well as a first-aid post, and a base for the auxiliary rescue party. The street fire-fighting committees were made up from the civilians in the area. They had a roster for patrolling during air raids. These street groups were issued with a stirrup pump, a bucket for water, and a device for picking up unexploded incendiary bombs.

After the retreat from Dunkirk soldiers were brought to Leeds to be billeted in Quarry Hill flats. At the time this was the largest block of flats in Europe. According to Lord Haw Haw, the Nazi radio propagandist, they were to become the Nazis' Northern Headquarters.

Before going to the flats they were rested in Accommodation Road and surrounding streets. Mum went out with the entire shop's monthly ration of cigs and handed them out to the troops. The street committees set to work organising tea and any sandwiches that could be produced. For my part I gave away all my comics and went round collecting foreign coins. I was old enough to notice the soldiers' dishevelled state and how tired and quiet they were, but I was too young to understand why.

During one of the air raids on Leeds, Richmond Hill School was closed down and in the same raid our shop and house were damaged. Keith was transferred to All Saints' School on Pontefract Lane, but it was several months before I was transferred to Ellerby Lane School. We were both destined to be evacuated to America, but our parents changed their mind at the last minute. One of those transport ships went down shortly after and I suppose we could have been on it.

The shop and house were both condemned in 1941 and we were allocated a house in Cross Gates: 93 Poole Crescent. It had a garden front, side and back. The council moved our furniture and belongings in the traditional way for areas like ours, namely in the green 'bug van' where everything was fumigated. We were to attend Cross Gates School. This made it four schools in three years, and in my case many months without one at all. Moving to Cross Gates was a bit of a culture shock. There were green fields to play in and the houses had gardens and not back yards. When we first went to school we were surprised to see children working in the school gardens. The teachers called us by our first names, which gave you a warm kind of feeling even if it was a surprise. I am sure that this helped new pupils to settle in and make new friends. I made two close friends that first year, John Atkin and Ernest Godly. While we went our separate ways in the late 1950s we have remained in contact to this very day.

Not long after we had settled in Cross Gates we went for a walk. We were crossing a bridge over the railway line when we spotted a little station. Mum said it looked nice and that she would like to work there. At that time she was working with Dad at the Marsh Lane goods yard wheeling sacks of grain. The man who worked at this little station, Pendas Way, was called up to the forces, so my Mum applied for the job and got it. Two shifts a day, eight trains a shift. She was station mistress, booking clerk and ticket collector rolled into one.

I was encouraged to join the scouts and became a member of Manston's St James's Church Scouts. Things were going very well until the vicar started to give us little talks about god. I asked him a question about something that was worrying me. I had seen a film where an RAF padre was blessing the bombers and I asked if the padres in the German airforce were doing the same, and if he thought this was wrong. He did not give me a satisfactory answer. I asked him again why vicars in both countries were wanting Christians to kill each other. He did try to get out of it by saying that what they did was to ask god to keep their men safe. I asked the very same questions at a church religious class. I got the same answer, and this time I added that if god were to keep both sides safe there would be no killing, so no war. The padre sent a letter to my Mum and Dad asking them not to send me again as I was a disruptive element.

The first job I applied for when I left school in 1943 was at James Gough's cabinetmakers in Regent Street. I was put to work – at the age of 14 – on wood-working machines. When Dad found out he said that I was too young to be working on machines and told me to talk to the union man. When I was told that there was no union he advised me to leave. I then followed the family tradition and started on the railways. This only lasted a few months because I failed the eyesight test. I wasn't up to railway standards.

I then went after a job at Archibald Ramsden's piano and organ tuners and repairers. I literally sat on their doorstep waiting for them to open for three mornings trying to get that job, but they wanted an experienced person. Some of the workers there recognised how keen I was and tried to intervene on my behalf, but to no avail. Dad had the idea of trying to get me into Neller Hall, the Military School of Music. This came to nothing, I think because of the war.

Then 1944 saw me starting work at John Barran's clothing factory as a trimmer in the cutting room. Before getting the job I was interviewed by the cutting room foreman. Mum went with me. The entrance to the offices was rather awe-inspiring: a grand staircase, polished wood walls, a handrail down the centre and a uniformed commissionaire behind a grand big polished wooden desk. He was known as the Major and, as I was to find out, ruled us youngsters with a rod of iron. Mum introduced us and the Major sent a message for Mr Thomas Boyes, the cutting room foreman. The only question I remember being asked was whether I went to church. My Mum immediately dived in and said, oh yes. I got the job and was told to report to the cutting room the following Monday morning. My real education was about to begin.

When I entered the cutting room I found it overwhelming. I was to learn that it was 110 yards long and 75 yards wide – as long and as wide as a football pitch. The roof was half glass. Alongside the cutting room were five floors the same size where the clothing was made up. You could get to these floors either by stairs or a lift that was positioned in one corner of the cutting room. Workers at each end of the room could go weeks without seeing each other.

At the end of the war in 1945 the young men started to return to the factory, bringing with them the memories of what they had seen and experienced. But most of all they had a determination that things were going to change as regards working conditions and wages. Before the war in 1936 a number of clothing workers in Leeds had joined the International Brigade to go and fight the fascists in Spain. This reflected a certain amount of left-wing and communist activity in the Leeds clothing factories. So now the pre-war militants returned with the younger men who had been called up at different stages during the war. These were the ingredients for the development of left-wing activity, not only in our factory but in all the other clothing factories in Leeds. By the late 1940s there were three union branches, each with 10,000 members and their own full-time secretary and elected branch committee. But what is more important, very strong factory organisations were being established.

The aspirations of millions of people were poured into the general election of 1945. A lot of hope and faith was placed in the Labour Party. When Labour's landslide victory was announced there was much genuine joy and celebration. Charlie Powell, one of the old fitters, had explained to me during the run-up to the election that in his younger days he had sold the Labour paper the *Daily Herald*. He said that in those days this was considered quite a revolutionary thing to do. When the result of the election was known he came up to me, shook me by the hand and said: 'We have done it! We have taken over. Do not let anyone take it away from you.' I did not fully understand what he meant but his sincerity and enthusiasm had an effect on me. So much so, that that evening when I saw a young man who had gone round our estate canvassing for the Conservative Party (me and my mates thought he was stuck up because his father worked in a bank) I shouted at him that we had taken over and they would never get it back. He chased me round Poole Crescent shouting something about letting Mr Churchill down. This was my first clash with the enemy.

I guess the Communist Party members would have agreed with him. After the war at a demonstration in London, they carried a banner with a picture of Churchill in one corner and a picture of Stalin in the other, with words like: 'Do not let anything separate those who have been joined together in struggle'. This featured on the front page of their paper the *Daily Worker*.

Another older worker in the factory, a band-knife operator, was close on retiring age. He had a great influence on me and many of the other youngsters in the factory. His name was Robert Armstrong. His grandfather had emigrated to Australia in the late 1800s, taking his son and toddler grandson Robert with him. Robert spent most of his time going from one mining camp to another, first with his grandfather and then with his father. Somewhere along the line Bob developed a great interest in history and geology and this led him to become an exponent of Darwin and the theory of evolution. He was always prepared to spend time with anyone to explain the difference between evolution and creation. Bob did not go down too well with the Communist Party members because he was a supporter of the right wing of the Labour Party. In spite of this I am sure that he sowed the seed that made me into a communist. Bob was living proof that you had to be more than a supporter of Darwin to be a Marxist.

My friends John and Ernest and I were having our first holiday away from our parents. We went to Butlin's holiday camp at Filey on the east coast of Yorkshire. It was early August 1945. One morning I went to get a paper. The front page carried the news of the atom bomb raids on Hiroshima and Nagasaki. I did not have any strong political beliefs at the time but this made me feel disgusted and horrified. All the papers, including the *Daily Worker,* justified the bombing. They said it would speed up the end of the war. It is now well documented that Japan was ready to surrender but the West had deliberately ignored this until they had dropped the atom bombs. This did not affect me sufficiently for me to join any political party or to go into a monastery. I simply carried on with my interest in Rugby League football and generally being a teenager until in August 1947 I was called to do my National Service in the Royal Air Force.

2

NATIONAL SERVICE IN POST-WAR GERMANY

I did my basic training at RAF Padgate. Looking back on it I think I was fortunate that it was summer, making the eight weeks more bearable. It was the usual square bashing mixed in with weapons training and cross-country running with and without kit. The positive side was that I came away fitter than I had ever been, as I noticed when I had my first game of rugby on leave. Then after a brief stay at RAF Honiley in the west Midlands and at the camp at Castle Bromwich near West Bromwich I was sent to do my trade training. This I did at a camp in Hereford. My 'superiors' had decided that I would make a good storekeeper.

This was winter 1947-1948, and what a winter. In the middle of the hut we had a round pipe-stove with the chimney sticking out of the back and going through the roof. We put our beds around the stove as best we could. We soon ran out of coke and coal. We decided to go to the Sergeants' and Officers' mess to ask if they had any spare fuel. They said that all they could let us have was a couple of bags. So for the next two nights at least we would be warm – this was my first experience of central heating. When that fuel was finished we drew up a roster of three in a team that would take it in turns to go out and forage for fuel. There were days that were just below freezing, with other days and nights with Arctic-like blizzards. Very soon we had burnt everything that was moveable within the perimeter of the camp.

I decided to liven things up at one of our afternoon classes.

After warning the lad who sat next to me, I said audibly, 'Don't be daft!' The teacher asked what the disagreement was. I then told him what the lad next to me had supposedly said, that there were one-man bands where he came from. 'Because I come from the north,' I said, 'he thinks I'm daft. There is no such thing as a one-man band. It would be impossible.'

National Service in the RAF, 1947-1949

After a bit of encouragement the instructor proceeded to explain how instruments were fastened to the arms, legs, back and so on. I finally got him to parade around moving his arm and legs up and down as a one-man band has to do. He then realised that he been tricked into giving the demonstration. I will say that – for a Sergeant – he took it very well.

So after my 'trade' training I was posted to that very select group of the Royal Air Force, 5352 Wing of the airfield construction unit, at the Hamburg (Fuhlesbuttle) airport. At that time it was being used by British European Airlines.

After two weeks' leave I set off for Hamburg, to the heartland of the 'enemy', as I thought. My journey took me from Leeds to London King's Cross, then over to Liverpool Street station, from there to the port of Harwich, ship to the Hook of Holland, then a train to Hamburg. I made this return journey three times over the next year and a half. Leeds to Hamburg had been organised by the Troop Movement department of the RAF. The last part of my journey, Hamburg to the airport, proved to be the most difficult. As soon as I got off the train in Hamburg I was literally on my own, and it was midnight.

I set off into the city. I had wandered about for quite a while when military police in a jeep stopped to ask why I was away from camp after curfew time. I explained that I had just arrived and was trying to find my way to camp. They took me to a point where they said I would be able to intercept a 'liberty truck' going to the airport. Then I had a bit of luck. I waved down a truck (a Thornycroft) and it was an RAF truck. The lads inside told me that there was no such truck to the airport. When I told them that I wanted 5352 Wing they said, 'Come aboard, welcome to the club'. By sheer chance this truck was the 5352 liberty wagon returning from a night out in Hamburg.

It was explained to me that while we worked on the airfield, we were billeted at No. 5 Motor Transport Depot, five miles from the airport at Langenhorn, where we slept and ate our meals. But we did not come under their direct discipline, meaning no inspections or parades. 5352 Wing did not have any bull at all; the officers and men were a law unto themselves. My first rebuke was to be told off by an officer for saluting him on the airfield. He said we were a working unit and we just had to get on with it. Most of the officers were engineers or architects and the Commanding Officer was a civil engineer with an honorary rank of Group Captain. We wore sleeveless jackets in summer or just open-neck shirts with RAF working trousers. In winter it was flying jackets, boots, and warm headgear. The only time we wore our issue headgear was when we went out of camp or off the airfield.

We were the envy of everyone at No. 5 MTD. The officers did not envy us; they just thought of 5352 as 'the rabble'. But we worked hard, and not eight to five like them. We worked very long hours and sometimes non-stop day and night. This included 'officers' and men. This was because we were involved in the 'Berlin Airlift'. The airport became a base for aircraft being used to transport goods to

Berlin. Some of the aircraft belonged to Freddie Laker and I suppose it was the beginning of the Freddie Laker airline.

The airport also had the responsibility of distributing PSP (perforated steel plates) and their fastening clips to areas where temporary runways had to be built. The PSP had to be loaded on to wagons, taken to the goods yards and loaded on to trains. Civilian labour was used, mostly made up of prisoners from the local prisons. Making sure a supply of PSP was always available, and the logistics of the transport and labour, was my responsibility, with my immediate officer signing the order papers etc.

My opinion of Germans was somewhat confused. On the one hand the RAF education on the subject was one of 'you're the boss so let them know it'. I found this a bit difficult as in my department I was in charge of some very mature and cultured people. All had been in the armed forces, from privates in the North Africa Corps to officers in the Panzers. One was an officer on a U-boat. Then there was the policy of the Communist Party: East Germans were socialists and West Germans were fascists. How simple and easy. I am pleased to say that I never fell for that one.

There were two older Germans. The elder of the two, Herr Franz Lange, had been too old for the forces. He was proud of the fact that he had read all the works of Shakespeare in English. Apparently he had been a teacher of English and European history. He resigned as a teacher before the war to avoid having to teach the Nazi version of European history. He took up office work at the airport where he stayed right up to the time I arrived to be his 'boss'.

One morning Herr Lange asked if he could have a word with me. Apparently his wife had asked him to tell me that she was prepared to do my washing. I knew that I would have to provide the soap and washing powder, and no doubt the family wash would be done at the same time. But I had no problem with that. Not long after, Frau Lange asked for my mother's address and I sent it to her as I could see no harm in it. What followed was something that at least made members of my family think, that is in regards to their attitude to 'the Germans.' She wrote a letter to Mum telling her not to worry about her son as she was looking after my clothes and any repairs I wanted doing. She told Mum that she had all her four sons killed in the fighting, and two grandchildren killed in the bombing of Hamburg. To paraphrase, she also said that the ordinary people were not to blame for the war but were used to fight each other on behalf of big business. Considering that I was wearing the uniform of the RAF that killed her two grandchildren her attitude was remarkable. No nationalism and patriotism was evident in her. This was a lesson to all of us and for myself another incident that helped to mould my attitudes and ideas in future life.

Erich Hagerdorn, another of the older Germans, had just scraped in for call-up and had become a prisoner of war at a camp in England. He worked opposite me at my desk. This man was a bit of a chess champion; every dinner time there was a game of chess going on, and if the game was nowhere near finishing then the board used to go away ready to start the next day. But if it looked as if a finish was imminent then the game would continue with me keeping watch in case an officer approached.

Erich invited me to stay for the weekend with him at his sister's flat where a bit of a family gathering was taking place. I gathered together as much food as I could to help fill the table. Unknown to me I was being watched by the CCG (Control Commission Germany). The anti-fraternisation rule had been slackened, but even so they thought my relationship was bad for discipline and I was told to cool it. I arranged to have a weekend off and I unofficially arranged to be off camp. Erich met me on the Saturday morning to take me to his sister's where the rest of the family were to meet. Unfortunately his wife and two daughters were over in the Eastern Zone so could not be there. There was a short train ride to the house. During that journey we passed through an area that had been a working-class residential area. For about five minutes, maybe more, both to the left and right there was nothing but rubble. Erich told me that they were still digging out the dead. I was glad that I had risked going out in my civvies, which was frowned on by the CCG and which the RAF police (snow drops) had instructions to discourage by periodically having a purge.

I expected to have a weekend where I was to be bombarded with stories of the war and the air raids. I did ask them about the firestorms; the description that they gave me was horrific. But it was obvious that it was something that they did not want to dwell on. Erich had been separated from his wife and two young daughters ever since his repatriation back to Germany. He was put in a camp near Hamburg while his family were in what became the Eastern Zone. Erich encouraged me to write to the girls so that they could practise their English. My last letter to them was just before I left Hamburg for demobilisation.

There was an occasion when a transporter loaded with a D8 bulldozer broke down at a place called Celle. I was dispatched to stand guard on it over the weekend. The place where it had broken down was a little village with nothing much there. A cottage doubled as police station and home for the village bobby. Saturday night was spent sharing a bottle of schnapps with the village bobby, a young man in his twenties. As a young soldier he had been stationed just outside Dresden. He was there during the fire raids. He explained to me that it was as if the air had caught fire. He was one of those sent in to do what they could. He very graphically explained to me what they were confronted with. People on fire, or simply smouldering from the initial effects of the heat. They found themselves having to shoot those with no hope in order to put them out of their misery. He was no Nazi, just a young man plunged into the carnage like millions of others, of all nationalities. Meanwhile another cab arrived to pick up the transporter and bulldozer. I had to wait until transport arrived to take me back to camp.

While waiting the young policeman told me that the Belsen concentration camp was close by and he volunteered to show me the way there. When it arrived we used my transport to get there. We pulled up outside the gates and walked into the camp. This was about two and a half years after the camp had been cleared and cleaned but many of the huts and buildings were still there. I tried to imagine what it must have been like. I had seen pictures of the camps but to be stood inside one, even if it had been cleaned up and was now no more than a monument to the racism and cruelty of the Fascist regime, was overpowering. Kramer, the camp Commandant (the 'Beast of Belsen'), was one of the accused at the Nuremberg war crimes trial. His defender said that he was kind to animals, loved his family, and simply adored his children. This man had lampshades covered with the tattooed skins of his victims.

Within a few months of arriving in Germany I had seen the result of the firestorm raids on Hamburg, been told of the terrible details at Dresden, and visited the site of the Belsen concentration camp. It was only in 1998 that I was told another detail of the Hamburg firestorm raids. A group of 200 or so men, women and children huddled together in the centre of the pitch at the Hamburg football ground in the hope that they would escape the flames. All that was left of them was ashes. The heat had been so intense that they had burst into flames. There would have been no escape anywhere on the pitch. In 1948 I watched Hamburg play on that pitch. Little did I know what had taken place there during the war. In comparison with the devastation of the residential areas the dock area appeared to be damaged very little.

It was years later when I first heard of Bomber Harris, chief of bomber command. Then in 1996-1997 there was an article in the *Skyrack Express,* a freebie newspaper that was circulated in East Leeds, with an appeal for money to build a statue to Bomber Harris in the forecourt of St. Clement Dane's Church. The appeal was made by Sir Harry Burton. I sent the following letter to the *Skyrack*:

Another view of Bomber Harris

> Just in case some of your readers, after reading the appeal letter from Sir Harry Burton, think that Bomber Harris was some kind of war hero, please allow me to make the following points.
>
> There were two attitudes in Bomber Command. To attack strategic targets. Docks, Shipyards, Armament Factories, etc. And secondly kill as many people as possible, with strategic targets taking second place. Harris was leader of the 'Kill Faction'. This meant fire raids and the blanket bombing of areas where there was nothing else other than the homes of people. Housing estates were his 'targets for tonight.'
>
> After the raids he would receive aerial photographs to study. A grid would be placed over the photographs and the target area divided into squares. This was done, not to study and estimate what damage had been done, but written into each square was an

estimate of how many were killed. The higher the estimate the more successful was the raid.

In Hamburg Hitler had met with great opposition. The fascists were fought on the docks and shipyards, with thousands taking to the streets to fight Hitler and his fascist thugs. Those not killed on the streets or in the concentration camps met their deaths when Harris ordered their homes to be bombed (is this the infrastructure referred to in Sir Harry Burton's letter?).

I saw the Belsen concentration camp, some two and a half years after the liberation. The horrors of these camps were brought home to me. The disregard for human life was fearful. I also saw the mile after mile of flattened streets and estates, destroyed not by accident but calculated, by firestorm and bomb.

It is difficult to find anybody who supports the rape of Dresden. A city of art, culture and beauty was destroyed and tens of thousands of its citizens killed in one night of bombing, a fire raid so intense that it was as though the air had caught fire. People on fire were being shot like dogs to be put out of their misery. It is said that more people died that night than by the immediate result of the Atom bombs dropped on Hiroshima and Nagasaki. I saw Hamburg and Belsen and had many eye-witness reports of Dresden, whilst doing my National Service with the RAF.

Come on Sir Harry Burton. You must know that Bomber Harris and his policy of killing civilians was an embarrassment to many members of Bomber Command and the Air Ministry. Erect a statue of Bomber Harris in the forecourt of St. Clement Dane's Church, London? How bizarre. Whatever happened to 'Thou shall not kill?'

You must forgive me for thinking that Harris's main aim was to cold bloodedly kill civilians.

Norman Harding (address supplied)

I received no letters back, but I did receive phone calls – from people telling me that they had family members killed either in battle or in air raids, all saying that the Germans deserved it, or simply indicating that it was revenge for the fact that they had lost loved ones in the war. It was also suggested that I had no sympathy for the British that were killed or for their families. Personally I regarded that as a great insult and was terribly hurt, especially when one of them was someone for whom I had always had a great respect because we could always discuss our differences without falling out. Compare Frau Lange's letter to my parents with the statement that 'the Germans deserved to die.' This of course includes the loss by Frau Lange of her four sons and two grandchildren. But she still had the humanity to send such a letter to my parents so soon after the war.

All the phone calls raised the question of whether I was a Christian. This I had to reply to in the obvious way. To paraphrase Samuel Johnson: 'If what you are saying is Christianity, then thank God that I am an atheist.'

The fascists never really took full control of Hamburg. It had been a very strong working-class city both before and during the war. There was a reflection of this in an incident when a number of German Jewish women were arrested and taken to the Gestapo headquarters in Hamburg and a group of non-Jewish German women demonstrated outside, demanding their release. No doubt the flag-waving, patriotic, our-country-right-or-wrong brigade in Germany would have been accusing those German women who were protesting of being traitors to their country. No doubt flag-waving patriotic our-country-right-or-wrong British would have said the same if it had happened in Britain.

In May 1948, all those of our wing who were not working on the airfield, along with the non-duty personnel on the camp, were confined to barracks. Those who were living in the married families' houses outside of the camp were instructed not to go anywhere near Hamburg. This was a mystery to all of us, except one young airman. I don't remember his name but let's refer to him as 'Lefty'. After we were dismissed from the parade where this announcement had been made, Lefty let it be known in the canteen, NAAFI, and anywhere else he could, that the reason for being confined to barracks was that there was to be a massive May Day workers' march through the centre of Hamburg, to coincide with a dock strike. Things like this weren't for our eyes, lest we be corrupted! On reflection I think Lefty must have been active in left-wing politics before he was called up. He told me that he had got the information from a youth group called the Young Falcons (I think that's the right name). Apparently he had made contact with them and attended their meetings.

Another thing Lefty used to do was to liven up our Sunday mornings. When the padre had finished his sparsely attended Sunday morning service, he would make a tour of the rooms trying to drum up support. Lefty used to follow him to question him on religion – and he was obviously an atheist. Finally Lefty challenged our Padre to a full-scale debate in the biggest dormitory in the block. Knowing what I know now, the Padre didn't have a chance. The following weekend we were summoned to a lecture by the education officer. It was to be on the East and West. Lefty was there and did a similar job on him. A week or two after that Lefty was posted to some remote spot in the Baltic, an island off shore from Scharbeutz.

He sure left his mark. There was a period when the food in the canteen went further downhill than normal. One day we arranged for one person to speak at every table. If one person spoke on behalf of a certain number of people you could be put on a fizzer (charge) for leading a mutiny or some such thing. When the duty officer came in and asked if there were any complaints (this was a daily occurrence) one airman at each table stood up. Each complained about the same thing, 'food quality and food quantity'. He promised to look into it. Nothing happened. After one particular bad meal I smuggled one out and had one of the technicians on the airfield take a photograph of it. This was then sent to the *Daily Mirror*. This forced an investigation at the camp and a conspiracy between the canteen Sergeant and the NAAFI manageress was uncovered: food was being transferred from the canteen to the NAAFI where it was being sold to the starving airmen. A kind of miniature airlift, you might say. Both of the culprits were transferred. I bet Lefty would have been proud of us.

Arnold Chemelevski (North Africa Corps) had told me that he had not seen any member of his family since he was sent to fight in North Africa. He assumed them to be dead. Then one day I was called out of my office to the reception counter. There was a young man talking to one of the staff who told me that the visitor had a letter for an Arnold Chemelevski. I called Arnold to come to the desk, where I left him and the letter bearer together. Within minutes they both came into the office. Arnold was in tears. This letter was from his mother and sister. While there was no news of his father, they were fit and well and living just across the border in the Russian zone, close to a crossing point at St Hubertus near Lubeck. The young man had told him that a meeting could be arranged if he could get to St Hubertus and across the bridge. The meeting was duly arranged. It was to be from Friday night to Sunday night. A weekend was best so Arnold did not have to answer questions about why he wanted time off work.

Some time earlier I had spent a few weeks at the camp at St Hubertus. During my stay I witnessed quite a lot of coming and going across the wooden bridge between East and West. On Friday and Sunday evenings civilians crossed from one side to the other without any hassle from the border guards, and on occasions there were no guards to be seen at all. The border between our camp and the Russian camp was a river and the bridge was close by.

The anxiously awaited weekend arrived. Two or three of us filled a rucksack with goodies. I had fixed myself up with a weekend pass to go 'see my friends at St Hubertus'. A Morris Cowley van had been arranged, and a driver from the German driving pool. For some reason we thought that it would be safer to have a German driver. We set off from Hamburg, headed down the autobahn to Schleswig Holstein and on to St Hubertus and the bridge, with a very excited Arnold. We parked about 800 yards away from the bridge. I walked with him up to the entrance and then gave him the rucksack so that the guard could see that I was with him. He walked over and off at the other end along with a few more. A guard from each side stood in the middle of the bridge chatting, and, I suspect, exchanging goods. Cigarettes and chocolate were popular items of barter. This happened at about 19.30 hours.

Having satisfied myself that he was clear, the driver and I made our way to the camp at St Hubertus. The German driver got himself sorted out and stayed in the section allocated for the German workers on the camp. As I remember I spent a pleasant but anxious two days waiting for Sunday evening. The two of us with the transport were there waiting at about 19.00 hours. It wasn't long before people started to arrive at the other side of the bridge. The guard on our side recommended that I go over the bridge, and let them see that I was waiting for Arnold, but warned me not to go over the boundary line as I was in uniform. When I saw Arnold I indicated to the Russian guard that I was waiting for him, so he was let through with no problem at all.

On the way back to Hamburg he told us that everything had gone smoothly. His mother and sister sent me their best wishes and thanks. When we arrived back at Arnold's home we went in for a drink. It was then that he told me that the majority of those crossing the bridge had work permits or some pass or other. The rest were just hoping to get through. For some reason both sets of guards were relaxed on this point at the weekend. I now think that to meet him on the other side of the bridge was a little foolhardy. Maybe I did take a bit of a risk. Anyway the German driver and I made our way back to the airport, where we parked up the van and then both got our heads down in the duty house with the duty crew so we were both ready for work on the Monday morning. The three of us were very pleased with the weekend's work.

My first experience with the bridge had been during my stay at St Hubertus earlier in the year. A report came through that a Russian soldier had been seen in Lubeck a few miles down the road. The duty officer sent an officer, an NCO and two airmen (I was one of them) in a jeep to Lubeck to sort out the invader. We finally tracked him down to one of the bars in town. He was sat among a group of Germans who were obviously having a good time. The Russian soldier was a young lad no older than myself; it was his birthday so he had decided to pop over to the West and have a few drinks with the locals. The officer with us wanted to make an issue of it but the much more experienced Sergeant suggested that we simply wish him happy birthday and get him back to the East. The Sergeant drove us to the bridge, we waved goodbye and off he went. Things seemed to be OK at the other side for the birthday boy and the guards were slapping him on the back and laughing. It looked as though they had been expecting him.

The Corporal in the pay office had quite a scam going. He had four airmen on the staff who didn't exist. He got the pay, the flight Sergeant got the cigs, I got the chocolate. The going rate for a bottle of champagne cognac was two bars of chocolate. I had ten bars of chocolate per week. The barter was done at the café Fiddler two miles down the road from the camp. The owner was affectionately known as 'Fritz the Fix'. I was a chocolate baron until the pay clerk was demobbed about two months before I was. The surplus airmen were posted one by one over a period of about four weeks and with some very creative bookkeeping the whole thing ran very smoothly. I mention the café Fiddler because a few of us spent many happy hours in the beer garden at the back drinking my chocolate.

My first Christmas in Germany was a very memorable one. It all started on 24 December. The CO invited everyone to his office for drinks. The officers and NCOs were allowed to drink sprits but those of us of the lower ranks were only allowed to drink beer. After two or three drinks we were all dismissed to go back to our place of work. When I arrived back at my office I found the German staff patiently waiting for me with a couple of crates of beer. They did not want to start without me. I was very touched by this. When we had finished they went home to their families and friends. I had been invited to visit some friends living in the married families' patch. I was passed on from one to another. At the last one, Warrant Officer Spooner's, I had a meal and a kip. Feeling somewhat refreshed after my meal and sleep I headed for the Fiddler armed with a few bars of chocolate kindly donated to me by Mrs Spooner. As I remember it I made a couple of calls on my way. I finally arrived at the Fiddler and swapped two bars for a bottle but saved the rest of my chocolate for New Year's Eve. I sat with a group of locals whom I had got to know during my previous visits. We talked about everything: our families, our work, sport. They practised their already decent English, and I tried out my poor German.

It was getting late and I would soon have to leave. Two of the men had gone to the bar to get some drinks. Fritz the Fix called me over to the bar and asked me to have a drink with him and the two men. He said something about it being a special drink. The bottle was taken from the back of one of the bar cupboards. He said it was a special kind of Schnapps. The four glasses were set up, the

RAF Christmas, 1948. I am seated second from right

drinks poured; we raised our glasses and drank to the future. Fritz the Fix smiled, I coughed, and the other two went away muttering something about 'V2 benzine'. I bid every one good night and made my way back to the camp. As I approached the camp I told myself to be quiet and I made my way round the perimeter fence to the spot where we climbed over. There was an arrangement with the transport section to leave a soft-top wagon on the other side so that we could drop down on to it and so to the ground. That night there was no truck left and I hit the ground with a resounding thud.

I must have shouted or something because the guards on duty ran over to where I was struggling to get to my feet. I was escorted to the guardroom at the front gate and was promptly stood in front of the long length mirror that was used by airmen to check their appearance before proceeding out of camp. I was told to tidy myself up. 'Not my fault', I said, 'it's those stupid idiots who forgot to put the truck in position.' 'Oh no it's not', they said, 'it's the fault of the stupid idiot who forgot that it was Christmas Eve and there was no time limit on the gate, so there was no need for a truck.' I was dismissed and sent to my bed. The tradition in the forces is that the officers act as waiters and serve the other ranks with drinks and their Christmas dinner. We were served with our meal and drinks. The duty officer did the toast, and hoped that we would enjoy the rest of the Christmas break. He also hoped that that the airman who came into camp last night by the way of the emergency entrance would remember that there would be no time limit on the gate tonight also.

The airlift was at its peak when I arranged a darts match with the civilian flyers and crew of Freddie Laker's Eagle airline. The planes were converted Lancasters or Halifaxes, ex-wartime bombers. The match took all weekend because sometimes we had to wait for the person we were playing to come back from a trip to Berlin. Instead of going back to the camp we decided to stay in the airlift mess so that we were handy for work the following morning. A good time was had by all.

The next morning, noticing that I was a little tired and had a faraway look in my eyes, the lads said that it would be a good idea if I had a little sleep in the office. While I slept, Erich took a telephone call and made some excuse for my absence. He was told that an officer was taking the de-Nazification committee on a conducted tour around the airfield and would be taking in my section. They were to be doing their de-Nazifying all week. Every German had to appear before the committee and on the basis of the interview would be de-Nazified. Erich and the rest decided that it would not be a good idea for the visitors to get the wrong impression, so I was bedded down in one of the many rooms. They locked the door and hid the key. The excuse for my absence for the telephone call and the visit was that I had gone to the petrol compound to do a snap check. The compound was told that if they received a message asking for me to say that I had just left to check on a petrol bowser on the other side of the airport and could not be contacted. Everything went smoothly. I learned afterwards that the North Africa Corps (Arnold) had masterminded the operation.

About this time an incident occurred that brought a great deal of tension on to the camp. Four of us were sat quietly playing cards and enjoying a drink of brandy in a house on the edge of the airfield. The house was used as a duty house and a weekend retreat for those who wanted to get away from it all. The duty German driver came and informed us that a number of jerry cans of petrol was missing. Now this could be very serious, as petrol was a very valuable commodity. Things became worse. Within minutes he was back panic struck; all the trucks' petrol tanks had been emptied. At first we had thought spillage added to evaporation could be used as an excuse, but not now. The German driver in his panic informed the Flight Sergeant in charge of the airfield transport. He panicked. He brought in the Special Investigation Bureau, the airforce equivalent of the FBI. Then we all panicked.

The person that I had taken over from had left me with a discrepancy of about 1,500 gallons of petrol. Our supply of petrol came from the RASC depot about ten miles away. I had been able to come to an agreement with the army lads that every time we sent our two tankers to be filled, the tankers would be empty but when the tanks were dipped it was recorded that there were 50 or so gallons still in there. This figure varied at each visit so as not to cause any suspicion.

Using this method I had been able to reduce the deficit to about 800 gallons, but with the visit of the SIB being imminent drastic action was called for. I made an immediate visit with our two tankers for our routine collection, including 100 gallons' surplus. I had to empty the tankers as soon as I returned into the underground storage tanks and go back first thing the next morning with an empty tanker on an unscheduled, non-recorded trip. They filled it from one of their storage tanks known as the 'petrol cow tank' that was used for emergency transfers. The organiser of this manoeuvre was a Corporal national serviceman from Dewsbury, near Leeds, my hometown. Once again, with help from my friends, the situation had been turned round.

The SIB investigating team finally arrived on camp, a Warrant Officer and a Sergeant. The first few days were spent moving around the airfield getting to know the airmen and German staff. They familiarised themselves with the layout of the petrol compounds and the method of distribution around the airfield. After about a week of this they started interviewing the personnel, starting with the Flight Sergeant who had brought them in to investigate. As I was responsible for the petrol compounds, I was the next in. It was soon obvious that the Sergeant was playing the hard man and the Warrant Officer was the 'reasonable' one. The investigation was to discover how and when 200 gallons of petrol went missing. At the time a few of us thought that the whole operation was like using a steam hammer to crack a nut. Was it an excuse to get on to the airfield in order to deepen some other investigation?

My biggest worry was that I was due to go on fourteen days' UK leave a few days after my interview. I really did think that my leave would be cancelled, but the 'kind' Warrant Officer gave me permission to go. Returning from leave, I had no sooner stepped on to the platform when one of my friends appeared at my side. He told me that they knew that when the German driver reported the missing petrol to the four of us we were drinking brandy. But they did not know where we had got it. We were not going to inform on the Sergeant who had sold it to us. Twice in my lifetime I have been met on a railway platform to be brought up to date on a situation; this was the first. The second was to be 29 June 1985, 37 years later. That story will come in a later chapter. My friend also told me, just before he slipped away, that there was a reception committee waiting for me. Sure enough as I passed through the gate from the platform our two SIB friends popped up, one on either side of me, and kindly gave me a lift back to the airport, where I was immediately sat down to be interviewed.

The German driver had made a statement to the effect that he had reported the missing petrol to the four of us as soon as he discovered that something was wrong. He had been asked the circumstances of his discovery. His story was that we had been playing cards and for a while he had been showing us how to play chess. Following this he had left the duty house to do a check on the vehicles, made his discovery, then returned to report it. A new problem now occurred; he had mentioned during the interview that the four of us were drinking brandy. As we were not officially on duty we could not be charged with drinking on duty. But we were charged for the simple act of drinking spirits. Other ranks were not allowed to do this. A 19-year-old officer would be allowed but a 50-year-old other rank would not. We were charged with breaking

King's Regulations. The charge was 'drinking brandy on RAF property'.

The Administration Flight Sergeant (the one who got the cigs) remembered that the previous year he put in an application for permission to decorate the duty house. He was turned down on the grounds that the duty house was not under the jurisdiction of the RAF. He gave each of us copies of the relevant document to make sure that whoever went in first had a copy. As it happens the four of us were marched in together. Our civvie CO sat between the two SIB chappies, with our friend the Flight Sergeant standing by the side of the table. We were informed by the CO that the SIB were only present as observers, and could not intervene. The Flight Sergeant was there to offer advice to the CO if he thought that he needed it. The charge was duly read out to us. The CO then asked if we had anything to say. As the appointed spokesman I pointed out that the charge was incorrect. We could not be charged with drinking brandy on RAF property when the building did not belong to the RAF. I gave the CO the document. He read it and gave it to the Flight Sergeant to read. He did a great job in pretending that he had never seen it before. 'Well, Flight Sergeant, what shall we do now?' asked the CO. 'Under the circumstances we can only drop the charges, Sir', he said. With that the charges were dropped.

Why spend so much energy on such a trivial matter? Many were asking themselves this question. We later found out that it was an excuse to stay around the airport. After spending many days rooting around the plant compound examining the bulldozers, graders, dumpers and such like, they finally told the officer in charge of the plant machines what it was all about. A bulldozer had been discovered working on a farm close enough to Hamburg to make it easy to guess where it might have come from. Somewhere among the masses of paper work they had found references to requisitioning parts for a bulldozer matching the serial number on the one found on the farm. But better things were to come to light; the bulldozer was being housed in what looked suspiciously like an ex-aeroplane hangar. The bulldozer was an RAF one but the ex-hangar's previous owner had been the Luftwaffe. It was obvious that the two objects had been together at the airport. The transaction had taken place in the first six months of 1946. The SIB acquired a list of all those who had been stationed at the airport at that time. As I remember it, none of us came under that category.

Early in 1946, something had happened that was still talked about while I was there. A trainload of cattle had been smuggled out of Holland into Germany. The story has it that an officer who had enough clout around the place was responsible, but he could never be pinned down. Some of the Germans who had been on the airport for a few years knew about it. This was not surprising as they were at the centre of events. The SIB discovered that one of the personnel around at the time of the disappearance of the bulldozer and the hangar was the same as the one that was at the centre of the rustling job. So the Sheriff along with his posse went off in search of the rustler.

Before they left they had one more job to do. It came as no surprise to me. I had been warned that they were more than angry when the brandy-drinking charge was dropped. I thought they would get us in the end. What I was not prepared for was that I was to be the only one of the four to be re-charged. I was in charge of the petrol, so I was responsible. I was charged with drinking brandy, and for not acting on the information that petrol had gone missing. The Flight Sergeant was powerless to help on this one and the CO had no option but to award me fourteen days in the guardroom. That is, to report with full kit for inspection early in the morning and in the evening (in between I did my normal work at the airport) and then carry out guardroom duties, with a short break about 21.30 hours, to prepare for a further full-kit inspection at 23.00 hours. For fourteen days, everyone pulled together to make sure that I had a full and polished kit for each parade. The North Africa Corps and the Panzers volunteered to clean and polish my webbing every afternoon.

A few days into my 'jankers' our area of the British Army of Occupation of the Rhine (BAOR) along with the British Air Force of Occupation (BAFO) were due to start military manoeuvres. Since all the trouble that we had gone through, my immediate superior officer, Group Captain Patton, in his wisdom had instructed me never to part with the keys to the compounds to anyone except himself, unless he authorised it. I had just had my evening jankers parade when a jeep pulled up outside the guardroom with a most obnoxious young flying officer who had been posted to us from Cranwell officers' training school. He was the type who waits for the driver to run round and open the door for him, who expects to be saluted. Nobody liked him. He marched into the guardroom with a purposeful step. He demanded that the Sergeant of the guard produce AC Harding. The Sergeant was ex-aircrew and did not take kindly to this nineteen-year-old sprog. He told him that I was in the back making tea and asked if he would like one. The young officer turned down the offer and repeated his request to speak to me. I heard all this through the hatch between the kitchen and guardroom. Not knowing what it was all about I made my way into the guardroom with the tray of tea with caution.

He asked me to hand over the keys to the petrol compounds. I told him that I was in no position to do that. He called me to attention and instructed me to hand them over. I told him that my senior officer, who was much more senior than himself, had instructed me not to give the keys to anyone without his authority. 'You must give me the keys. The manoeuvres start at midnight', he said, 'and we need fuel for the vehicles.' I remember distinctly that I was starting to enjoy the situation and decided not to budge from my position. Even so, I was not 100 per cent sure of my ground. He carried on demanding, and I continued to repeat my reasons for not doing so. By this time he was shouting at the Sergeant of the guard to do something. He said it was not his problem. This seemed to irritate the young sprog even more. He went on saying that our vehicles would run out of fuel and we would be the laughing stock of the manoeuvres. This point had already crossed my mind. I suggested that the best thing to do was to waste no more time and go and get my superior officer to come and collect the keys, or to bring a signed authorisation giving me permission to hand them over to him.

After about half an hour my officer turned up and told me to get him the keys. It was arranged for me to be taken to the airport so that I could get the keys out of the safe in my office. With a broad smile he said thank you, then gave the keys to the sprog who dashed off to play soldiers. Then Group Captain Patton, reputed to be the best plant mechanic and operator in the 5352 Wing of the airfield construction unit RAF, waved cheerio and said if anyone wanted him he would be in the officers' mess, 'trying to keep clear of these damned manoeuvres'.

I had now become well established both on the airfield and at our host barracks. I finished my jankers. The SIB, who had been about as welcome as a fox in a hen run, had finally departed. Normal trading could now resume. All ranks started the usual practice of bringing goods for barter to my section for distribution. I discovered that unfortunately we had one theodolite surplus. I had to put it on one side until I could work out how to balance the books on this particular item. This problem was a recurring one.

There were three forms that were well used in the RAF.

1. Certificate Issue Voucher (CIV 173) for issuing surplus equipment you have to the camp in the sky. By its very nature this was very rarely used.

2. Certificate Receipt Voucher (CRV 174) for receiving equipment you don't have, from the same camp in the sky. Very well used. And

3. Certificate Exchange Voucher (CEV 175), a magic form which very usefully by-passed the camp in the sky and could convert items such as shoes to boots, trousers to coats, and even beds to wardrobes.

Get the drift? One minor problem was that you needed the signature of the equipment officer. The problem of the surplus theodolite was solved in the old-fashioned way. I flogged it on behalf of the syndicate.

I was by now only about three or four months away from my demob. Any thoughts that I would be able to simply pass this period away without problems were soon to be dashed. I was called into the office and Warrant Officer Spooner outlined what he had in store for me. The previous day he had been approached by the officer who was in charge of stores at our host camp. Apparently he was told on the grapevine that enquiries were being made at BAFO HQ regarding the running of his department and the movement of goods and equipment under his direct control. This included everything you could think of: all types of clothing and equipment for just about every kind of work carried out on any big RAF camp. On top of all that he was responsible for everything needed to equip the houses in the married families' quarters outside the camp. This household equipment was stored in a huge warehouse a few miles away.

We had been asked, because we were a 'practical outfit', if we would use our skills and experience to help out, as his lads were new to the game. There was to be a full audit of the books and stock covering the whole spectrum of items. I will never forget the smile on Spooner's face when he told me that as our work on the Berlin airlift had slowed down he had volunteered me for the job. There were only three weeks to do it before the auditors arrived. I made it clear that the officer would have to sign everything put in front of him for the operation to run smoothly. This was agreed. I was to start immediately. We chose a decent size office to work in. The one with the most experience was to work with me. The rest, about six of them, were to do the counting and checking. Taffy and I were to work on the ledgers, which we had brought into the office and piled up in the corner. Each of us had a good supply of the three conversion vouchers that I have mentioned previously.

During this period we had our own clothing and equipment distribution service. We had the best-dressed airmen in BAFO. Boots were swapped for nice shiny shoes. The few of our lads who lived in married quarters found that their old furniture could be exchanged for new. We worked feverishly and we were ready two or three days before the auditors arrived. Not all the books balanced – it would not do for everything to be too clinically clean. The auditors were there for three or four days. Everything was found to be in order. As soon as the auditors had left Taffy and I were called into the office, and a very relaxed and relieved officer wanted to show his gratitude by sending the two of us to a forces' leave hotel at Scharbeutz on the Baltic coast. We insisted that all eight of us should go. We were driven there on the Friday afternoon and collected on the Monday morning. Another job well done.

The next weeks were spent carrying out routine work. Then one morning I received a telephone message from the orderly room that my demob number had come through. This meant that in two weeks' time I would start my journey to the demobilisation camp just outside Blackpool. Warrant Officer Spooner said, 'Why hang around here for two weeks?' and gave me a clearance sheet to go round all the different sections. Once I had a signature for a section as far as they were concerned I did not exist. A couple of hours later I was back in his office for his signature for the final clearance. After that I could pack my bags. Instead of having to use the traditional kit bag I was able to use a canvass holdall and a wooden suitcase lined with an army blanket that had been made for me by the German staff in my department. I also had a parting gift, an ash tray turned out of a solid piece of wood engraved with the Hamburg coat of arms and a message saying: 'To Norman from his friends at Fuhlsbuttel'.

Transport would be waiting for me at 07.00 hours the following morning to take me to St Hubertus (Lubeck) where I was to spend the remaining time waiting for my travel pass and arrangements to come through. On arrival I was given my clearance sheet. I cleared myself from all sections except the pay and canteen sections. I only existed on pay day and at mealtimes. So I had nearly two weeks of virtual holiday.

Summer 1949. I was out of the RAF and back home. Two weeks' leave and then back to work in the clothing factory. At this point I was twenty years old. In retrospect I am convinced that the experiences that I had gone through played a large part in moulding my attitudes for the rest of my life – well over 50 years.

3

FINDING MY FEET POLITICALLY

When I left the factory in 1947 the lads had returned from the war determined to make changes to wages and conditions. The older ones who had been militant or members of the Communist Party before the war greatly influenced the younger ones who returned from the war and wanted changes to be made. When I returned in 1949 it was easy to see that the Communist Party had made big strides into the John Barran's clothing factory. This was also true in the rest of the Leeds area. Right up to 1956, the year of the Hungarian Revolution, the Communist Party could muster 30 delegates, comprising members and supporters from the garment workers' union, to the Leeds Trades Union Council. Until about 1953-1954 I was considered to be a contact, so I was always on their list, though a contact who had to be handled with care, as I later came to understand. For instance Bert Ramelson, the Communist Party Yorkshire Area Organiser, held Friday night education classes at his home in Quarry Hill Flats. I was never invited. Another feature of the local political scene was Bert Ramelson's Friday lunchtime open-air meeting in front of Leeds Town Hall.

From 1949 into the early 1950s I was encouraged by members of the CP to join the factory library. You paid sixpence per week and then took it in turns to choose a book to add to the library. My first book was an exposure of the Ku Klux Klan: *I Rode with the Ku Klux Klan* by Stetson Kennedy. Another was *Peekskill: USA* by Howard Fast, the story of an attempted assassination of Paul

Robeson. During those early years I read a number of books by Upton Sinclair, John Steinbeck and Howard Fast, along with many other books that came to my notice. By 1952 I had become a regular reader of *Tribune,* the Bevanite paper. I was receiving every week a colour magazine called the *Soviet Union*, which was sent to its readers direct from Moscow. This was as far as it went regarding any attempts to recruit me. I was recognised as a Bevanite. Then the CP made their move. I was asked if I had ever thought of joining the Labour Party. I hadn't even given that a thought. I was encouraged to make this move. I was constantly told that people like me were needed in the Labour Party to help those fighting to defend Bevan from the attacks of the right wing. This must have been a strong argument, as I agreed to join.

After reading my *Tribune* every week I would pass it on to my Uncle Will. He had been greatly influenced by the Independent Labour Party, had supported the Russian Revolution of 1917 and was a great admirer of the Soviet Union. But his resolve was weakened by the zigzagging of the CP just before and just after the war had started. He was no union-jack waver and here was the CP wrapping itself up in it. I made one of my usual weekly visits with the *Tribune* to Uncle Will. After a few minutes he said that he had a book that he would like to give me, a book that he obviously valued very dearly. He went upstairs and came down with a book wrapped in brown paper. 'Read this', he said, 'it will do you more good than *Tribune*'. It was the unabridged version of John Reed's *Ten Days that Shook the World*, untouched by the hand of Stalinism. As my political understanding developed the more I valued that book. But I was to make a great error in judgement. About 1957-1958 a university student who was doing a thesis on the Russian Revolution asked me if I could lend him any literature that would help him. Thinking that he must be a serious student, I loaned him my *Ten Days* and a two-inch thick file on Stalinism from 1945 onwards. That was the last I saw of them. I now feel that loss very dearly. I was greatly impressed by this book and like my uncle I saw a way forward and became a supporter and defender of the Soviet Union. My eyes shone with the vision of ploughs instead of guns, combine harvesters and tractors instead of tanks and weapons of

In the cutting room at John Barran's, 1952

destruction. I took my *Ten Days* to work and lent it to CP members for them to read. The response I got was the same from each one: take no notice of what it says about Trotsky, his role was to betray the revolution. That was the first time Trotsky's name had been mentioned to me. That meant that my first opinion of him was very negative.

I continued to be active in the Labour Party, doing the best I could to get militant resolutions passed at the Cross Gates Ward Labour Party meetings, attending my trade union branch meetings and going as a delegate to the Leeds Trades Council, where I felt more at home than I did at Labour Party meetings. To them I was just a willing grafter, and fodder for election work. At one council election I took a day off work to campaign for the return of our candidate, Councillor Jackson, only to discover that the candidate himself not only did not take a day off work but, to rub it in, had worked an hour's overtime. At the next ward meeting he rose to give thanks to the ward workers, going on to say that he was a socialist locally, nationally and internationally. At that I intervened saying 'but not on election day'. I said, 'Your internationalism goes as far as the Leeds branch of the United Nations, the centre for international capitalism.' With that I walked out of the meeting. I kept my membership but I did not do any more work.

Even then, at a time when I was most vulnerable, the CP did not make any move to recruit me. I was in somewhat of a political limbo, just getting my weekly dose of comfort from the *Tribune*. One Sunday afternoon when I was about to go out to meet my friends there was a knock at the front door. Only strangers come to the front door. So it was with 'I wonder who this can be?' going through my mind that I answered the door. I was confronted by a young man and woman. They asked if they could speak to Norman Harding. That's me, I said. I asked them in and they introduced themselves as Paula and Ray Bradbury, members of the Cross Gates Ward Labour Party for the past few months. Ray had been elected as secretary. He told me that going through the ward minutes he had come across my name as the mover of resolutions that they both agreed with. Would I consider going back to the ward as an active member again to work with them and similar-minded people. This sounded much different to when the CP encouraged me to be active in the Labour Party and left me on my own. Here seemed to be a chance that I would be able to be with and work closely with others. I agreed to go back. But, I said, you might not like my politics, I am a firm supporter of Nye Bevan.

My life was never to be the same again. I was invited to their house after the next ward meeting for supper. They asked me what books I had read. I told them, but when I told them that I had read *Ten Days that Shook the World* they became very interested. I think they must have felt a bit disappointed when I followed this up by saying that Trotsky had betrayed the revolution and that he was in my eyes a traitor to the working class. But to their credit they must have recognised that I was ignorant of the politics of Trotskyism and Stalinism, that Trotsky was just a name that I had read in the book, and if he betrayed the revolution then he had to be opposed. This meant that I supported the revolution.

In the course of the next period I was introduced to Labour Party members who were also sympathetic to the politics of *Tribune*. Meetings were held on a regular basis to discuss such topics as the 1917 Bolshevik revolution, the rise of Stalin, the policy of peaceful coexistence, and its link to socialism in one country. The literature that I found myself reading were things like Lenin's *Last Will and Testament* and *The Revolution Betrayed* by Leon Trotsky, *Socialism on Trial* by Goldberg and *Negroes on the March* by Guérin.

The *Socialist Outlook* paper lost a libel case and had to pay heavy damages. This paper had a wide readership in the Labour Party. The driving force behind it were the members of the Trotskyist Group that had cells mainly in England and Scotland. The *Socialist Outlook* Readers' Group took in quite a wide periphery of contacts from the political left, with varying degrees of commitment. It did not take the Labour Party long to ban members from giving any support to the fight to save the paper or to have any connection with the paper.

At a meeting where the paper's supporters were discussing the campaign to save the *Socialist Outlook* the varying degrees of commitment soon came to the front. One notable leftwinger in Leeds was Councillor Douglas Gabb, Secretary of the East Leeds Constituency Labour Party (one of the most left-wing in the country). He suggested that there should be two layers of supporters: one openly campaigning and another one working quietly, kind of keeping their heads down. And he thought that he should be one of the latter. He would support (in general) left-wing resolutions but took no action on them. He made sure that he was never in any danger from the Labour Party bureaucracy. He was always Denis Healey's agent at parliamentary elections.

It was during the latter end of the struggle around the *Socialist Outlook* when I had come into contact with the Trotskyists and one of the first things they asked me to do was to sell raffle tickets to raise money for the paper. Well, I was an innocent, diving in where angels fear to tread. I actually approached Communist Party members to buy raffle tickets to support a Trotskyist paper! At this particular time it had not become obvious that I was coming under any political influence from the Trotskyists, so on the basis of unity and defending the left wing in the Labour Party I did manage to sell about three pounds' worth. After all, I said to them, it was you who encouraged me to join the Labour Party in the first place. But of course the day had to come when I made my first move that alerted them to the fact that the CP cardholders in the Labour Party were not the ones that I was talking to. In fact those worthies had their heads down so low that no one could see them. The move I made was on the question of the Moscow Trials. I also took my copy of Lenin's *Last Will and Testament*. Right from the beginning it was not a private thing between the CP and myself; I made it very public. I forced the discussion at tea breaks and also in the canteen and at the various spots that they gathered at after dinner.

The Trotskyist Group decided that it was time to get me to work in the Labour Party. Ray Bradbury proposed at the ward meeting that I become one of the delegates to the East Leeds monthly meetings. These meetings could be quite lively. On occasion resolutions from the various wards were on the agenda dealing with proposed national policy. The next step was to be delegated to the Leeds City Labour Party. Like the Leeds Trades Council it was a very well attended meeting. The Leeds City Labour Party had delegates from Labour Party wards and constituencies, trade union branches and many more affiliated bodies, plus the Labour Party councillors and aldermen. The Trades Council was made up mainly of delegates from the trade unions. My union, the National Union of Tailors and Garment Workers, had 30 delegates, and the vast majority were CP members or supporters.

I shall always remember the first time I moved a resolution. It was at my union branch, the Leeds No. 2 Branch of the NUTGW. Under the item 'correspondence' there was a letter from the General Secretary informing all members that the National Executive Committee was to enter into discussions with the Masters' Federation for a wage increase of sixpence an hour for both men and women. I will now go through the different stages of this wage demand, because it brought about my first big public split with the CP, and the Stalinists' policy of peaceful coexistence started to take on some reality for me, resulting in me being invited to join the Leeds Trotskyist Group. I moved that we welcome the claim for a wage increase and that we strongly endorse that the claim was for an equal increase for men and women workers in the industry. I called on the NEC to stand firm on their demands. This was passed. I felt that by getting in before the CP had time to move anything would, in a way, be part of starting to get myself known to the branch members. This type of move and getting involved with the struggles inside the union proved to be very valuable in the years ahead when the CP attempted to brand me as a 'Trotskyist reactionary' or 'anti-communist'.

At the next branch meeting (meetings were monthly) we had the first report-back of the discussions with the Masters' Federation. It was simply to inform members that there had been an offer of twopence-halfpenny for men and two pence for women. We were told that the NEC had rejected this offer as an insult. I again moved support for the report and I remember stressing the word 'insult' as regards to the offer. The talk in the factory about the offer agreed that it was indeed an insult.

For the next branch meeting the union meeting hall in Circle House was full. Much interest had been generated around this wage demand. I asked the branch secretary not to give his report under the item of correspondence but to have it as the first item on the agenda. The firm cries of 'yes!' convinced our secretary that this would be a very good idea. The report told us that the firm stand of our NEC had resulted in a result. We had been offered threepence for men and twopence-halfpenny for women. As soon as the secretary had finished his report I raised my arm to speak. But at the same time so did Stan Hives, the leading CP member in the factory, the party Branch Secretary and a member of the Leeds and Yorkshire District Committees. Without any hesitation the chair called on Hives to speak. What followed was a shock to everyone in the room, except (of course) those who were in the know. Those attending the meeting could be put into categories:

(a) Hardcore CP members
(b) CP members
(c) CP sympathisers
(d) Interested union members
(e) Those who supported the union leadership, right or wrong, and
(f) One future member of the Trotskyist Group (myself).

The ones in the know were the CP hardcore and the union officials who were on the platform.

Hives started by saying, 'I move that this meeting of the No. 2 Branch accept the National Executive Committee's recommendation that the union say yes to the offer of the Masters' Federation of threepence for men and twopence-halfpenny for women.' He went on to say that it was obvious that the NEC had fought for our initial demand of sixpence all round and had taken the fight as far as they could, so we had to be realistic and accept the offer. The seconder made a similar mealy-mouthed speech. I immediately rose to move a second resolution rejecting the offer. The chair refused this and said that I would have to move an amendment to the resolution. We all know that this is an old trick. The trade union bureaucrats are well schooled in such tactics; they try to lose the amendment in a fog of confusion. I replied by saying that the resolution was impossible to amend and that it would be more democratic to have two opposing resolutions so that the members had a straightforward choice.

I asked for this to be put to the vote. It was and I won. Those against were the CP hardcore; the rest of the CP was split roughly down the middle, as were the interested members. Then of course there was the union right wing. I was allowed to move my resolution. I remember the points that I made but not necessarily in the right order. I reminded the meeting that Hives had supported the demand for a struggle to take place so that the membership could achieve their demand of sixpence all round. I demanded to know from Hives what had changed, for him to make such a sudden about-turn. Had he grown soft on the union right-wing leadership or had he decided to sell out? I went on to discuss the economics of the offer and showed how it had already been swallowed up by the latest food increases; I had many points of this nature prepared. It was Hives and his betrayal that had forced me to try and think on my feet. I made sure that everyone in the room recognised that he considered himself to be a communist and what he had done was an insult to the principles of communism. I used this issue of insult to bring in the point that at the previous meeting the union leadership, the CP and the rest of the meeting had agreed that the offer of twopence-halfpenny for men and twopence for women was an insult. 'We are now in a position where according to the union leadership and a leading Communist Party member the difference between an insult and something acceptable is a halfpenny.' Their offer did not even include an equal rise for men and women. I ended by saying that the attitude of the union leadership and Hives was a much bigger insult to the membership.

During the discussion on the two resolutions it became very obvious that the hardcore was unashamedly giving its full support to the platform, meaning that Hives had not acted on his own; his move had been a decision taken by the Communist Party. However it had not been taken by all of the membership, and certainly there was opposition to the move. During the debate many of the interested members spoke and my comments regarding the insult had been taken to heart. The chair brought the debate to an end and suggested that movers of both resolutions should waive the right to reply as time was getting short. He won that one and took the vote. The Hives resolution took the majority of the votes. All the right wing voted for Hives.

Many of the Communist Party members voted out of loyalty. An indication of this was that after the meeting there were heated discussions between CP members in the Yorkshire Hussars in Eastgate. My resolution took the majority of the interested members who were in attendance, but most importantly six or so Communist Party members voted for my resolution. Later that night I discovered that the other two Leeds branches had also voted to support the offer. This meant the whole Leeds District, so I suppose you could say that the union had the support of the union branches in Yorkshire. The same story was repeated all over England where the CP members spearheaded the support for the union leadership. Their line was that the leadership had done its best, so let's be realistic and accept the offer. They even sank to the depths of congratulating our 'leaders' in their success.

But there were rumblings in the factories. There were 30,000 members in the three Leeds branches. The union leadership, and the CP, must have realised that to short-circuit the rank and file's rumblings they would have to get the offer accepted at mass meetings of members, especially in Leeds, Manchester and London. About ten days after the call for acceptance mass meetings were held. The

John Barran's factory committee was encouraged to call a members' meeting in the canteen a few days before the Leeds mass meeting.

In the meantime I had been discussing all my moves with my late comrade Jack Gale, and also other members of the Group. John Archer recommended that I see a contact of his (an ex-CP member and retired clothing worker). John had come across him at a meeting of the Leeds branch of the National Council of Labour Colleges. The most important bit of information that I got from him was that over the last few years the Communist Party had been trying to get the ban lifted that barred CP members from holding official posts in the union. Then everything dropped into place. They were trying to do a deal with the union at the expense of the union membership. Stalin's policies of 'peaceful coexistence' and 'socialism in one country' brought to bear right down to factory level.

At the factory meeting I moved to reject the offer saying very much the same as I had said at the union branch meeting, except that I introduced the issue of the CP trying to prove to the union what a bunch of responsible members they were. I said that if the Communist Party wanted to have a campaign to lift the ban on them holding office I was sure that they would get the support of thousands of union members throughout the country. I was sure that this was the principled way to fight the issue and not to use the union members' wages to buy their way in. I made my remarks directly to Hives. The presence of a large CP factory branch (and a larger still *Daily Worker* readership) made sure that between them and the right wing the vote went for acceptance. Even so I was sure that the vote did not represent the gut feeling of many.

The mass meeting went very much the same way as the factory meeting, except that the vote against accepting the offer was a larger percentage of the vote. The positive sides were that I was able to speak to about 1,000 members, calling on them to oppose the acceptance, using mainly the economic questions of the cost of living, and that a halfpenny was the difference between an insult and a reasonable offer. I was also able to speak directly to practically the entire CP union membership in Leeds. I again raised the question of a principled fight to get the ban lifted, which would get huge support, instead of using the wage increase to buy their way in. I added, 'You have done the leadership's dirty work. The ban will have iron bars on it.' As they found out, nothing changed.

I was invited by Jack Gale to a meeting to discuss the experiences of the last few weeks. The members of the Leeds Trotskyist Group attended the meeting. Their names were John Archer, Mary Archer, Jack Gale, Celia Gale, John Walls, Lance Lake, Norman Atkinson, Ray Bradbury, Paula Bradbury and Bob Pennington. The main thing that came out of that meeting was a decision to have a public meeting in one of the rooms at the Trades Club in Upper Fountain Street. The subject of the meeting was to be 'Trotskyism and Stalinism' and the speaker Jack Gale. The big surprise of the night was that Hives and two or three other members of the CP turned up. Jack did a great job that night and the notes he prepared for the meeting were duplicated and handed out. Mine finished up as a well-thumbed document. The contributions by Hives were aimed at discouraging the uncommitted that were there. His points were that we were ultra-left, anti-Soviet. His parting shot was that the subject of Trotskyism versus Stalinism did not exist: there was no such thing as Stalinism, what was going on at the meeting was Trotskyism versus communism. This was 1953 or 1954.

Forty years later at a 'Hands off Iraq' demonstration I reminded Hives of this statement. There were others on the demonstration who had been members of the CP in the 1950s. A few of them had actually worked in my factory. I asked those who would talk to me what their opinion of Stalinism was now. Going over the questions that I was raising in the 1950s in the light of the current state of the Communist Party and the ex-Soviet Union was, I suppose, a very subjective thing to do. But I sarcastically told Hives to cheer up; the break-up of Stalinism was the best thing that had happened in the fight for communism since 1917. I had taken a lot of stick from them in the past and I just wanted them to know that I was still around, live and kicking.

One Sunday in early summer 1954 Ray and Paula Bradbury and I were walking home from an 'ideal homes' exhibition in Roundhay Park. Paula walked in front with Ray's sister so that he could talk to me. He was very keen to discuss with me the lessons of the CP sell-out on the question of the wages struggle. He then told me that he been told by the Leeds Trotskyist Group to invite me to join them. He explained that it was not just a case of a few like-minded people coming together to discuss politics. The Group was part of an organisation that had branches all over the British Isles. Leeds met not only as a branch but took part in meetings attended by all the branches in the north of England. An annual conference was held where important decisions were taken, and a Central Committee elected. This was our national leadership which in turn elected the national secretary, the leader of the British section. We were also affiliated to the Fourth International.

I agreed to join and was very excited at the prospect of being able to work in an organised way against the Labour Party right wing and the Stalinists. I was invited to meet Jack Gale, the Leeds branch secretary, so that he could explain to me, among other things, the importance of security: no one was to know who the members were. They said I was being recruited because through the struggles in my factory I had started to understand the politics of Stalin's policies of 'peaceful coexistence' and 'socialism in one country'. I now believe that the reason should have been that in the process of *taking part* in the class struggle I had come into conflict with the Stalinists and the right wing, which meant I started to understand the importance of our opposition to the CP policies of peaceful coexistence and socialism in one country. But it was not enough to be anti-Stalinist, as I was to learn in a more profound sense in later years. The context was that the Russian Revolution took place in isolation from the rest of the world, and had created the conditions for the rise of Stalinism and its opponents, the Left Opposition. Stalinism betrayed working-class struggles all over the world, and hundreds of thousands of working-class fighters were executed either by bullets or in Stalin's labour camps. Yes, we were right to fight to understand this degeneration and to oppose it. But socialism is about building a future society, based on new social relations, not just about fighting degeneration. To be just anti-Stalinist is a million times wrong. It is the same as saying that getting rid of religion will get rid of the problems of the world. This method will never get rid of anything. The reasons have to be understood and that means a

Marxist understanding of the social relations in the context of the development of society.

It was a Saturday night and I was about to attend my very first branch meeting. I had no idea what to expect. The Leeds Group meetings were held at Jack and Celia's house just off Chapeltown Road. Ray and Paula took me there on public transport; no one had a car in those days. Celia let us in and invited us into the front room. Although this was 1954 I can still remember who was there: John Walls, John and Mary Archer, Lance Lake (Councillor), Norman Atkinson, and two dockers from Hull who arrived soon after, closely followed by three Nigerians: Jonas, Warrie and John (Slim).

Jack was sat in a great big armchair that almost swallowed him up. He introduced me to the meeting and welcomed me as a member. The opening contribution was to be a report from the Central Committee that was held the previous weekend. This was to be given by John Archer. Everyone was seated except John, who reclined on the floor in front of us. He was supporting himself on his right arm with his pipe tobacco tin in front of him. He scraped the old tobacco out of the bowl of his pipe, knocked the residue out into the tin lid, refilled his pipe then laid his pipe down. Looking round at each of us, he closed his eyes momentarily and said, 'Comrades, I bring you greetings from the centre'. What happened after that has faded from my memory.

Two months or so after my first branch I attended my first national congress of the Group. It took place in a chapel hall in Frith Street, London. I was checked in at the door by Ted Knight (later leader of Lambeth council and known as 'Red Ted'). My credentials for attending had to be cleared by our Central Committee members before I was allowed into the hall. The content of the conference meant very little to me as I did not understand most of what was being discussed, although I do remember one statement that Gerry Healy made: 'Who knows? Maybe one day Catholics will denounce the Pope, and the Communist Party will denounce Stalin.'

From then on I took every opportunity to discuss with the Communist Party members the history of the Russian Revolution.

By now everybody knew that my differences with the Communist Party were not from an anti-Soviet position. On many occasions I had to reject the support of anti-communists; I constantly supported the Russian Revolution and the need to overthrow capitalism and not try to reform it.

My daily routine was to call in at Jack's, who was now living close to me in Cross Gates (in the house previously owned by Ray and Paula who had moved to Hull) to discuss the events of the day and the discussions in the factory. At one point I was trying to get Hives and company to have a discussion in the canteen on the question of the changes that had taken place in society over the centuries. I remember the question coming up, that man is naturally greedy and you can't change human nature. I used to really enjoy myself with this one. The can't-change-human-nature brigade used to expound this theory as though it were some kind of advanced philosophy that I just could not get into my thick skull. One dinnertime I placed a salt pot in front of them and asked them why was it there for them to use free of charge. Why didn't they put it into their pockets every day to take home, and why didn't they go home every night and fill every utensil with water? This would happen if these commodities became scarce for one reason or another. Then presumably 'human nature' would change and they would become 'greedy'. Conditions are the basis for human nature, and not something that you are born with.

Not long after the events in Poznan in 1956 Jack came to see me one Saturday afternoon. When I answered the door he was stood there with a deep grin on his face. We sat in the kitchen and he proceeded to tell me an incredible story. He had picked up his telephone and before he dialled he realised that there was a conversation taking place. He covered the mouthpiece and listened in to the conversation. It went some thing like this. Man's voice: 'Isn't it terrible what is happening in Poznan?' (The Russians were attacking workers in the streets in Poland.) 'Yes', said a girl's voice, 'it wasn't like this when we went there. We will have to meet to discuss this and decide if we should raise it in the party.' The young woman was apparently a bus conductress and they arranged to meet in Briggate when she had finished her shift.

At the allotted time Jack and I went to Leeds and waited in Briggate for a bus conductress to meet a boyfriend. Jack had already suggested that I should be the one to approach them. When boy did meet girl I approached them not knowing exactly what I was going to say. I excused myself for butting in and said I thought I had seen them at a Young Communist League meeting (I was once taken to a meeting by a friend) and were they in the YCL? (We did tell them at a later stage how we had come to meet them in Briggate.) Yes we are, was the answer. I then introduced them to Jack. They did not seem to recognise him, so we were OK. After a brief talk it was suggested that we went for a pint and a natter. I think they thought that they had made two contacts. The boy's name was Vince Lacey; he was about 18. The girl's name was Shirley Brady. Shirley was lodging at Cliff Slaughter's. We assumed that because Cliff was a prominent member of the CP his phone was tapped and we knew that Jack's phone was tapped. We thought that when Vince rang Shirley the two phones were connected by some tapping error. The fact that Jack picked up the phone at that exact moment must put the odds at millions to one.

It did not take long to get a discussion going. We told them that we were on the left in the Labour Party and active in the Young Socialists. One of the policy questions that we discussed was the abolition of conscription into the armed forces. We were pushing for this in the Labour Party YS, while the CP's policy in the YCL was to reduce conscription. Vince and Shirley agreed with us that it should be abolished. To our great surprise they were able to get the two of us invited to a YCL meeting where conscription was going to be discussed. On the night of the meeting Jack had to go to a meeting in Manchester. So I was to be on my own in the inner sanctum of the headquarters of the Leeds and Yorkshire CP, the Northern Star Hall, named after the Chartist paper *Northern Star*.

Charlie Labelski of the YCL led the discussion. Two points stood out from his contribution: one was that cutting conscription was more likely to be accepted by the government because they could still get troops to trouble spots now that aeroplanes had taken over from ships. The second point was that the call for abolition was an ultra-left position which would not succeed and was put forward just to look more left than the Communist Party or as deliberate ploy so that conscription would remain in place. He held up an ashtray and then proceeded to show us what ultra-leftism really was. He placed his finger on top of the ashtray and moved his finger round to the left saying if you keep going you finish up on the right. I said his demonstration had more to do with the earth being round. I also asked him if it meant that if you kept going right, you would finish up in the YCL.

We did make inroads into the YCL nationwide and influenced many of their members well before the crisis of 1956, the Hungarian uprising. In fact we had a fair amount of support for abolition of conscription at the YCL annual conference. The CP was greatly worried. The first hint of this was when Hives told me that he had been talking to a friend of mine. 'Who is that?' I asked. 'Vince Lacey', he replied. 'Never heard of him', I said. We warned Vince and Shirley to be very careful who they talked to.

On the occasion of the 21st birthday of the YCL paper *Challenge,* a social was held in the Northern Star Hall. Jack, Celia and I were invited to attend by Vince and Shirley. The looks on the senior members' faces were as though the farmer had invited the fox into the henhouse. But they need not have worried; we had already decided not to do anything that would make things awkward for Vince and his supporters who were there. One of the girls, a leading member of the YCL, used to spit venom at us when we turned up on a Thursday night to sell *Keep Left,* our youth paper. She once waved Harry Pollitt's pamphlet *The five fingers of Trotskyism* which had a picture of a hand with a name for every finger and one of the fingers was fascism. In 1956 she left the YCL and joined the Co-operative Party.

When the dancing got under way I decided to do my bit for peace and bravely went where no Trotskyist had been before and asked her to dance. To my surprise she accepted. Nothing was said but at the end of the dance I said thank you and here's to the revolution. Charlie Labelski said that I had just taken a big step for unity. We were having a drink of tea when Vince came up to us and told us that some leading YCLer thought that we getting too friendly with many of the members, and had sent for Bert Ramelson, the

CP Yorkshire full-time organiser. He came in with his wife Marion, had a brief talk with someone and then came across and told us to leave.

Vince came over with a group of YCL members including two or three young miners. One of them was Arthur Scargill, who later became President of the National Union of Mineworkers. They said that if we were thrown out they would have to be thrown out with us. To avoid any further trouble we agreed to leave and said that we would be across the road in the pub. Within minutes Vince and his mates joined us for a discussion without any interference.

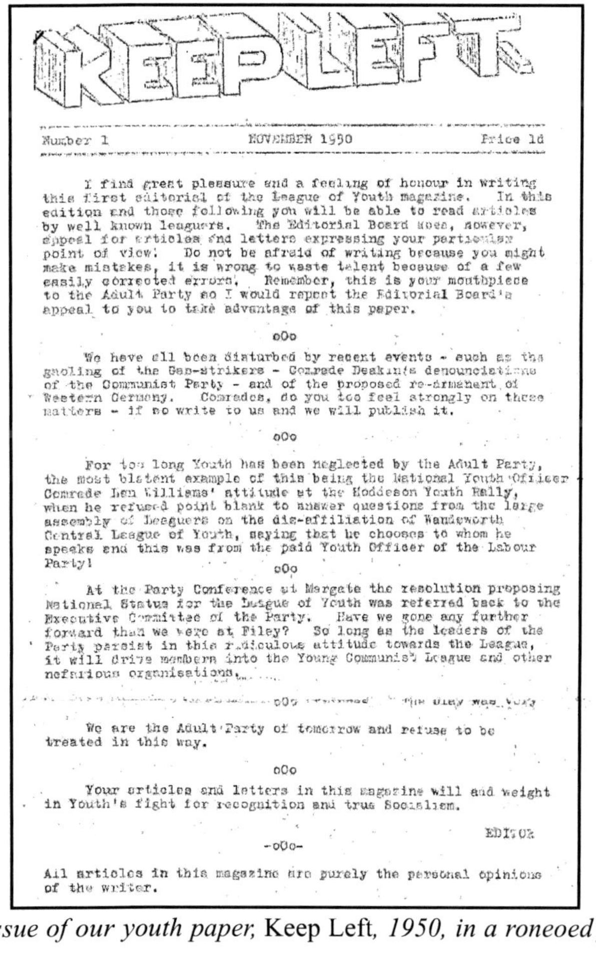
KEEP LEFT

Number 1 NOVEMBER 1950 Price 1d

I find great pleasure and a feeling of honour in writing this first editorial of the League of Youth magazine. In this edition and those following you will be able to read articles by well known leaguers. The Editorial Board does, however, appeal for articles and letters expressing your particular point of view. Do not be afraid of writing because you might make mistakes, it is wrong to waste talent because of a few easily corrected errors. Remember, this is your mouthpiece to the Adult Party so I would repeat the Editorial Board's appeal to you to take advantage of this paper.

oOo

We have all been disturbed by recent events - such as the gaoling of the Gas-strikers - Comrade Deakin's denounciations of the Communist Party - and of the proposed re-armament of Western Germany. Comrades, do you too feel strongly on these matters - if so write to us and we will publish it.

oOo

For too long Youth has been neglected by the Adult Party, the most blatant example of this being the National Youth Officer Comrade Ben Williams' attitude at the Hoddeson Youth Rally, when he refused point blank to answer questions from the large assembly of Leaguers on the dis-affiliation of Wandsworth Central League of Youth, saying that he chooses to whom he speaks and this was from the paid Youth Officer of the Labour Party!

oOo

At the Party Conference at Margate the resolution proposing National Status for the League of Youth was referred back to the Executive Committee of the Party. Have we gone any further forward than we were at Filey? So long as the leaders of the Party persist in this ridiculous attitude towards the League, it will drive members into the Young Communist League and other nefarious organisations.

oOo

We are the Adult Party of tomorrow and refuse to be treated in this way.

oOo

Your articles and letters in this magazine will add weight in Youth's fight for recognition and true Socialism.

EDITOR

-oOo-

All articles in this magazine are purely the personal opinions of the writer.

First issue of our youth paper, Keep Left, *1950, in a roneoed format*

4

MY EARLY DAYS IN THE TROTSKYIST MOVEMENT

Within a few months of my first Leeds Group meeting I went to a northern aggregate meeting in Manchester. Attending were comrades from Newcastle, Hull, Leeds, Liverpool and Manchester. It was my first meeting with these comrades. Some of the names I remember are Jim Allen, Joe Ryan, Peter Kerrigan, and Jim Swan; there were many more and most of them were industrial workers.

From the day I first made contact with the Group our main activity was to organise against Stalinism and the right wing of the Labour Party. I think it is true to say that in my experience work in the unions was on the agenda only as much as it exposed the trade union and Labour Party right wing politically, as well as the Stalinists. In this way we somehow saw ourselves as presenting the Trotskyists as an alternative leadership for the working class. This does not mean that Trotskyists did not take part in and indeed lead struggles in the working class. We did just that, before, during and after the second world war. But how did we see our participation in these struggles? Was it a way of forging an alternative leadership from the struggles that take place at the very heart of capitalism? Or was it looked upon simply as a way of exposing the present leaders and posing the leadership issue as one of proving to the working class that the social-democratic and Stalinist leadership in the workers' movement was wrong and the way forward was to join the Trotskyist Fourth International? Just a step away from saying 'take your pick and if you don't pick us then you get the leadership you deserve'.

I joined the Group at the back end of the faction struggle with Pablo. Michel Pablo was a Greek comrade who foresaw centuries of Stalinism. In line with this he had a policy of collaborating closely with the Communist Party. While the politics of that struggle were not in the forefront of my mind it was obviously in the forefront of the minds of those comrades who had been involved in that struggle. But some comrades could not put it in perspective in our relationship with the working class. At a monthly delegate meeting of the Leeds Trades Council a discussion was taking place on some aspect of policy regarding the relationship of the Trades Council to a campaign launched by the electricians' union (ETU) on wages. I saw that John Archer had indicated that he wanted to speak. When the chair, Councillor Jones (a very just and efficient chair), called on him to speak, our late Comrade John Walls whispered, 'Oh dear . . .' John Archer then proceeded to give the delegates of the Leeds Trades Council a lecture on Pabloism.

I was so horrified and embarrassed that at our next Group branch meeting I reported that I had moved a resolution at my union branch on the question of the National Amalgamated Stevedores and Dockers Union (the Blue Union) versus the Transport and General Workers' Union. It was to be forwarded to the Trades Council and to the Leeds City Labour Party delegate meeting. I was to move the resolution on behalf of my union branch at both of these meetings. I proceeded to explain to the meeting why I thought it wrong for Comrade Archer to make the contribution he had made at the last Trades Council meeting. I then suggested that he should not make a contribution on my resolution at either of the meetings. At the end of the meeting John left more quickly than usual and the other comrades explained to me that no one had ever dared speak to John Archer in such terms before. Apparently in my innocence I had offended him and damaged his ego.

In 1955 the district office of my union decided to organise a weekend school at Scarborough. There were to be two lectures spread over the weekend to be given by a lecturer from the Workers' Educational Association. Number one was to be the decline in strikes in the USA since 1945 and the reasons why. Number two, why workers in the Eastern Bloc and the Soviet Union would never rise against the regime.

Our comrades in the American section produced a weekly paper the *Militant*. The fact that we had comrades in the USA producing a weekly paper had quite an impression on me. I was always pleased to receive the latest issues and found it a great advantage to have information from reading the *Militant*. I was able to point out at the first session that big class actions were still taking place in the USA, such as the big strike at the Westinghouse Plant, and to list strikes that were taking place where the National Guard had been called out. That meant guns against the pickets. The lecturer's line was that all that had ended in America, that peace in Europe (the end of the war) had been followed by peace between the unions and the bosses. Because of this the people of America had benefited. Shades of MRA (Moral Re-Armament), a very rich organisation financed by employers. Shop stewards and the like were wined and dined in luxury and educated to believe that employers and employees should live in harmony for the betterment of industry. At the break I produced copies of the *Militant* that carried these stories for those attending the weekend school to read. The district secretary pulled me on one side and said that it was wrong of me to embarrass the lecturer like this: 'We are here to learn from him.'

After the break we had a very lively discussion. At the end of the first day I told our lecturer that I was looking forward to tomorrow's session. Our educator approached the working class in the Soviet Union in the same subjective impressionist way. I remember him clearly saying you have to believe what you see. In the Soviet Union and the Eastern Bloc you had a regime that had such a grip on the working class that it would never again be able to defend itself. All protest and strike action was now out of the question. My contribution was basically to say that the history of the struggle of the working class throughout the world showed that it had strength so great that it would rise against its oppressors. And that included the Soviet bloc. This school took place before the Twentieth Congress of the Communist Party of the Soviet Union at which Krushchev's speech denounced Stalin, and before Poznan and the Hungarian uprising. Following these events I tried to contact the lecturer without success. In retrospect I think my reason for wanting to contact him was for subjective reasons. I just wanted to say 'I told you so'. I certainly went out of my way to remind the Communist Party members of the discussion at the school. The only defence they could put up at the school was: 'It's all lies. It's Western imperialist propaganda.'

One hot sunny day I suggested to Ray and Paula that we pop up to the local for a pint. A couple of friends of mine that worked at the Temple Newsam pit were in there. A family member of theirs, some long lost uncle or something, was there from America and had looked them up. We drank our first pint listening to him telling everyone how stupid we all must be to fall for the idea of 'communistic medicine'. On top of that he found out that he had two relatives working in a communistic coal mine. He was a real loud mouth. His family was extremely embarrassed. Then he started on the trade unions. The turning point was when after all this he said, 'Why don't you two lads come back to America with me? It's the land of the free.' I did try to be nice to him and explain to him the benefits of the National Health Service and other socialist principles. I then excused myself and went home to get myself some facts on the question of freedom in the USA. I was soon back and he was still raving on. I outlined to him some of the recent events in America, giving dates and places where the state had tried to force freedom on to workers by using armed troops and police. He was not pleased. 'Just who are you boy?' I told him that I was the Labour Party candidate in the election that was just taking place. 'And where do you get this information from?' With that I pulled out a copy of the *Militant.* He obviously recognised the paper and became very angry. With that he said, 'I have travelled all this way and the first pub I go in I meet a *Trot*!' At this point the landlord suggested that it would be a good idea to drink up and go.

I cannot speak for everyone in the Group, but in 1954-1955, I thought that Trotskyism had the answers. I could support the Bolshevik revolution and speak of Lenin and Trotsky in the same breath, support the gains of the Russian Revolution while denouncing Stalin at the same time. We were in a position that made it possible to defend the Soviet Union from a principled position. But in retrospect I feel now that being a Trotskyist made it possible for me to be a communist without having to embrace the stigma of Stalinism. Did we embrace this as a kind of protective ring around us, which was at the same time preventing us from getting out? There were exceptions when we felt that we were on safe ground, such as 1956, when it was possible for us to step outside.

Following the closing down of the *Socialist Outlook* (our paper at this time) we worked through the columns of the Bevanite paper *Tribune*. This paper was no stranger to me as I had been an avid reader for about three years before joining the Group. In fact it was through reading an ad in *Tribune* that I became aware of the existence of *Keep Left*, the Group's paper inside the Labour Party. This paper went from being a duplicated sheet to a printed broadsheet. In the 1960s it became very influential in the youth sections, which scared the living daylights out of the Labour Party. Because of this the Labour Party decided to produce its own youth paper, *Advance*, to counter the popularity of *Keep Left*.

A prize was to be presented at the annual conference to the Young Socialist branch with the largest circulation. The winning branch was duly called to the platform to receive their prize and accolades from the Labour Party leadership. The secretary of the branch was asked to explain for the benefit of all the other youth branches how they were able to have such a large circulation. To rapturous applause and laughter he told them that they put a copy of *Advance* into every *Keep Left* sold. A few years later we won a majority of seats on the national committee of the Young Socialists. But I will leave that campaign and the work of the Labour Party dirty tricks' department for later.

In 1955 we were still working hard in the Labour Party. Wherever it was possible we took on tasks of being ward secretaries, youth officers (I held this post in the East Leeds constituency), local council candidates, election agents, etc. The most outstanding success in Leeds was when one of our members, Ron Sedler, with Mary Archer as his agent, took the Harehills ward seat from the Tories, who had held it for years. We had our own well-thought-out policies with housing and rents the main plank in the platform. Both council and private landlords were targeted. Halls were filled for public meetings – unheard of in other wards. The Tories circulated a leaflet attacking Ron and Mary and the Harehills ward Labour Party, saying that Ron was not a proper Labour Party candidate. They called on the Labour Party to expel him and close the ward. No doubt the Labour Party would have liked to do this but it was not that easy in those days. The Labour Party election victory had been a resounding success and left the bureaucrats very angry and embarrassed. We continued our work, increasing our delegates to Labour Party constituencies and the Leeds City Labour Party. We also made a lot of progress getting candidates from trade union branches and the Labour Party to the Leeds Trades Union Council.

Then came the huge events of 1956, a year to remember: the Suez Canal crisis, Khrushchev's speech at the Communist Party of the Soviet Union Twentieth Congress denouncing Stalin, and then the sending in of Soviet troops and tanks against the Hungarian workers.

Our activity around the Suez crisis was to defend the right of Egypt to nationalise the canal. It was easy to get resolutions passed throughout the labour movement opposing the invasion by Britain in the Canal Zone. There was a Conservative government with Eden as the prime minister. But there were always those who opposed the invasion but did not support the nationalisation of the canal. We got the arguments 'we built it so it is ours' and 'the Arabs will not be able to administer it properly'.

The Labour Party called for demonstrations throughout Britain. These were to be held on a Sunday. On the Saturday we sold *Tribune* in Briggate and campaigned for the Leeds demonstration. On this particular weekend I had been invited on the Saturday to the wedding of friends of mine, Danny Keneally, the son of a Leeds councillor, and Helen Murray, also the daughter of a Leeds councillor and Hugh Gaitskell's election agent. Danny and Helen had arranged the seating so that a Communist Party friend of his and I were to sit on either side of Hugh Gaitskell, the leader of Her Majesty's loyal opposition. Danny was to make some comment about this during his speech. He was unable to do this as neither Gaitskell nor I could attend because of the crisis. I called into the register office to see them and give them their gift. Both of Helen's parents were very angry that I had put politics before the wedding. Not with Gaitskell: me.

After the reception Danny and Helen came to Briggate, where we were campaigning, to give us their support. Then off they went for their honeymoon, which started with taking part in the London demonstration. All our contingents throughout Britain carried placards opposing the war and supporting the nationalisation of the canal.

It was a cold February evening. I was walking along Vicar Lane, Leeds when passing the market entrance I spotted the placard of a newspaper vendor of the *Yorkshire Evening Post*. It read 'Khrushchev denounces Stalin in secret speech'. I must have said something out loud as a couple of passers by thought that I was talking to them. Khrushchev had raised the question of opponents of Stalin being executed, tortured, sent to labour camps or simply disappearing. To question the infamous Moscow Trials resulted in arrest or worse.

When we had raised these questions previously with Communist Party members we always understood the betrayals of Stalin. We were not anti-Soviets opposing Stalin; we were communists opposing the betrayals of the Stalinist bureaucracy and their representatives in the world's Communist Parties. But as far as they were concerned the truth always came from the Communist Party of the Soviet Union and in turn was passed on to the membership. Within two hours of seeing the placard I was at a meeting of the Leeds branch called for the sole purpose of discussing this issue. I knew from previous discussions with John and Mary Archer and Lance Lake just how difficult it had been for Trotskyists before and during the war, physically being thrown out of meetings and branded as fascists by the Communist Party and their many fellow travellers in the Labour Party. The CP judged you by your attitude to the line that came out of the Kremlin.

The three of them had waited a long time for a break like this so it was understandable that they were a little excited at the news. But the two who were sitting on the edge of their seats just aching for clocking-on time the following morning were John Walls, AEU (engineering union) convenor of stewards at George Mann's factory, and me from John Barran's clothing factory. Jack Gale was in a similar position, as there were two Communist Party teachers at the school where he taught. We were strongly advised not to go charging in shouting 'I told you so'. We had to remember that this particular discussion was going to be around for a very long time. We had a certain knowledge of the origins of Stalinism and the history of the Russian Revolution. In addition to this we knew what the CP members had been lied to about – the communist opposition to the Stalinist regime and the crimes of Stalin. The work that we had already done in the YCL and CP and the contacts that we had already made would give us a good start for future developments. So we went into our places of work knowing that we had to keep calm and let things unfold and not be pushy. Difficult, but discipline prevailed.

A few days before I had loaned a CP fellow traveller my copy of Lenin's *Testament*. In this Lenin warns against Stalin and writes in favour of Trotsky. The CP line had always been that this was a forgery. But now, as well as the other revelations, Khrushchev admitted the testament's authenticity.

I arrived at work, went into the cutting room, clocked on, went to my bench, folded up my coat in its cover and put it under my bench. I can see all this as though it was yesterday. Les Dixon as usual had brought in the *Daily Worker* and had left mine on the bench. I started to read it. There were five or so CP members within earshot of me and others were scattered around the room. The bell went for us to start work. Two or three minutes had passed when the CP supporter to whom I had lent the pamphlet turned round and speaking directly to Stan Hives, one of the leading CP members in the factory, said: 'So this is not a fake after all!' Silence. Then Peter Jackson, a YCL member known to Vince, came up to Hives and asked him if this meant that Khrushchev was a Trotskyist. Then the fellow traveller said out loud that Norman had been saying these things about Stalin for the past two years: 'I now accept that he is right. You [Hives] said that it was all anti-communist and anti-Soviet propaganda and all lies. What do you think now?'

With that, the foreman Bill Long got up from his desk and left the room. I overheard Les Dixon, a CP member, ask what the hell was going on. I suggested that we should have a debate in the canteen at dinnertime; the word soon got around. I was going to have to be very careful to separate myself from those who were simply anti-communist and would simply poke fun at the CP members. There would obviously be many seriously worried about events but who would still have loyalty to the Party. These could well be the best contacts to make. I wasn't sure that a discussion would actually take place, thinking that the Communist Party members would want to have a discussion among themselves first. After all, this was a huge question for them and it was only the previous evening that the story had hit the streets.

During the morning I had been thinking about how to approach the discussion and when the debate did happen, I had a few ideas prepared. The first thing to remember was that those who had joined the CP had done so to achieve communism. I gave my support to the 1917 revolution and made sure that it was understood that I opposed the Stalinist regime because it persecuted the countless thousands who had made the revolution possible and that Stalin, to defend his position of power, was prepared to sell out the international working class. At this point I reminded everyone of the way the CP had sold out our fight for a wage increase in our industry. The only defence Hives could put up was that I was an ultra-left and was trying to sound more communist than the Communist Party. They had very little to say in the party's defence. Frank Stockdale, CP member and deputy shop steward, said that we had very little time and that this was not a yes-or-no issue. I agreed and suggested that we should continue later and that they would have a better idea what to say after the Yorkshire Area meeting of the CP the following weekend. This had the desired effect: how come he knows before us? Stan Hives looked very uncomfortable so I added: 'Maybe he doesn't know about it yet.'

Writing this is like getting an instant playback. I even remember that I was so keyed up that I forgot to put my coat on and had to borrow a pen from Gilbert Taylor.

We never did have another discussion; it was a case of taking

At my bench in the cutting room at John Barran's

every possible chance that came our way to have discussions with anyone. We had acquired a list of CP members in the Leeds area and we toured all over knocking on doors, selling copies of the Twentieth Congress speech and hoping for a chance to talk. I worked in partnership with Jack Gale. We got a lot of discussion but we also got doors slammed in our face. We agreed that a slammed door did not always mean absolute hostility but might be simple party loyalty. In some cases this proved to be correct. On top of all that was happening in the CP, we had been able to gain massive support at the YCL conference for the abolition of conscription to the armed forces as opposed to cutting it to twelve months.

Over the next months we continued with the pressure by being regular visitors to wherever Communist Party members gathered, mainly the CP headquarters at Westminster Buildings and the Trades Council Club in Upper Fountain Street. We used the contacts we had to influence the discussions in the Communist Party branches. Then it filtered through from King Street, the CP national headquarters, that the recent developments had been as a result of the intellectuals having too much influence, making it possible to keep the truth away from the membership. 'Mistakes have been made,' was the general cry, 'We will have a thorough examination of the facts and make sure that these mistakes don't ever appear again.' To reinforce this a debate appeared between Emile Burns and R Palme Dutt in the *World News and Views* about relations between the leadership and the membership. I was given a copy and was told the party was now getting to grips with the real problems that had been responsible for the contents of the Twentieth Congress speech.

CP branches were having regular meetings on this question. The members appeared more settled and some were more prepared to discuss. They felt more confident because they thought they had the answers to our questions. We were insisting that what had been revealed at the Twentieth Congress was only the beginning. The objective situation that was behind the speech would continue to create even more and bigger crises. As part of their re-vitalisation plan a Yorkshire rally was called in the lecture hall of the museum. As this was also a public meeting it was easy for us to get tickets. We felt very important as we were allocated our own personal stewards.

The YCL choir treated us to a few songs before the meeting got under way. The most important speaker of the night was to be Willie Gallagher, the veteran Scottish communist and working-class fighter. Years before I had read his books *Rise Like Lions* and *Revolt on the Clyde*. I was impressed. When he had finished speaking Jack Gale asked him what had happened to a comrade of his, Rose Cohen, who had vanished while living in the Soviet Union. Bert Ramelson intervened and said that type of question was not in keeping with the rally. I am sure that Willie was relieved at not having to comment on the question. I said that maybe it was just one of those mistakes that had been made. It is said that she had 'opened her mouth too much'. She had been a very close friend of Harry Pollitt, general secretary of the Communist Party at the time. In 1937 when Rose Cohen was being purged Pollitt intervened on her behalf very strongly, making him very unpopular. Rose Cohen was never seen again.

The situation in the Labour Party was changing. The Communist

Party cardholders and supporters in the Labour Party were moving closer to the right wing of the party, making their peace and becoming anti-communists. Some even became local councillors. A few became MPs. This was repeated all over Britain. This tendency grew following the Hungarian uprising. At the same time we were gaining more and more respect because of our principled opposition to the Communist Party and the Labour Party.

In October 1956, just eight months after exposing the crimes of Stalin, Khrushchev sent in the tanks against the Hungarian workers. The Communist Party was in a state of shock following this. The immediate response from the CP was that that MI5, the CIA and the fascists had stirred up the Hungarian workers to rise against the communist state. They were desperate for guidance from the leadership. Once again there were intense discussions taking place. The worker comrades in the CP were horrified. When strikes took place in Britain the media always worked on the lines that the strikers had been worked up by communist agitators. We all know that workers will not simply strike because they are told to. There have to be conditions prevailing to get the workers angry to respond to leadership. These criteria also applied to the workers' uprising in Hungary. News was filtering through not only from the media but also through working-class channels that workers' councils and a central committee were being set up in Budapest. The theory that it was a fascist-led uprising was blown out of the water. Reports came through of demands for ending the secret police, for workers' control in industry, the right to elect management in industry, and above all for the defence of the nationalised relations that existed in Hungary. These demands and many more were in the resolution passed at the central workers' council in Budapest. This was no right-wing coup!

The CP was devastated and it was hitting the worker members very hard indeed. They were not going to be bought off with the line that this was because of some mistake made by the intellectuals. This was tanks against the working class. To try and hold the situation the membership was asked to be patient as they were sending the *Daily Worker* journalist Peter Fryer to Budapest to get the real facts of the situation. Peter Fryer did go to Budapest, but the *Daily Worker* refused to print the reports that he sent back about what he witnessed and what his enquiries uncovered. This was like throwing petrol on the flames. All over Britain members were refusing to do their *Daily Worker* deliveries; one was Frank Stockdale, a leading member in my factory. Albert Field, who had the biggest *Daily Worker* round in Yorkshire in the mining area of Castleford, also refused. Albert was a very dedicated communist and did not hesitate to take up the fight against the CP leadership. From experience I knew that he drove comrades all over Yorkshire and further afield. He collaborated very closely with Cliff Slaughter in going around Yorkshire talking to and organising Communist Party members against the CP leadership. Albert was very much a free spirit; he had a van and found work wherever he could.

One evening Albert drove a sales team around the Castleford area. Halfway through the sale he left us to go and buy some scrap metal. When he returned we had finished off the sale. He told us that on the way home he had another call to make. We could hear the scrap metal being unloaded and after about five minutes he got back into the cab and gave me a fist-full of pound notes. I said that was a bit of good work, buy and sell in the same evening. Yes, he said, especially since it was bought at the front gate of a factory and sold back to them at the back gate. He pushed his cap further up his head and grinned from ear to ear.

On his arrival back in England Peter Fryer was in great demand to speak at large meetings of the Communist Party. Leeds was no exception. The Leeds Trades Hall was booked and, as expected, it was packed. These meetings widened the rifts that were already in evidence in the CP.

In Leeds, with the work and contacts that we already been able to make in the CP and YCL, especially in the period following our stroke of luck with the overheard telephone conversation, the Group decided that we should take the discussion into the wider labour movement. I was to move a resolution in my trade union branch with the intention of sending it to Labour Party sections, but more importantly to the Leeds Trades Council. It was here that the Leeds trades union movement was represented at its monthly meetings. The Communist Party had a very large delegation from union branches. The main points of my resolution were opposition to the tanks being brought in against the workers, and a list of the points made by the Budapest central strike committee.

The CP was very busy preparing for this meeting of the Trades Council. A meeting of Leeds members was called where tactics were discussed and a line thrashed out. No mock discussion between Burns and Dutt would satisfy the members this time. We were told of their line of attack by our contacts who were at the meeting. It was to be on two fronts: 1. Western intervention had been the cause of the growing opposition to the Soviet Union and the workers' unrest. Any arms that the workers had been able to acquire had been provided by Western imperialism, as opposed to arms being provided by dissident groups in the army. 2. All the opposition to the tanks being sent in was being encouraged by right-wing reactionary forces. Anti-communists were using the situation to attack the Soviet Union. The Soviet Union had to be defended.

Ramelson told the delegates that the right wing and Catholic Action would support my resolution. All communists and supporters had to close ranks and defeat Harding's reactionary and anti-communist resolution.

When we were told of these decisions it confirmed the points that we had agreed should be made:

1. Defence of the Hungarian workers and their property relations;
2. Defence of the Soviet Union;
3. Defence of the Bolshevik revolution of 1917; and
4. Support for workers in struggle all over the world.

I thought that points three and four would help to push the right wing into supporting Ramelson. This was a situation where political principle was more important than simply winning the vote. I had met with Jack Gale, John Walls and John Archer to go over my speech and the points that I was to make.

I was very nervous as I went into the Trades Hall that Wednesday night. In all modesty I did feel that I was defending all those millions who had been slaughtered by the Stalinists and capitalists alike. Ramelson was the most capable man in the party and a very dominant figure. John Walls was already there at our usual table.

The hall slowly filled; it became obvious that this was going to be the biggest Trades Council meeting for a very long time. Before the meeting started Bert Ramelson came over to me and asked if for the sake of unity I would accept his amendment. It simply said that we were all worried about the events in Hungary and that an international delegation should be sent to try and resolve the situation. This I rejected out of hand. It made me more determined. I realised that he was a very worried man and I started to feel more relaxed.

The meeting started under the chair of Councillor Malwyn Jones so I knew that I would get a fair crack of the whip. When we had reached the appropriate place on the agenda he called on Brother Harding to move the resolution. John gave me words of encouragement. I had ten minutes to make my points. I moved the resolution and covered all my points. John seconded. The main attack, as expected, came from Ramelson. He was very agitated and concentrated on the point that the events were being orchestrated by world imperialism and that the Soviet Union had intervened to counter the danger of fascism. He pointed at me from the other side of the room and said: 'This is something you failed to mention.'

I was asked to reply to the discussion. I finished by addressing my closing remarks to all of the delegates: 'I don't want any fake tears for the Hungarian workers. A vote for the resolution is a vote for the international solidarity of all those workers who are in struggle. It is a vote defending the right of the workers in Russia to have their revolution in 1917, as it is the right of the Hungarian workers to fight against Stalinist domination.'

Tellers were elected, the vote taken and the resolution narrowly defeated. The vote was interesting. Sufficient CP members voted for the resolution to cause the CP concern. How many members voted against out of loyalty to the Party is hard to say. But the right wing voted for Ramelson, encouraged by the 'do you want fascism in Europe again' line, and of course because they were against the working class fighting for their rights. I knew that Ramelson would have been watching to see who voted for and who against. I shouted across the room: 'Who got the right-wing votes, then?'

The following days a winter of discontent descended on the

Communist Party and members were showing more and more displeasure in the leadership The CP once again tried to lay the blame at the feet of the intellectuals. Hives spoke in a very hostile manner, saying: 'What do those intellectuals at the university understand about the problems of the working class?'

1957 was to be another very eventful year with many expulsions and resignations from the Communist Party.

In the first half of July 1957 the Labour Party organised a youth rally in Hyde Park (they never learn). They had arranged for quite a large contingent from Sweden to attend. Because Hyde Park is a royal park we were not allowed to sell or give away literature. This of course would suit the Labour Party as it meant that we could not sell *Keep Left*. As always it was left to the *Keep Left* Young Socialists to bring the contingents that would swell the rally. It upset the Labour Party when they found out that we had translated our statement that was in *Keep Left* into Swedish. A team was to give these out to the Swedish contingent. While doing this Jack Gale and I were arrested but released when we promised not to give any more out. The promise meant nothing as we had run out of leaflets anyway.

That evening a number of us volunteered to make some placards for a picket, at Vivienne Mendelson's flat. It was here that I was introduced to a young man by the name of Royston (Roy) Bull. He had recently made himself known to the Young Socialists in London. He appeared to be keen and said that he was coming to Leeds university at the start of the term and that he would like to stay in touch. I took many steps to make contact with him without any success. There was no sign of Roy Bull. Then one day in the factory Hives told the members that at last there was someone at the university whom the workers could trust and who would be speaking to the branch at the weekend. The name of this CP representative was Roy Bull, and he was a venom-spitting anti-Trotskyist. There was many a confrontation with him. On one occasion he was present on the barge that the students had on the river Aire. There was a very heated discussion and Cliff Slaughter, who had now joined us, offered to baptise him in the river. He was strongly advised to leave. I was in no doubt that he was the most venomous anti-Trotskyist that I had ever met. I can't remember when he disappeared from the scene altogether.

Fifteen or so years later I was about to leave the Workers Revolutionary Party Centre in London when in came one of our journalists, Stephen Johns (Hammond), closely followed by Roy Bull. Party leader Gerry Healy took them into his office. I hung around and when they had left I went in to see Healy and told him what I knew of Bull and said that I did not trust him. Bull had told Healy that he been in the Communist Party, had gone to Moscow, become disillusioned and returned to England and taken a job with the paper the *Scotsman* in the London office. Then, through the journalists' union branch, he had met Johns, who in turn introduced him to our paper, the *Workers Press*. I am of the opinion that Bull vanished from the university and went to Moscow where he received some kind of special training – and came back and found his way into our paper. I did in fact tell Bull that I did not trust him. Not without cause, I might add. Healy later said that he understood why I did not trust Bull, but that I had to give him a chance.

Now back to 1957. The factory management had obviously noted that the Communist Party position in the factory had been weakened, so they decided to put a ban on the *Daily Worker* being brought into the factory. When this decision was relayed to the factory committee we immediately called for a meeting in the canteen. I approached Hives and said that I would move a resolution saying that the *Daily Worker* would continue to be brought into the factory as this was a democratic right. I suggested that this would be better than asking the management to withdraw the ban. They agreed. The resolution was passed. It was also agreed that we would not officially tell the management of the decision and simply continue bringing the *Daily Worker* into the factory. It did cause a bit of confusion in a few people's minds that I had defended the Communist Party in this way, after all that they were saying about me. I simply told them that it was a case of working-class solidarity.

Jack and I were out every night possible with our new large format *Labour Review,* taking every opportunity to visit anyone we thought would talk to us. On one occasion I was travelling home to Cross Gates on the tram when one of the two men on the seat behind me said, 'It will be terrible if we have to admit that John Archer has been right all the time.' When they got off the tram I followed them. They went down Harehills Lane and turned into a street just past the Hillcrest cinema. I noted the street, went home and arranged for a canvass of the street with *Labour Review*. This issue had a yellow cover and in large black letters on the front cover were the words 'The Moscow Trials'. The two CP members were located. We did have a discussion but they said that they were going to stay loyal to the Party. When in the future we called to see them we never received a hostile reception. Later in the year we received an invitation to send someone to speak to the Harehills branch of the Communist Party. Barbara Slaughter, one of those who had recently left the CP, went. Discussion forums where dissident CP members and ex-members along with other groups in the labour movement could discuss the questions that had arisen over the last period had sprung up all over Britain.

The popularity of the forums led to a conference being organised at Wortley Hall near Sheffield on the weekend of 27-28 April 1957. Representing the Group were G Healy, Ellis Hillman, Jack Gale and me. There were others who were our comrades there but for the time being they were still in the CP. The session was opened by Professor Hyman Levy. This was a very important conference where many of those present took their first step to take different political positions. I will list those that spoke in the debate, taken from issue No.1 of the *Newsletter*, 10 May 1957, edited by Peter Fryer:

G Healy, Jack Gale, Mercia Emmerson, Jim Roach, Ken Coates, Raya Levin, Peter Worsley, Tom Kaiser, Adrian Gaster, John Daniels, Dick Goss, Alan Lamond, H Kendall, Bert Wynn, Jack Britze, Harold Silver, Eric Heffer, John Saville, Max Hamilton, Jerry Dawson, T Cowan, Harold Ruben, Jeff Barker, John St John, David Wood, John Fairhead, Martin Flannery, Pauline Harrison, Joe Young, Lawrence Daly, Peter Fryer, Roydon Harrison, Ralph Samuel, Edward Thompson, Raymond Challinor, Paddy MacMahon, Johnnie McLoughlin, Michael Segal.

I returned to Leeds knowing that I had heard and met many exceptional people.

THE NEWSLETTER

Edited by Peter Fryer, 1 Seymour Terrace, London, SE 20. Subscription 10s for 12 issues, post free.

a service to socialists

Vol. 1, No. 1 May 10, 1957

COMMENTARY

As was made clear in the circular announcing its publication. THE NEWSLETTER has no sectional axe to grind. Its main purpose is to provide socialists with news and documents which they will not find adequately treated elsewhere. It is addressed in the first instance to what a speaker at the Wortley Hall conference of the Socialist Forum movement called 'anti-Stalinist Marxists': that is to say, those who have left the Communist Party since the Twentieth Congress of the CPSU; the oppositionists who are remaining inside that party to fight; and the large number of socialists inside and outside the Labour Party who have many fundamental aims in common with these Marxists.

This first issue gives particular prominence to two things: the situation in the Communist Party since its recent Congress; and the Wortley Hall conference. It does so because the decisions that communists are taking in these first few post-Congress weeks, and the deliberations of such gatherings as Wortley Hall, are shaping the future of the Marxist movement in Britain for years to come.

THE NEWSLETTER has no intention of becoming obsessed by the crisis within the Communist Party, now deeper than ever. But the resignation of such a lifelong militant as Don Renton is immensely important. Here is the answer to the sneers about 'spineless intellectuals' who have 'lost their nerve'. Renton is a man of exemplary courage, zeal and devotion to principle. What have Gollan and Pollitt to say to this man who has walked out of the party in disgust, not because he has ceased to be a communist, but *because he remains a communist*? Renton has quit because the leadership evaded and will continue to evade all the questions of principle which the Congress ought to have faced. As long as these leaders continue with the old methods and policies those who are true to principle, true to their life-work, true to their records of service to the working-class movement, will stream out of the party. This is the lesson that Congress report-back meetings all over the country are driving home.

★

THE question arises: what are the ex-members to do? It is not THE NEWSLETTER's job to answer this question for them. But as well as reporting what they *are* in fact doing, our columns are open to an exchange of views. Can a genuine communist movement be built in Britain? What part have the Forums, these arenas of lively controversy, to play? Should we join the Labour Party? Or should we set up something new? These are the questions that readers and readers-to-be are discussing. Their letters will be welcome.

WHY I LEFT THE COMMUNIST PARTY

by Don Renton

(who was described by Harry Pollitt in 1954 as 'a fine example to all of us by his devotion to the cause of Communism' and by Wal Hannington as 'a fearless fighter for the working class and a most sincere and loyal member of our party'.)

SIX MONTHS before the Khrushchev revelations at the Twentieth Congress I raised the issue of the absence of collective leadership in the CPSU at a meeting of the Scottish secretariat.

I argued that the CPSU could not be all we had cracked it up to be if Khrushchev's account of how the breach with Yugoslavia took place was true.

I challenged the trials in Eastern Europe, declaring that Khrushchev's account of Beria's activities brought under suspicion the 'evidence' under which Communists were persecuted. Later Rajk, Kostov, Gomulka and others were 'rehabilitated'.

No discussion took place in the party. I came to the conclusion that our party leaders knew what had been going on both in the USSR and Eastern Europe, but deliberately concealed the facts from the membership.

At the recent party congress I was shown letters from Pat Dooley about Czechoslovakia, written several years ago.

In both this case and that of Dr. Edith Bone I am convinced that the party Centre knew what was happening—but they refused to act.

They say they were shocked by Khrushchev's revelations. I believe them. They were shocked that Khrushchev let the cat out of the bag—but that the cat had been kept in the bag did not concern them.

I remain loyal to the principles which brought me into the party. I cannot be 'loyal' to leaders who have abandoned those principles.

Don Renton's career

Don Renton joined the Labour Party when he was fourteen and the Communist Party when he was seventeen—28 years ago. He served in the British Battalion of the International Brigade, was wounded at Jarama, and spent months in Franco's prisons.

Sentenced to 30 years' imprisonment, he was rescued by an exchange of prisoners.

'Spain,' he says, 'was only an incident, and a brief one, in my career, with nothing heroic about it. Other and better comrades died in the hands of the fascists, and what is worse in the hands of brother communists in the Soviet Union and Eastern Europe.'

In London in the late thirties Renton took part with J. B. S. Haldane in dangerous breathing-apparatus tests after the Thetis disaster, and worked untiringly as a leader of the unemployed. With them he took part in lie-down demonstra-

(continued on page two)

NEXT WEEK'S NEWSLETTER . . .

. . . will contain the first instalments of two important series:

Talks with Soviet Leaders on the Jewish Question by J. B Salsberg. These famous articles, now to appear for the first time in any British publication, have been specially translated from the Yiddish for The Newsletter.

The Last Two Years in Poland by Stanislaw Kowalski, our Warsaw correspondent. Kowalski is a young Polish journalist who has been in the thick of the struggle for democratization.

First issue of The Newsletter, *May 1957*

In the first edition of the *Newsletter* there is a letter from Don Renton explaining why he left the Communist Party. He had joined it in 1929, fought in Spain with the International Brigade, and spent some time in Franco's prisons before becoming full-time organiser in Edinburgh. He left because the CP no longer represented the principles for which he joined. There were hundreds of similar cases.

In retrospect there were sectarian attitudes within our group. Although I didn't recognise it, this revealed itself once when I was staying at Bert Karpin's house during a weekend northern aggregate.

I had been outlining our work in Leeds with the YCL and CP following the Twentieth Congress speech and Hungary. He was putting coal on the fire at the time. He put down the coalscuttle and said, 'I don't know why you bother. They're all Stalinists.' At the Sunday morning session of the aggregate I let it be known that I was opposed to this line of thought. Karpin in his defence just said that maybe it was possible to recruit one or two. He was not challenged in any way.

For my holidays I used to have one week at our annual camp and the second week helping in the printshop. Formerly a stable, it was down a cobbled alley off Venn Street, behind Clapham High Street. The entrance was through two big metal green doors and then another very solid door into a narrow white-washed passage.

In the first room on the left you would see Tony Banda working at his compositor's workbench. Coming out you would hear the jingling and clanking sound of the hot-metal Linotype machine. Under the stairs to the store room was what passed as an office — just enough room for a small table, with a light bulb hanging from the steps. On the table was a telephone and just enough room for someone to work. Anyone going in or out of the comp room had to squeeze past whoever was sitting there. The passage opened out into the printing area with a Heidelberg flatbed printing press. There was just enough room to walk round the press but down the side, directly opposite the passage, there was enough room for a bench where three or four comrades could sit and work, collating pages of a book and such like. At the far end was another door that led down a short open passage, with a door to the flat upstairs. In later years I 'lived' in one of the rooms. It was announced in one *Newsletter* that the following edition would be smaller because of a construction change in Plough Press: a door between the comp room and the printing area. A small thing, but it made things easier.

I spent many a long day and night happily working at the bench on whatever was being printed at the time and talking to my comrades The high point of the night would be when we went out and had a sausage sandwich at the stall in Venn Street.

On the first weekend in August 1957 I was at this bench, from where you could see directly down the passage. The doorbell rang, someone answered the door, and in walked a very smartly dressed man. I was introduced to Harry Constable. Gerry Healy, who was in the printshop at the time, said: 'Come in, Harry, we have been waiting for you.' A discussion took place around the need for action on the London docks in support of the strike taking place at Covent Garden Market at the time. Mike Banda was to take the car and go with Harry to visit other dockers' leaders. Healy said: 'Go with them, Norman, you'll find it an experience'. We met a number of leaders from the different docks.

The following morning, at 05.00 hours, I went with Ted Knight, Vivienne Mendelson and others to join the picket at Covent Garden. The others had been on the picket line before but this was my first morning. Later Ted and I went to the Transport and General Workers' Union office to see the Covent Garden branch secretary Bernie Holland and arrange for Harry to come and see him and the strike committee that morning. They were delighted at the thought of support from the London docks.

When Harry arrived we went to the union office. Bernie was already there, the table was cleared of newspapers and off-cuts from the printshop were laid out as notepaper on the table. Picket leaders and the strike committee were sent for and trays with mugs of tea were brought in. It was agreed that Ted and I could stay. Bernie outlined the history of the strike and agreed that it was now time to get support from other sections of workers. Harry concentrated on gathering as many facts about the strike as possible. He told the committee that he would be back in touch with them later in the day. The room emptied, the men went back to their posts, and the windows were opened to let out the haze of smoke.

By mid-afternoon I was in the strike office getting details for a leaflet that was to be duplicated that evening for the next morning's picket. The telephone rang. Bernie answered and said something like 'great news'. Then he told a steward to get round the pickets and tell them that Constable had got Tooley Street docks to refuse to handle fruit and veg in support of the market men. This was a great boost for the pickets and set off a chain of support around the docks. In the *Newsletter* of 17 August 1957 Hugh Scannell (West

India Docks) outlined the solidarity between the London dockers and the market men and any other sections of workers who found themselves in struggle for wages and conditions of work. That was why the dockers' and stevedores' union, NASD (known as the Blue Union), was supporting the market men. London, Liverpool, Birkenhead, Manchester, and Hull docks had already declared their support for solidarity action. At Canary Wharf (London) a fruit ship had been declared black so the owners had sent the ship to Oslo, but no docker would handle it there either. All the way up to Leith dockers would not handle produce destined for Covent Garden.

The officials of the Transport and General Workers' Union and their closest friends in the Communist Party were completely discredited in the eyes of the strikers. One such official tried to weaken the will of the strikers because of a writ that the Covent Garden owners were taking out against the dockers. Tommy Walker, leader on Butler's Wharf, let it be known that the only document they were interested in was a union card and the obligation it imposed on trade unionists.

The 4,000 market men fighting to keep conditions that had been squeezed out of the employers over years were being betrayed at every turn by their leaders. National Secretary Frank Cousins, darling of the Communist Party, was sunning himself on holiday. Because the strike was unofficial they did not get a penny from the union. The bosses had prepared well for the strike and had a well-drilled army of scabs, mainly their clerical staff, even though young members of the Clerical and Administrative Workers' Union were there early every morning to dissuade their members from crossing the picket line. One of them, Vivienne Mendelson, spoke at the rally of market men and dockers in Trafalgar Square. She received a tremendous welcome and was applauded, especially when she said Cousins should have been there.

When he did come back from his holiday, Cousins spent a long time closeted with Mack (the knife), the bosses' leader. A recommendation for a return to work was plotted. Since the dockers had decided to return to work only when the market men went back, these two knew the strike had to be ended quickly. The number of dockers taking supportive action was increasing at a rate of 2,000 a day. Cousins addressed a meeting of the market men and persuaded them to accept the recommended offer by a small majority.

At a mass meeting of the strikers the press was banned but special dispensation was granted to the *Newsletter* so Ted and I were allowed to stay. Communist Party members protested and demanded that we should leave. The stewards defended us, saying we had earned the right to be there. Things looked as though they could turn nasty so we decided to leave. We did not want the meeting side-tracked. Harry arrived to speak as we were leaving. We explained the situation and he agreed with our decision. He had been up all night trying to put some backbone into Bernie Holland and the strike leadership. When the strikers understood the conditions of a return to work they voted by a large majority to continue the strike. I can only imagine what impression Harry made on them, dressed smartly, as always, in a suit. Cousins received applause, but Harry got a standing ovation.

However, when support was at its highest point the market men's union leaders finally convinced them to go back to work. Harry wrote a pamphlet, *Lessons of the Covent Garden Strike,* which I still have. It was also reproduced in the *Newsletter* of 24 August 1957.

Harry Constable earned the right to be referred to as a leader of leaders. He won great respect as a working-class fighter and played a part in every struggle on the London docks after 1945. In 1951 the Labour government charged him and six other dockers with conspiring to incite an illegal strike. London dockers Harry Constable, Albert Timothy, Edward Dickens, Joe Cowley and Liverpool dockers Robert Crosby, Joe Harrison and Bill Johnson were threatened with prison, but their release was met with widespread rejoicing. It had nationwide publicity and made an impression even in my clothing factory. Harry was respected as a working-class leader by many Communist Party members even though he was known to be a Trotskyist.

While writing this section I learned that Harry died in December 2000. He will always be remembered. Goodbye Comrade.

5

THE SOCIALIST LABOUR LEAGUE

The SLL (Socialist Labour League) was founded in 1959, and was a deliberate attempt to transform ourselves from the small circle – the Group – that we had been. The initial recruitment was enormous. Our willingness to take on the right wing and the trade union leadership attracted many to our ranks. A number of the contacts we had made organising the National Rank And File conference applied for membership, and since 1956 we had recruited a number of militants from the ranks of the Communist Party.

One such comrade was Brian Behan, brother of the author Brendan Behan and leader of many a struggle on the London building sites. In 1960 Brian Behan proposed that we should leave the Labour Party and launch ourselves as an open workers' party. We held a Yorkshire aggregate of all our members (as did all other areas) to discuss this question. Behan did have some support in the area, but the proposal for the open party was decisively rejected. But neither were we going to surrender the *Newsletter* and the SLL in order to snuggle up nice and cosy as a 'pressure group' in the Labour Party. We chose instead to take the fight to them. However those who supported the call for an open revolutionary party ended up diving into the deep end of the Labour Party pool and came up spluttering. It was really an example of how sectarianism and opportunism can come from the same source.

Over the next years we went on the offensive. We took on Gaitskell and Nye Bevan (who had completely gone over to the

Moscow line). Bevan said that 'we could not go into the negotiating chamber naked'. We fought for unilateral disarmament in the Labour Party and in the wider movement. The demand that Britain should unilaterally disarm grew in spite of the united opposition of the Labour Party, the trade union right wing and the Communist Party. It was a great day when at the Labour Party annual national conference at Scarborough, unilateral disarmament won the day. It was a very angry Right Hon Hugh Gaitskell who told the conference that he would 'fight, fight, and fight again against this decision'.

On the other hand we continued to defend the gains of the past struggles. We defended and used Clause Four of the Labour Party constitution, continuously struggling for socialist principles. Alongside we continued to participate in the struggles of the working class. Our activities brought a constant flow of new recruits into the Labour Party and the SLL. The bulk of these were youth who took up activity in the Labour Party wards and in some cases became ward officers. But the main activity was setting up Young Socialist branches throughout Britain. The Labour Party and the trade union bureaucracy were running scared of the success we were having. It must have appeared to them that we had tens of thousands of members because we were everywhere.

The youth we were recruiting were thrown into the fight in the Labour Party, not just to be used as election fodder but as political working-class fighters. The National Executive proscribed the Socialist Labour League, and soon after banned the *Newsletter*. The Labour Party bureaucrats all over Britain flexed their muscles and prepared to get rid of these annoying socialists from their ranks. In Leeds we were the first to suffer a concentrated attack. Leaving work one night I was making my way down Chorley Lane to catch a bus round the corner in Park Lane. Someone ahead of me had bought a paper from the seller at the corner of the street and was shouting up to me that I had been expelled from the Labour Party. Sure enough on the front page of the *Yorkshire Evening Post* was a banner headline saying 'Nine Leeds Labour Chiefs Expelled'. There were some photographs, mine among them.

Arriving home I spotted a car parked outside our garden gate and as I approached the driver got out and asked me if I was Norman

Harding. He told me that my parents would not let him into the house and that they had appeared a little nervous. I was not surprised as they had been told from many sources that I would be getting into trouble because of the company I was keeping. I told him that I would not make any statement until the nine of us had met to discuss the issue. He said he was an active member of the National Union of Journalists and assured me that he would only report what we told him. He gave me his telephone number, and I said that he would be contacted if we agreed to make any press statement. (He was true to his word and we were able to work with him many times over the years.)

When I got to the back door, Mum and Dad were there to meet me. They were worried because the paper had not made it clear why we had been expelled and, as Mum put it, 'People will think that you have been fiddling the funds'.

The expelled got together that night. They were John Archer, Mary Archer, Jack Gale, Celia Gale, Cliff Slaughter, Barbara Slaughter, John Walls, Ron Sedler, and Norman Harding. The Leeds Nine. Ron Sedler, a solicitor, explained that we had been expelled illegally. We had not been informed of any charges or given a chance to defend ourselves. This was an infringement of natural justice. An appropriate letter was sent to the Leeds Labour Party. The result was that we each received a telegram telling us we were no longer expelled. In the next post we received a letter laying down charges: being associated with a proscribed organisation, the Socialist Labour League, and selling the banned *Newsletter*. We were to answer these charges at the next City Party meeting. Each of us would make a statement and be allowed to have one person to speak in our defence. Tom Jackson (of the handlebar moustache) spoke in my defence. I was expelled and he went on to become General Secretary of the Post Office workers' union.

For two or three nights I slept with a notepad by the side of my bed. I would awake with some point or other, jot it down and go back to sleep. It was a Wednesday night when the 'trials' were due to take place. The night before I must have gone over my blasted speech a dozen times, then on the morning gone over it again. I donned my motorcycle gear and set off for work on my BSA

Bantam Major 149cc. I knew that I was focused on the meeting but I did not realise just how much. I pulled up at the kerb but did not get off the bike because when I looked around I realised that I had pulled up outside the Leeds Trades Hall. Instead of going straight down into Park Lane from the Headrow I had turned right into Upper Fountain Street and arrived for the meeting twelve hours early. Funny, but scary just the same.

We all made our speeches. I made points about fighting for the principles of socialism and defended Clause Four. I made the point that as the Conservatives had their representatives in the Labour Party, such as Mathews, why couldn't the socialists? The vote was taken on each of the accused. John Walls, an engineering shop steward, received the smallest vote for expulsion. This was after he had called the Labour Party leadership a load of rascals and traitors. He told them to get on with it and do their worst. Maybe the delegates were touched by his honesty. We were all expelled but later Ron Sedler applied to renew his membership. At a meeting where he was to be considered for re-admittance we organised a picket outside of about 30 YS members demanding that he should be let back in. He was readmitted.

The SLL and the *Newsletter* continued the work in the labour movement. Over this period everyone expelled was replaced by many, many more. Those who were expelled worked twice as hard as before. The Labour leaders had thought that by expelling our leadership their problems would be solved. They were so wrong. Young Socialist branches took on a new life; they were springing up like daffodils in the spring. The youth that were already in the Labour Party were tired of being envelope fillers and found a political voice in this fast-developing youth movement. Students from the colleges and universities moved around starting branches where none had existed before. From this activity the local Labour Parties were flooded with new, young and enthusiastic comrades. Our campaigns were against youth unemployment, the Tories, and the Vietnam War. The two main groups battling it out in the Young Socialists were the 'official' Labour Party around *Advance* and ours around *Keep Left*. It was soon obvious that we were steadily building a very influential part of the labour movement. The annual

East Leeds Young Socialists

conferences of the Young Socialists were beginning to experience a culture shock. Each year more and more delegates were young unemployed and other radicalised sections of the youth.

I had a Hillman Husky and every weekend I would take a team of youth out to the small towns around Leeds to recruit and start new branches. Many of our student comrades took on the responsibility of building and developing new branches. Comrade Guyton built a very large branch on a housing estate near Sheffield. On one occasion it organised a demonstration of a couple of hundred through the estate against youth unemployment.

The campaign around youth unemployment and the Conservative government did not go unnoticed. Harold Wilson, who was hoping to be the next prime minister, knew that these youth would not put on soft gloves if he moved in at Number 10. As you can imagine he was a very worried man. Then through the pages of *Keep Left* we moved up a gear and started to work with the intention taking the Young Socialists out of the hands of the Labour Party by winning all the regional seats of the national committee with one of our comrades as national secretary. That was one hell of a campaign. In or out of the Labour Party it was all hands on deck. Those of us who had been expelled had to work under cover with greater caution than ever and at the same time work harder.

The trades councils called a national demonstration and a lobby of parliament on the question of unemployment. *Keep Left* called for support. In Leeds we told the Trades Council to put us down for three coaches. The coaches were to make their last pick-up at the top of Morritt Avenue, Halton, so that the cars could be parked outside the Gales' and the Lakes' houses. Anyone who has been involved in organising transport and getting everyone to the transport on time will know how difficult a job that is. I had the job of making sure that everyone from the east Leeds area was shuttled over to the coaches from various points. We were to leave no later than midnight. For weeks our comrades had been working flat out to make this a success. It was one of those periods when I would go for days without seeing my parents, up in the morning to go to work and home long after they had retired for the night. I made my last trip with the Husky, put the passengers on to the coach, then went to park outside Jack Gale's. The next thing I knew I was being awakened by Comrade Parsons, an NUM (National Union of Mineworkers) comrade from Castleford. I had parked and immediately fallen asleep.

Lambeth Trades Council had invited Leeds, among others, to have breakfast in a hall just off Euston Road opposite St Pancras Station. This was a welcome respite before going to the assembly point. Bert Ramelson, the Communist Party Yorkshire Organiser, was seen tucking into his food. Cliff Slaughter went over to him and said, 'I hope the Trotskyist food does not choke you.'

I was told during breakfast that I was to be one of the speakers at the rally at Central Hall, Westminster after the lobby. I was sitting at a table with Kevin Fitzpatrick, Tricia Sorbie, Brenda Ingleby and other comrades from the university. I commented to them that I was feeling pretty exhausted. I said I thought that the way I felt I would be in no fit state by the time of the meeting. Brenda brought me a glass of water and a couple of pills. I don't know what they were but later I felt quite refreshed.

The demonstration was huge and attracted lots of attention from the onlookers, many of them tourists. At one stage I found myself walking alongside the Liverpool contingent when a dozen or more broke ranks and surrounded one of the onlookers. They had recognised one of the characters from an American TV series called *Wagon Train*. It was Wishbone the cook. He talked with them and put money into all of their tins. I gave him a leaflet for the rally. Before he turned to leave he said to me, 'What a shame, what a waste.' He was seen later outside parliament and at the rally.

Carrying banners and placards within a certain radius of parliament was banned. There was a snowball's chance in hell of this being observed. Thousands were milling about outside St Stephen's Gate. The approach roads were a mass of banners and chanting and cheering demonstrators. It was a most exhilarating sight. A Young Socialist climbed up the wall at St Stephen's Gate. When he had reached a respectable height there was a tremendous cheer from the vast crowd as he secured a red flag and copies of *Keep Left*. A window above opened and Barbara Castle stuck her head out, waving her Labour Party membership card and shouting, 'I am one of you'. She was invited to jump down and join us. She neither came out nor jumped down!

Remembering that I was to speak at the rally I found a spot on a wall to prepare my notes, a very inspiring spot among the banners and the constant barrage of demands being put on the Right Hon gents inside. The demonstration began to disperse as the time came for many to catch their transport. They did not move off as disorganised groups but as a demonstration with their banners held high. I made my way with other comrades to the Central Hall wondering how many would attend the rally. To fill this large hall would still only be a very small percentage of those attending the day's events. I made my way to the front and on to the stage. The only other speakers I can remember were Dave Finch (chair) and Liz Thompson, one of the Rand family, who along with their entire Young Communist branch joined us after the events of 1956.

Dave opened the meeting while I took stock of the audience. The hall was packed with people standing down the sides and along the back. Dave leaned over and told me to get ready as I was next. My notes were three headings with notes under each: 1. Agitate; 2. Blast the Tories; 3. Fight will continue under a Labour government. The rally was a huge success. Now we had to get back to Leeds, see everyone back home and hope to be able to go to work the following day. As I was leaving I was told that Healy wanted to see me. He said that he was going to do a speaking tour of the north of England and he wanted me to be the supporting speaker. He added that he was impressed by my work in Yorkshire. I took this to be a great compliment.

Once again we were able to extend our influence in the Young Socialists and strengthen our existing branches. Now the fight for control of the YS national movement was on. At the 1964 YS annual conference the main job was to make sure that we were strong enough in all the regions of Britain to win the nominations for representatives on the national committee. The Labour Party leaders were aware that they were in danger of losing their YS organisation. Wilson could not tolerate the thought that with Labour expected to win the next election there would be a youth movement prepared to take him on. He also knew that we had the experience, ability and enthusiasm to rally huge numbers of working-class youth, and we were gaining increasing support in the constituency Labour Parties. The dirty tricks department was determined to do all in its power to sabotage this conference. The big weekend came and the Friday night, and what a night it was. We had four coach pick-up points in Leeds. Supporters and members started at about 20.00 hours getting all the youth under various roofs ready for the next step of getting them to the coaches. As a precaution we had arranged for the coaches to arrive at the pick-up points an hour earlier than necessary and for all four areas to ring Jack's as soon as the coaches arrived. Jack and I were there to receive these messages. The news was the same from all four: no coaches. Jack rang the coach company's office and was told that a member of the YS had rung to change the pick-up points of two of the coaches. They told him where the new points were. The other two coaches turned up all right at the arranged places. We concentrated as many of our cars that we could on the old points and shuttled the youth over to the new pick-up points. We told expelled members to keep away from this operation, as we were sure that the Labour Party would be

Above is the march leaving Marble Arch. In front of the banner are YS National Committee Majority members (from l. to r.): Mike Farley, Dave Ashby (chairman), Sheila Torrance (vice-chairman) and Bob Hamilton. Below are some of the pensioners who joined the march.

Pensioners march to lobby Parliament

London, Thursday

HUNDREDS of old people demanding

by Newsletter reporting team

and Young Socialists from Liverpool, Wigan, Bolton and Manchester.

Twenty Young Socialists

The Newsletter*, 6 February 1965, reports the march*

watching very closely. Two coaches set off on time and the problem ones set off half an hour late.

We were successful in winning the vast majority of the regions and so had a majority on the national committee. Dave Ashby was elected as national secretary: we had done it. This we did at a time when the SLL was proscribed and the *Newsletter* banned and YS members could be and were expelled from the Labour Party for associating with expelled members. When future historians write up the history of the Labour Party this will be regarded as one of the biggest defeats suffered by the Labour Party (excluding general elections), and far greater than a defeat at their annual conference on some resolution or other. We had taken away their youth movement. But of course Wilson and his Labour Party leadership were not keen to be looking down the barrel of the YS cannon. At every opportunity they made attacks on the YS branches and the constituencies that they were associated with.

We kept up the pressure. One of the things we did was to organise a national demonstration and lobby of parliament in support of the demand for an increase in pensions. This was to be a combined demonstration of youth and senior citizens. During the build-up to this demonstration it became obvious that there was a strong bond between young and old. The youth looked after the pensioners on the coaches during the journey to London from all over Britain. This was not just our YS members but youth who had decided to go on the demonstration. It was the same kind of relationship that you find in families between grandparents and grandchildren. Although the length of the demo was only a short distance, transport had been arranged for anyone who could not walk the whole way. Even so the majority opted to walk. The youth, with the dress and hairstyles of the day that the media associated with 'trouble' and 'hooliganism', acted in a way that many of the onlookers found baffling. Many of the police walking at the side of the demonstration looked puzzled at the sight of pensioners being helped along by a youth on either arm.

On arriving at the St Stephen's entrance a queue was formed to go in and lobby the MPs. There was an attempt to only let in pensioners and exclude the youth. This was soon nipped in the bud.

Mrs Anderson led a number of irate pensioners to the door and kicked up such a fuss that they had to continue letting in the youth.

I wanted to get inside early to be around with others to keep an eye on things. The police on the door were quite keen to stop queue jumping. I asked Marty, an American student from Leeds, to go with me to the door and put on a deep American accent and explain that we were on a tourist schedule. It worked a treat and we were let in with a smile. I gathered a group of lobbyists and sent in a request card asking the Right Hon Denis Healey to come out and meet his constituents. The card was taken in by one of the liveried gentlemen. One youth said, 'Don't they wear funny clothes', much to the amusement of those who heard. The Right Hon finally appeared and went straight into attack mode – 'I will only speak to the OAPs and all you others can get out' – telling the OAPs that the 'others' were Trotskyists 'trying to take over your protest'. Healey was told in no uncertain terms by the pensioners that in that case they too were Trotskyists, because without the Young Socialists they would not be having this protest. 'Throw them out and you will have to throw us out first,' they said. The Right Hon soon found out that they were not going to be fobbed off with the usual parliamentary language, phraseology without any meaning, talking without saying anything. After about ten minutes he moved away, saying that he had some important business to attend to. He should never have said that. OAP Mrs Anderson, who had been a shop steward in her Leeds clothing factory, wasn't going to let him off lightly. She was after him like a greyhound after the hare. She tried to follow him into the inner sanctum but was stopped by the men in fancy dress. He left with 'so you don't think our pensions are important' ringing in his ears. She made an impression that day, as she did later at the Young Socialists' annual conference.

There were many tired people travelling home that night. Those who could not be dropped off at their homes were taken home by cars.

6

THE CAMPAIGN FOR NUCLEAR DISARMAMENT

Along with the other members of the Leeds branch I became active in CND (the Campaign for Nuclear Disarmament). My first activity was to take part in the first Aldermaston March in April 1958. I was immediately made part of our sales team. Comrade Hendrie (the Major) and I were top of the sales chart with approximately 500 hundred items of literature each. This became my role for all the future Aldermaston Marches.

At the end of each day the sales team was exhausted. If the day's march was fifteen miles, then we would walk 30. I remember one year at the end of one of the days I sat on a wall and when the transport arrived to pick me up I could not get off; I had literally moulded to the shape of the wall. Because of this I was taken to a comrade's house close to where the march was to restart the following day to have a night's rest in a proper bed, with an added bonus of the following morning off. This dream was shattered about 08.30 that morning. There was a phone call from Bob Pennington telling me to go to the Royal Festival Hall and sell at the Paul Robeson concert that was taking place there.

At one of the rest points on the Aldermaston March in 1963, I was selling our literature when I was approached by a member of one of the other left-wing organisations. He said that he had in his possession a document that had been leaked from one of the government departments. He asked if I would like to read it. My first reaction was to be careful; was I being set up? I decided that if this was a leaked document, set up or no set up it would be worth reading. The document made reference to the existence of RSGs (Regional Seats of Government). These were deep bunkers positioned in strategic positions around the country. It outlined the importance of these RSGs if central government was out of action for any reason. This was the first day of the march and the *Newsletter* was due out the following morning (Saturday). I immediately sent one of our messengers with this document to the London office. An extra page was put into the paper with a reprint of the document. We never sold so many *Newsletters* in one day as we did that Saturday. We sold it on the slogan 'Wanna Buy A Secret?'

One year on the march on a very hot sunny day a crowd of building workers was standing on the side of the road as I walked past a pub. What caught my eye was the pint that one of them was holding. The sun was shining on it and making it sparkle; it was love at first sight. He must have noticed me looking longingly at the glass, for he held it out and told me to drink it. I put it down in one. Now that's what I call working-class solidarity.

The marches were very hard and strenuous, but very exhilarating. Tens of thousands took part. One year, on the last day of the march, we had a very large contingent with the Socialist Labour League banner leading it. As we rounded the corner at Parliament Square to go down to Trafalgar Square, our contingent was stopped and held up. As soon as the end of those in front had started to enter the square we were allowed to continue, so in fact we were leading a section of the march down to the square. The public address was introducing the contingents into the square. You could almost detect it choking him when he had to say, 'And here comes the Socialist Labour League'. That day there were an estimated 100,000 at the rally in Trafalgar Square.

No one who took part in the Aldermaston Marches could fail to pay tribute to the excellent organisation that made the marches possible. When the march arrived at its destination at the end of the day the marquees were already erected and sections of the march were directed into their allocated marquee. Food stalls were waiting, portable toilets erected and medical facilities ready for anyone who needed attention. The following morning as soon as the march was under way the clearing up squads went into action. One team started the mammoth task of taking down the marquees, loading them into trucks and then going off to the day's finishing point and re-erecting them. The latrine squad had a specially equipped tanker and the disposal was by arrangement with the appropriate council. The catering squad loaded all their equipment into their truck and headed for the lunch-break destination. The final act was for the clearing-up team to spread themselves across the area each with a plastic waste bag and collect every piece of litter in the area. The fields were always cleaner when the march left than when it arrived. A truck collected the bags and disposed of them at the dump. This operation was repeated at every stopping place. The population along the route had been told to expect a march consisting of dropouts, and to expect the fields to be left in a mess. The locals were impressed and that made it easier for the future marches. Mind you the enemies of CND were angry because they could not use rubbish and bad organisation to denigrate the march and so had to concentrate on the aims of CND. By the same token the media tried to create the impression that the march was one big drug and sex orgy. This type of opposition is, of course, still going on whenever young people get together in mass activity.

We were soon to be involved in turning CND towards the trade-union movement and unilateral disarmament. This inevitably brought us into conflict with the Communist Party and the 'left' in the Labour Party. At the annual conference of the Labour Party at Brighton in 1957, Nye Bevan, leader of the left-wing group organised around the weekly newspaper *Tribune*, had just returned from Moscow convinced that their policy of calling for Britain to keep nuclear weapons was the correct one. The thinking behind this was that if Britain did not have the Bomb we would be at the mercy of American imperialism. He threw in his lot with the Communist Party demand for summit talks to bring about disarmament. Bevan spoke at the conference in support of the National Executive opposition to Norwood's resolution, moved by Comrade Vivienne Mendelson, calling for unilateral disarmament. His call was 'we must not go naked into the conference chamber'. Then came the spectacle of Bevanites heckling Bevan.

The Communist Party went full steam for the policy of summit talks. In fact they judged your socialism by your attitude to summit talks. Believe me, using this as a yardstick there were many strange socialists around. We also experienced the nauseating nationalism that the Communist Party plunged themselves into. The Leeds Trades Council, under the influence of the Communist Party, organised two busloads to go and demonstrate outside the American airbase just outside York. John Walls and I went along to the demonstration. The CP members had Union Jacks pinned to their hats and/or their coats. A number of them carried Union Jacks and waved them as though they were fighting the American War of Independence all over again. The favourite slogan was 'Yanks Go Home'. This type of thing went on for a number of years.

Yorkshire CND organised a demonstration in Scarborough on the east coast. Leeds Trades Council had agreed to take part, which meant of course that the Communist Party was preparing to take part, even though the main theme was to be for unilateral disarmament. They turned up with their Union Jacks and summit talk posters. The Trades Council had agreed that its banner should be carried on the demonstration. Yorkshire CP full-time organiser Bert Ramelson and I were to carry it. It was a very large and successful demonstration, with many people calling for unilateral disarmament. The only remark that I remember making to Ramelson was that 'there were a lot of American imperialists on the demo'. (One of the reasons why the Communist Party opposed unilateral disarmament was that this would 'leave us at the mercy of American imperialists'.)

At the next May Day demonstration in Leeds I saw what could only be described as Stalinism personified. Once again the Communist Party turned up with their Union Jacks, but this time with large flags of many of the UN countries. The scramble was not around the Soviet Union's flag. It was to see who would have the 'honour' of carrying the Stars and Stripes and the Union Jack at the head of the other flag carriers.

Bert Ramelson, by far the most able of the CP members, used to hold an open-air meeting in Victoria Square outside the Town Hall every Friday lunchtime, which was a feature of Leeds political life. One such lunchtime he was speaking on summit talks. I kept interrupting and asking him questions. At a certain point an old lady who had been listening turned on me and started to berate me something shocking. There was always a policeman near at hand to keep the peace and he came over to see what the trouble was, and so did Ramelson. She told the policeman that I must be 'one of them communists' because I was having a go at the speaker, pointing to Ramelson.

There is a very serious point to this story because the media, along with the right wing, were running a campaign to convince everyone that the Communist Party controlled CND. Unilateral disarmament was linked to the CP and Moscow. The idea that CND was a CP front organisation was used quite deliberately by the state machine and not without some success. In many discussions on the question of 'ban the bomb' I was accused of being a stooge of Moscow. But it was always easy to prove to them that they were the ones who supported the policy of the Communist Party, opposed to unilateral disarmament.

It would be naïve to think that the government and the media did not know or understand the struggle against the CP's efforts to swing the CND away from unilateral disarmament. That they did know was confirmed in October 1999 when a TV programme exposed Vic Allen, a Leeds university lecturer, as an agent in CND acting for the Stasi secret police of East Germany.

But it wasn't just East European security agencies which spied on CND. On 10 May 1958 the *Newsletter* had a report that Harry Newton, the shop steward for the Leeds electricity meter-readers' branch, had been dismissed instantly, accused of insolence to a 'superior'. Harry Newton had a letter published in the *Newsletter* on 2 August informing the readers that his dispute had come to a successful conclusion. He thanked his workmates for their solidarity in standing by him and supporting him financially and campaigning for his reinstatement. He finished his letter by saying, 'I think my case illustrates once again that whenever we workers unite together almost anything is possible.'

During the late 1950s and the early 1960s Harry Newton was around CND and the Communist Party. Later he did some work with the NUM and became a Workers' Educational Association lecturer. While watching the spy programme on BBC television in 2002, featuring Vic Allen, a familiar face appeared on the screen: Harry Newton. The viewers were told by the narrator that Mr Newton spied on CND in Leeds on behalf of MI5. So we had two of them in there, one for the East and one for the West. I wonder how closely they worked together. Any financial contributions that came our way from Mr Newton were very welcome. Like everyone else he had to pay his way. Newton died some years ago so unfortunately we are not able to pursue him for compensation. As for Vic Allen, his activities have to be looked at. He made a visit to Nigeria and finished up in a Nigerian jail but he took two of our comrades in with him. They were both leaders in the national union that represented workers on the waterfront. Both of them would have been known to the authorities as Trotskyists. Allen was an Stalinist agent, reporting to the Stasi of East Germany. The question has to be asked, what happened in Nigeria?

The family that lived next door to my father's parents asked Dad to be godfather to their young son. That youngster grew up to be Detective Sergeant Harold Robinson of the Leeds CID. I first met him in his official capacity when he led a raid on a Leeds pub where many of the Leeds left gathered on a Thursday night to listen to Eddie O'Donnell's Trad Jazz Band. I assured him that Biggs (the train robber who was on the run at the time) wasn't in the pub, and he told me all they were interested in was under-age drinking.

Leeds CND organised a rally outside the Town Hall as part of a propaganda and recruitment drive. Not long after we had started members of the Young Socialists selling *Keep Left* pointed out that they had noticed a couple who looked out of place. I moved around watching them and noticed that they did not seem to know anyone. I approached and asked if they would like to buy a copy of the *Newsletter*. They declined saying that they already supported the cause. I responded by asking them to buy one for the *Police Gazette* and their files. I moved away and asked someone who had a camera to go and take their photographs and tell them that it was for our files.

Shortly after this a figure appeared from around the corner of the Town Hall: Detective Sergeant Harold Robinson. At that moment the two would-be Pinkertons moved away and made their way round the Town Hall to come up behind the chief. I followed them at a discreet distance. The three of them were talking on the corner near the police station. Have you ever been in a situation where you know that you are really going to enjoy a situation, a moment that you want to savour and implant in your memory forever? That's how I remember feeling. I crept up behind them and I said, 'Hello, hello, hello, what have we here?' As I walked past them I said to Detective Sergeant Harold Robinson, 'They're no use to you now; we have their photographs.' After that messages were got to my parents via a relative telling them that I was heading for trouble. One such message said that I was involved in dangerous and illegal political activity. This had the desired effect on my parents, who became very concerned and tried to convince me that I had come under the influence of troublemakers.

Jack Gale and I were both convinced that our phones were tapped. One night we were discussing the question of the police activity around the CND. I can't remember how we got on to the idea but we decided to try and put one over on the police, especially Detective Sergeant Harold Robinson. Only Jack and I knew of this, not even Jack's wife Celia knew. We planned a telephone discussion where we would discuss the details of a bogus previously-arranged CND Rally in Victoria Square in front of the Town Hall. Jack and I telephoned each other from different parts of Leeds. We had a series of telephone conversations which suggested that contingents would be coming from various areas, such as Bradford, Huddersfield and Sheffield. On the allotted day Jack and I went into Leeds and stood on the top of the Town Hall steps. I think we had arranged the time of 13.00 hours for people to start arriving. One or two police officers kept walking past the bottom of the steps. This was normal as the police station was just on the corner. Then we noticed that the same copper started to pace up and down. He was joined by two more; I think one was an inspector. We went into the Town Hall and walked round until we arrived at the back door. There were no signs of activity outside. Then we spotted the peaked-cap bobby who was at the front of the Town Hall walking past the end

Talking to Leeds University students in the Fenton Pub, Woodhouse Lane

of the street; we followed him past the entrance to the library and turned the corner into Great George Street. There it was: a bus full of police officers, and just behind it a minibus with half a dozen of the CID branch of CND with their branch secretary Detective Sergeant Harold Robinson.

I must say I was very surprised that the plan had worked. I thought that they would be too sophisticated to fall for it. I would have expected them at least to be able to check it out one way or another. It is also possible that the police did not know of the activities of Harry Newton.

There they were as large as life. We went back to the front of the Town Hall and noticed that the police stationed there were becoming very restless. So back we went to the buses. Three or four of the occupants were standing on the pavement deep in discussion. One of them was our favourite Detective Sergeant Harold Robinson. As we approached he spotted the two of us. As we made to pass I asked him what was going on. He said something like, 'You tell me; where are you going?' 'To the library', I replied, 'There is nothing happening today so we thought we would do some research.' We did not look back, so I can't say what happened next.

Through the auspices of the Young Socialist newspaper *Keep Left* we organised a weekly jazz night at the Old Red House public house. There was a nice big room upstairs with its own private entrance making it easy to take entrance fees from those attending. There was also a bar so people could be contained in the one room. One night we had Dominic Behan as the star guest, but mainly it was a Trad Jazz night, usually with Eddie O'Donnell. We had these jazz nights for six or eight weeks and in that period of time we built quite a regular attendance from around the labour movement. Then one night we were raided by the police. We should have seen this coming at least an hour before. There were two couples sporting sweaters and wearing CND badges. They had not been before and were not known to anyone there. Also before the raid someone pointed out to me that a bloke with ginger hair was trying to encourage a member of the Young Socialists to have a drink of beer by offering to buy him a pint. The YS member, Barry Brier, did not drink, but more than that he was under age. Ginger was downing pints as though there was no tomorrow, and when the raid came he was well under the influence of drink. As soon as the inspector led in the might of the Leeds police force the police spies went over to where they thought there was an under-age drinker. I realised that I had considered the jazz night as a night out. As Leeds Area Secretary I felt that I should have spotted the tell-tale signs.

The first thing I did was to point out to the inspector that the only person who was under the influence was one of his own men. I also explained to him how Ginger had tried to encourage Barry to drink beer and had failed. I said that this was a lousy way to get a result and smear a young man's reputation. To my surprise he agreed with me and asked who it was, so I pointed out the Ginger cop to him. I went over to Ginger with the inspector and others confirmed that my accusations were correct. Ginger was told to take no further part in the proceedings and that he would be dealt with later. Ginger let me know that he wasn't very pleased with me.

We were all told to stand in two lines and give our names and addresses to a police officer. In the room were two young students from the Middle East who were obviously very uneasy and when it was their turn they refused to answer the questions. The police officer reported this to the inspector who in turn brought them over to me. I explained to him that these two young men lived under a very repressive regime and this type of thing frightened them. The inspector told me to tell them to give a name and address, and repeated 'a name and address'. So a couple of students who were members of ours sorted them out with a name and address. The inspector then closed down the night's entertainment, apologising for spoiling the night for everyone. He muttered something as we left about how ridiculous the whole thing had been. 'There must be someone got it in for you lot.'

When we got outside I was on the pavement with Cliff Slaughter and I saw Ginger on the other side of the road with two of his mates, pointing at us. The two mates ran across the road, bundled Cliff into a car, and took him off to Millgarth police station. A few of us went to the police station to see if there was anything we could do. We were in luck; our 'liberal' inspector was there. We explained to him what had happened, and thought that it was a case of Ginger's mates getting the wrong man. Cliff was let out a little later. After that whenever I was on a demo I kept my eyes open for a copper with ginger hair.

Over the years our work in Leeds was to take as active a part in CND as we could, helping to organise and taking part in demonstrations, outdoor and indoor public meetings, leaflet distributions at factory gates and the Leeds city centre, and getting resolutions about ending the manufacture of nuclear weapons raised in as many organisations as we could, especially in trade union branches. Not one ward or constituency of the Labour Party was left untouched. We played a big part in turning CND to the labour movement. The main opposition to this turn came from the Communist Party. At one Leeds meeting of CND and supporters a representative of the Communist Party said: 'If we don't stop this concentration on the labour movement we will scare away our supporters from other areas, such as church groups and the middle class supporters.' Say no more.

7

WORK IN THE TENANTS' AND LABOUR MOVEMENT

In 1957 I became a member of the Cross Gates Tenants' and Householders' Association. One of the first things that I took on was to organise a Christmas party for the children on the estate and one for the pensioners. One of my union branch committee members was on the committee of the Cross Gates Working Men's Club. He arranged for us to have the use of the concert room for both events. For the children's party I was responsible for organising the games. There were the best part of 200 youngsters (am I glad that we did not have the worst part!). Jelly and buns all over the place. The noise was … well what can you expect when all are enjoying themselves?

For the pensioners, the recycled teenagers, the meal was in the afternoon and we were to have a concert in the evening. Dad took on the task of getting artistes. To do this he went to the monthly audition night that the club turns have. A couple of his old pals from his club days were there and they helped him to get together enough volunteers for what turned out to be a very good show. Dad and I did the job of being the MC. Dad did three spots, one from his vaudeville repertoire; for the second he played and sang a couple of Fats Waller songs; and he finished with a couple of his Richard Tauber favourites, accompanied on the organ by one of his old mates who had worked with him in the past, song plugging in the music shops. It was soon obvious that he hadn't lost any of his old skills. The concert room was packed, with well over 300 people there, including many of the club members who had come into the room to listen.

Some time after the show Dad had a series of heart attacks and had to curtail his activities; I was glad that I had been able to be there and hear him. I hadn't been able to spend much time at home and it was to be even less in the future, so it was nice that Mum, Dad and I were able to work on this activity together.

Around about this time Leeds City Council was determined to increase the rents. We were opposing this in the Labour Party and building up quite an opposition to the rise. The Labour Council was proposing the increase and the Leeds City Labour Party monthly delegate meeting rejected the proposal. The proposer of the resolution to reject it was an inconspicuous member of the Cross Gates Ward Labour Party, of which I was secretary. The whole plan had been worked out at a meeting of our delegates two evenings before. From the minutes and the housing committee report a question would be asked that would bring about a response that would in turn bring about an opening, allowing this new delegate, who was unknown to the chair, to speak. He was sat at the back; he was slightly built so he was just a shape to the chair, who maybe thought that he would be asking a nice friendly question. The chair pointed to the back of the room. The new delegate stood up, made a very short contribution and then moved the rejection of the proposed increase. One small speech by man, but a huge lecture for mankind. I formally seconded the resolution. There was a very lively debate, Council group versus the rest, much to our delight.

When the rent increase was rejected the housing committee chair, Alderman Hammond, screamed that this was a disgrace and suggested that she would be a laughing stock, made to look a fool. As we did not want any fools in the leadership of the Leeds City Council, Jack Gale moved that we would accept her resignation. As I remember there was no shortage of seconders. At the time it was in the constitution that the delegate body could overrule the Labour Council group. The *Yorkshire Evening Post* made a big issue of the fact that the trade union and Labour Party delegates had overruled the Leeds City Council.

At the June 1957 meeting of the Leeds City Labour Party, the following resolution was passed and sent for inclusion on the agenda of the annual national Labour Party conference:

> 'This Conference declares that the basic industries must be nationalised in order to secure the best use of raw materials and labour. It therefore instructs the NEC to include the confederation plan for engineering as part of the Party's programme for the coming General Election and to give these measures of reorganisation of industry under public ownership high priority in the work of the next Labour Government.'

Four weeks later at the next delegate meeting it was the Labour Party's turn to elect the Lord Mayor. Once again the Leeds trade unions and Labour Party delegates did not agree with the Council group choice, so a very well respected, retired member of the engineering union and Labour Party was nominated, Tom Jessop, the father of Marion Ramelson, a full-time Communist Party worker. Even though the right wing packed the meeting with new and recycled 'delegates', once again the right wing was defeated. This was too much for the conservative element in the party to stomach, especially those in the national leadership. There was a 'send the gun boats' attitude around. The following year the big guns moved in from London to find a way of changing the constitution. It also showed that they were very scared of the strong left-wing movement that was developing not only in Leeds but all over Britain.

To continue the struggle to fight for better housing and to keep up the pressure on the housing committee, I was able to organise a meeting in the main hall of the Leeds Town Hall through the Leeds Tenants' Association, of which I was secretary. The purpose of the meeting was to unite the Leeds tenant associations behind a campaign for better housing conditions and for no more rent increases. Money to pay for this was to come from the nationalisation of the building industry and allied trades. I was to introduce the resolution as secretary of the federation. The secretary of the Middleton Association was the chair and the guest speaker was Jean Temple from the Northeast (Tyneside) Tenants' Associations.

Opposition to the reference to nationalisation came once again from the Communist Party. They said the resolution would be defeated because many in the audience would be frightened off by any hint of left-wing politics. The CP moved that the resolution should be voted for section by section. I almost fell for this. It was the intervention of Jack Gale that saved my bacon. The resolution was discussed and then voted on in its entirety. The only votes against were the Communist Party members. It was quickly pointed out to them that they were the only ones to oppose the call for nationalisation. It was also agreed that the resolution would be presented to the full Leeds City Council at their next meeting in the Civic Hall. The delegation was to consist of the secretaries of each Leeds tenants' association and I was to make the statement to the Council on behalf of the federation. As expected, the only positive thing to come out of this was media coverage for our demands.

We had big meetings not only in Leeds but also in places like Bingley, Shipley, Castleford, Wakefield and many more. The one that gave me the greatest pleasure was the one organised by my own Cross Gates Tenants' and Householders' Association in the main hall of the Cross Gates School. All three Labour councillors had been invited to attend and defend or oppose the Labour Council's decision to increase rents. One turned up, Councillor Jackson. The hall was packed out, with people standing at the back and down the sides. Our association chair Mr Caldwell was in the chair; Councillor Jackson represented the Labour Council group and I was speaking as Cross Gates and Leeds federation secretary. Jackson spoke as though he was pleading for his life. In a way I suppose he was. He blamed everyone but the Labour Party. At one stage he tried to appear militant by blaming the 'money-grabbing bankers and the greed of the building industry'. When he finished, one of the tenants congratulated Jackson for putting his finger on the real culprits. Would he now call on the Labour Party to put those industries under public ownership for their wealth to be used for the benefit of everyone? Jackson spluttered some kind of an answer. He mentioned something about supporting Clause Four and that he had joined the Labour Party to be a socialist internationally, nationally and locally (I wish I had a pound for every time I had heard him say that!). People like him disgusted me, as did Denis Healey MP, who once told me that if I behaved myself he would help me to make progress in the Labour Party. I told him to get lost. I said that I thought he was pathetic.

I think I must have let Jackson get to me because I remember going for the jugular. I finished my contribution by asking the audience to approve sending twelve delegates to the Young Socialists demonstration at the Labour Party conference in Blackpool at the expense of the association. This was passed. I think this must have been the last straw for Jackson. He excused himself from the meeting and left rather quickly. The meeting then elected the twelve delegates. It was also agreed that the meeting give its full support to the Leeds Tenants' Associaton deputation (that came out of the Town Hall meeting) when I was due to make a statement at a Leeds City Council meeting.

The Cross Gates twelve went to Blackpool for the demonstration with a banner we had made especially for the occasion. Apart from the Leeds leadership the only other person to come anywhere near us was Comrade Paul Jennings. He spoke to members of our delegation and took photographs. London knew of our success in getting such a deputation, the only one of its kind on the demonstration. I feel that Paul had more idea what work has to be done to get such a deputation. It just did not drop out of the sky. I did wonder at the time why Comrade Gerry Healy had not come to talk to the tenants. It was only a passing thought and was soon lost in the back of my mind or, as usual, rationalised away by saying that he was a very busy man and had more important things to do.

The other work that I was involved in was helping with the production of the Rank and File paper the *Miner*. The main miners involved around this paper were Jim Swan, Jimmy Allen, Joe Ryan, Joe Fitzgerald, Ron Morgan, Trevor Parsons, Curly Owen and Frank McCabe. Albert Field used his talents and enthusiasm in getting the *Miner* distributed in Yorkshire. The paper became extremely popular in the coal-mining communities and scared the living daylights out of the union leadership and the National Coal Board. There was a leadership developing in the coalmines of the same calibre as was developing on the docks. One was Jim Allen (who later became a well-known playwright for television) and another whom I knew exceptionally well was Joe Fitzgerald.

We organised a meeting in Joe's area. When Joe came into the room he said: 'Where the hell have you lot been? I have been looking for you for years.' Joe told me of a pit-top meeting where safety improvements were being discussed. Joe thought this could be a good time to start the process so he stepped forward and emptied his water bottle on to the coal dust, indicating that he was not going down the pit. The others followed his example. From then on Joe Fitzgerald became the most respected miners' leader we have ever had in Yorkshire. He was unfortunately killed in a motor cycle accident going to his shift at the pit.

The Communist Party was prominent in the leadership of the NUM at the time that the *Miner* was being published. Will Paynter, a CP member, had taken over from Horner as General Secretary. He later joined a government-employer consultative committee.

The paper and the miners supporting it became quite an embarrassment to the union bureaucracy. Moral Re-Armament (MRA) decided to intervene and do as much damage as they could. MRA preached 'brotherly relations' between workers and employers and that goodwill and friendly negotiation can overcome difficulties between employees and employers. A very rich organisation with big donations coming from big business, MRA was able to impress and corrupt. Their main target appeared to be shop stewards and rank-and-file militants. Their leading figure was a Professor Buchman.

We were having a national meeting in London and our miner comrades were going to be there. While we were on our way to London representatives of MRA were visiting the wives and families of our NUM comrades, a good example of their tactics. When visiting one of our comrade's houses, after giving the wife the friendly soft talk, the MRA rep discovered that she had not been able to visit her mother for a number of years because she lived down south. He immediately arranged for a nice big, posh, chauffeur-driven car to take her to see her mother. She was understandably overjoyed at this and became quite taken up with this idea of peaceful collaboration. On the miner's return from

London, the MRA made sure he received a cold welcome and provided his wife with the means to put continuous pressure on him. Where the MRA had been able to get into a house it made things very difficult for our comrades.

While I was working at John Barran's clothing factory, the shop steward, Gilbert Taylor, did not turn up for work one Monday morning. No message was forthcoming explaining what was wrong. There was no Gilbert on Tuesday, Wednesday – he was away all week. Still no news all the second week. What was strange was that there had not been a sick note or any communication whatsoever. Even stranger, the management appeared not to be bothered by this disappearance. After two weeks, on the Monday morning, in pops Gilbert. Naturally he was greeted by: 'Where the hell have you been this last two weeks?' He replied by saying that because of a family problem he had been given permission to be absent for two weeks. Midway through the morning he was called upstairs to the office to see Biddle, a leading director of the board. We were still in dispute regarding the management's refusal to recognise the cutting-room committee. This had previously been custom and practice. As soon as Gilbert came down he called a cutting room meeting.

He said the management had agreed to recognise the cutting-room committee, with one proviso: that the meetings between the cutting-room committee and the management be called 'joint consultative' meetings. The meetings would only be there for consultation, and no pressure was to be tolerated in order to get demands met. This was to apply to both sides. It was quickly pointed out that the management had already put pressure on us by saying that we had to agree to their terms to get the committee recognised. Gilbert then put his position to the meeting. It went something like this. 'Listen chaps I think it is about time the workers and management stopped fighting each other. I am convinced that more can be achieved by good honest negotiation and good will than to be constantly at each other's throats.' Even the Communist Party members could not swallow this one, but they thought it was just a case of Gilbert being off caught off guard by the management. I knew immediately where he had been for the last two weeks. The

Me in 1958

MRA had a large plush hotel in Switzerland where they entertained trade union militants, especially shop stewards. They had a fleet of aircraft to fly them there and limousines to pick them up at the airport and to take them on jaunts while they were there. These details had been made public just after our mining comrades had been targeted by MRA.

I took a deep breath and said that I had a question to ask. He said: 'Yes what is it?' I asked him if he had met Professor Buchman while in Switzerland over the last two weeks? He was obviously very shaken by this. I realised that I had hit the right button. I went on to explain that it was not a case that he had been caught off guard. The management had arranged for the MRA to contact Gilbert, and to work on him. The MRA would have convinced him of the correctness of their ideas and then invited him to go to the 'education centre' in Switzerland. They would have arranged for the management to give him the two weeks off. 'Am I right, Gilbert?' He said: 'Yes, and I think it is the right way.' Frank Stockdale, Geoff Emsley, Ronnie Jackson and other CP members supported my motion that we reject the management's proposal. Gilbert Taylor resigned and Frank Stockdale, the deputy, took over as steward. The fact that I had been able to say where he had been for the last two weeks did give me a little kudos. Gilbert said: 'You have been doing your homework, how did you know?' 'By what you said,' I replied.

There was a TV programme called *Who Goes Home?* (which has some kind of significance with the House of Commons: after a session the Speaker calls out, 'Who goes home?'). The programme was chaired by Bevins who, I think, was the editor of the *Daily*

Herald at the time. It was always clearly stated in the introduction to the programme that it was live and spontaneous. The idea was to have a Labour and a Tory MP from the same area. The audience was made up of representatives from organisations in their constituencies.

One of the series was to come from Leeds; the two MPs were Denis Healey and Sir Keith Joseph. Just in case any reader does not know who is who, Joseph was the Tory and Healey was Labour, the Hon MP for East Leeds. So obviously East Leeds Constituency Labour Party was invited and we were allocated ten tickets. Councillor Douglas Gabb was the secretary of the East Leeds Labour Party. In his infinite wisdom he distributed all ten tickets to known Trotskyites and supporters. Whether he would have done this if he had known that in the future it might jeopardise his chance to be 'his most worshipful' we will never know, but he did it. Ten Trots, asking questions to Denis Healey, on a live TV programme! We did not have the heart to refuse the invitation.

When it became known in my factory that I was to appear on the television in *Who Goes Home?* Hives and company told everyone that this was my chance to prove that I was a socialist and supporter of the Soviet Union. To do this I had to ask Joseph and Healey if they were prepared to support the call for a summit conference in the name of world peace. I refused. This call for a world summit conference was all part of the Stalinist policies of 'peaceful coexistence' and 'socialism in one country' which worked something like this: to safeguard his position in the USSR (where 'socialism' was supposedly being built in one country) Stalin was prepared to maintain 'good relations' with the capitalist world (peaceful coexistence) by betraying workers' struggles in the rest of the world, using the various national Communist parties to bring this about. This was the 'Moscow Line'. So I told them I would support a summit conference if they would have it on the summit of Mount Everest in a snowstorm.

Along with the representatives of the other organisations we were transported from Leeds to the television studios in Manchester. On arrival we were directed into a room next to the broadcasting studio. There were drinks and eats laid out on a table and we were told to tuck in. While we were doing this, Bevins was moving round explaining just what type of questions he would like. He wanted questions that would make it appear that the two MPs were really in opposition to one another. We knew exactly what he meant and we had prepared some questions that would do just that. We were expected to play the game of kidding the viewer. Bevins was really impressed with our suggested questions, which would make it easier for him to engineer a right old ding-dong. What Bevins did not know was that the questions we were going to ask were in our other pocket. When it came to planning to get certain results from a meeting we were a match for him. After a while we were asked to finish our food and to make our way into the studio. We all had to walk past the platform where the two would-be protagonists were already sitting. Healey looked at us and said: 'Lord save me from my friends'. I turned and looked him straight in the eyes and replied: 'Forgive them, father, for they know exactly what they're doing.' I really do enjoy moments like that. I have been told that I have a sense of humour and eye for the moment. I hope I never lose it.

The chair made his opening remarks and introduced Joseph and Healey. Then he asked for the first question. He pointed straight at Jack Kleinberg, who was an optician. He was supposed to be asking about the NHS and the question of free spectacles. The question they got was: 'What do the two MPs think about the demand to withdraw British troops from Cyprus?' No way was there going to be a ding-dong over this one, not even a ping pong could be expected. They both gave some kind of a parliamentary type of answer. Whether or not the chair thought there had been a misunderstanding, he selected another member of our group. The question he asked was on nuclear disarmament. 'Do you support the demand advocated by CND that Britain should stop manufacturing nuclear weapons, or do you support the policy advocated by the Communist Party that says Britain should keep the bomb so that we can keep our independence form the USA?' There had to be another Houdini escape by the platform to get out of that one. But not before the 'soviet' bureaucracy, the Communist Party, Healey and Joseph had all been tucked cosily in bed together.

We were only to get one more question in. This was based on

the concept of nationalisation and the continuing compensation being paid to the ex-owners of the coalmines and railways. There were six or seven questions that night and we managed to get in three. The rest were shared out between the Conservative Party and other organisations. When it was all over, there were further drinks and light refreshments. Bevins wasn't very pleased with our group. He said we had deceived him. Jack said that if we had done what he wanted us to do, we would be guilty of collaborating to deceive the viewers. 'You told the viewers that it was spontaneous and live and that's what we did.' Bevins was very angry but what could he do? He could not complain, as all he could achieve would be to make himself look foolish.

I have another Dennis Healey story. Later when I was in London working full-time in our print shop one of my jobs was to collect the Sunday papers as soon as they became available. In exceptional cases when I could not get round Fleet Street one place I used to get the papers was at a paper stall in Victoria Station. I had just put my hand on a copy of the *Times* when another hand tried to take the same paper. We looked at each other; it was Dennis Healey. 'Ah, Norman Harding, East Leeds Labour Party,' he said. I knew just what to do. I looked at him for about three or four seconds and then replied: 'Yes, but who are you?' The girl on the stall had been waiting to see who would be taking that copy of the *Times* and to get her money. I got the paper and said goodnight.

Every year the workforce at Barran's put on a pantomime the weekend before Christmas. Thursday night was for relatives, nurses from the local hospitals, pensioners and so on. Friday night was for the employees and the management. As near as I can date it, in 1958 the production was to be *Dick Whittington.* As usual, many of the chorus and townspeople were members of the Communist Party. At a point in the proceedings Baron Fitzwarren had a shipload of merchandise that had arrived at the docks. At this time there happened to be a much publicised dock strike in London. The producer Len Waite thought that it would be good idea to be up-to-date and introduce this into the panto. The Baron called all the townspeople together and announced that there was a strike at the docks and he would need volunteers to unload his ship. As soon as the townspeople took a step forward to follow the Baron to the docks, I stood up and shouted from the audience 'Don't cross the dockers' picket line! They are your brothers! Don't be scabs!' Geoff Emsley and Les Dixon took up the cry from the stage: 'I will not cross the picket line.' The majority of the townspeople went off stage left instead of stage right. Loud applause from the audience, except from the two front rows that were occupied by the Barran family, board of directors and management. The curtain was closed to allow a clean start to the next scene.

There was always a do after the panto. The usual dancing along with a bit of Christmas cheer and youngsters hiring out their bike shed key, half a crown a time. There were always one or two humorous moments. Gilbert Taylor (who was still shop steward at the time) fell asleep on the train, missed Micklefield station and ended up in Hull. Frank Stockdale made a number of attempts to mount his bicycle and finally managed to get his feet on the right pedals and went off down Chorley Lane. He turned left on a short cut that took him into Victoria Square and had the misfortune to fall off his bike right outside the police station. He was late home. I shared a taxi with Dick Whittington's cat and Widow Twanky. I was obviously put off at the right place on the corner of Poole Road and Cross Gates Road, where Mr Atkin, the father of my friends John and Marion, spotted me attempting to count the stars in the sky. He escorted me round the corner to 93 Poole Crescent and saw me safely inside. Anyway that's the story I was told.

The founding of the Yorkshire Symphony Orchestra, the YSO, was a very positive development. With it came a determined drive to make the concerts available to as many citizens as possible. Once the orchestra had been welded together under the direction of Nikolai Malko we had in Yorkshire an extremely accomplished orchestra. A wonderful scheme was introduced to hold what would be called 'industrial concerts' in Leeds, Bradford, Huddersfield and Halifax on Thursday nights. Special programmes were printed for each concert. The contents gave details of the composers and pointed out which passages to listen for. It also explained the meaning of such words as coda for the benefit of those of us who were just starting to learn about such things. Each of the four had a concert once a month, with all four Councils helping to fund the YSO. The factories were circulated and asked to send a request for tickets. The price was two shillings and sixpence irrespective of the position in the Town Hall. In our factory the personnel office sent a sheet round all the departments asking for all those who wanted to go to sign it before every concert. About twelve of us were regular attenders, mostly from the cutting room. Like other factories, we ended up having our own regular block of seats.

There was to be a special treat: Malcolm Sergeant was to conduct 'A night with Delius' at one of our concerts. The usual list came round and the regular names were put down. On this occasion I ordered two tickets as my father had said that he would like to go. The day before the concert we all received our tickets from the personnel office, only this time the personnel officer brought them herself, and not her secretary. We had not been allocated our usual seats, as there had been an overwhelming demand for tickets. She apologised and said that it had nothing to do with her. When we arrived we understood what she had meant. Down the two sides of the Victoria Hall there were a series of alcoves each with three or four seats facing inwards so that you were looking across at the rows of seats. You had to twist your neck, in our case to the right, to see the orchestra. Generally these seats were not used. To make matters worse, right across from us in our usual seats were the chairman of the board as well as a number of heads of departments. I was fuming because I was sure that some of them did not know the difference between a bassoon and a bass drum. It was a good night as far as the music went; the piece I remember best was *The walk to the paradise garden*. The closing notes just seemed to slip away from you; even when the vibrations had stopped you could still hear them in your head. The impression was that the applause was delayed as though the silence was part of the music.

The next morning on our arrival at work we had not cooled down one bit. It became clear to us that the management taking our seats represented the class divisions in society, and we should act accordingly. As a member of the cutting-room committee I was asked to approach the shop steward and ask for an immediate meeting of the committee. The purpose of the meeting was to receive a complaint that we had been discriminated against. The management was sent a message telling them that the act of taking our seats for themselves and pushing us into the side seats was considered to be an act of snobbery of the worst kind, and if we didn't get an apology by noon a deputation would go to the media and tell them just what had happened. We would down tools until they got back, when the whole situation would be discussed. At 11.45 we received an official apology saying that it had been a mistake to act in this way. It would never happen again.

I became a great admirer (from afar) of June Mills, the principal oboist. A social was to be held in the Town Hall so that the public could meet the orchestra. I decided to attend to extend my interest in the oboe. As I entered the hall I was given a magazine that contained photographs and pen pictures of members of the orchestra. Turning the pages I saw that there was a bassoon player by the name of David Mills, whose wife played the oboe. I sure wasn't going to play second fiddle to a bassoon player so I turned my attention to the free drinks and food.

At the height of the popularity of the YSO there was a growing resentment from the so-called elite because the concerts were more and more being frequented by factory workers. In some cases 'overalls were seen to be stuffed into plastic bags', according to a letter in the *Yorkshire Evening Post*. At one of the invitation concerts held on Saturday nights, Eileen Joyce was to play Grieg's piano concerto. The first part of this had been made popular as the theme of a well-known film. When she had finished playing the well-known part, the majority of the audience started to applaud. The conductor turned, held his hand out to the soloist who stood and acknowledged the applause. She returned to her piano, the conductor faced the orchestra raised his baton and continued with the concerto. What more could the 'elite' want to prove that the concert hall was no longer their property? The expected letters were sent to the *Yorkshire Evening Post*: 'What will Eileen Joyce think of us?' 'Stop the subsidy from the Council; those who want to attend should pay a higher price for the tickets.' The letters must have been brought to the attention of Eileen Joyce because she sent a letter to the paper disassociating herself from 'those terrible people'. One of the points she made was: 'When at a football match you don't only applaud when a goal is scored. Good approach work is also appreciated'. She added, 'Music is there to be enjoyed. I support what the YSO is doing to this end.'

The pressure continued and then the opportunity arose for the Tories to heighten the campaign against the industrial concerts and the subsidies. Tito Gobi was booked for one of the invitation concerts. He finished his programme. When the applause died down he announced that as long as we wanted to stay he would continue singing. It really was a night to remember. It went on so late that the transport department had to put special buses on to every part of Leeds. The Monday edition of the *Yorkshire Evening Post* had blazoned across its front page 'Overtime for busworkers to take home concertgoers'. From then on the Tories exploited the mistaken, snobby idea that classical music is for the upper class and 'if they want it let them pay for it. Why should we?' The end result was that all four Councils withdrew the subsidy. The industrial concerts finished and shortly after that the YSO was disbanded. The 'Glyndeborne set' had won. The pretentious, peacock-strutting, cultural parasites would rather destroy music than share it — music that has the power to take hold of your emotions and create in you sadness, joy, contentment and excitement. I suspect that many of the anti-YSO brigade did not understand this. The bitterness and hatred that I have of a society that creates such divisions is the reason why I became a communist.

In 1958 I was nominated for inclusion on the list of prospective candidates for the municipal elections. The Halton Labour Party ward invited me to stand as their candidate. This was a powerful Tory ward so I stood little chance of winning the seat. Not one member of that ward lifted a finger to help, saying it was more important to work in a marginal ward. My brother Keith and I were a two-man electioneering team. Keith and I attended the count and, as expected, the Tory was announced the winner. The candidate was immaculate; he looked as though he had come straight out of Austin Reed's window, while the two of us did not have time to wash and change. We had been dashing around on my motorbike all day and must have looked very dishevelled. The returning officer called on the Tory to make his acceptance speech. Then I was called on to reply. I was taken completely by surprise. I was very tired and feeling very hostile towards my overbearing patronising opponent. I thanked the returning officer and the tellers. I then apologised to all the decent people of Halton for failing to get rid of the Tory candidate. I then vowed that I would not rest until every Tory had been kicked off the Leeds City Council. Apparently that wasn't a very nice thing to say. This fact was brought to my attention by the returning officer who was also a leading Labour Party councillor. I was hauled in front of the executive committee of the Leeds Labour Party and severely reprimanded. The Executive's disapproval of my conduct was recorded.

Over the next period I continued to campaign for socialist principles and sold the *Newsletter* wherever possible, including at the Labour Party conference in Scarborough. There was to be a CND demonstration on the Sunday with a contingent of Young Socialists made up from all our branches nationally. There was always a lot of activity on the Saturday before conference when the compositing of resolutions took place — always a good time to sell literature. It was decided that Doria Arram (Pilling) and I would go over on the Saturday morning to sell at the compositing. We took all the literature for the weekend activities with us. As expected we made a great impact and had a very good sale. One thing we were selling was a pamphlet called *The Future of The Labour Party* priced at twopence. My slogan was, 'Who will give me twopence for the future of the Labour Party?' We sold all day and kept up the pressure on the delegates constantly going in and out to fight for their points to be included in the composite resolutions.

As a bonus the usual pre-conference rally was held on the Saturday night. Doria and I had noticed that a number of our supporters and members had arrived on the Saturday evening so we organised a sales team. To our great joy and satisfaction by 21.00 hours we had sold every paper, every pamphlet, every magazine, and given out all our leaflets relating to the following day's demonstration. Then the reality of the situation hit me. We had nothing to sell or hand out on the demonstration the following day. I telephoned Jack to round up as much literature as he could and to contact London and get the YS coach to bring supplies of literature with them and, if that failed, to see what the areas could do. I rang Jack back at 22.00 hours; he told me that London would be bringing fresh supplies and that the 'Centre' wasn't very pleased with me: I should have calculated the literature to cover both days. I would be spoken to when they arrived. Jack told me to ignore them; what we had done was correct.

Sunday's demonstration was a big success; television and the press interviewed members of the YS national leadership. Our literature stock had been replenished and a good sale was had by all. All that was said about selling everything on the Saturday night was something about paying more attention to detail. I can only remember saying that I thought I had done that by raising the alarm when we sold out.

The *Newsletter* called for a national industrial Rank-and-File conference on 16 November 1958 at the Holborn Hall, London. There was a tremendous campaign for this all over Britain, resulting in the attendance of 500 working-class militants. During the build-up to the conference Gerry Kitchen and I went to Sheffield for the weekend to work with the striking busworkers. We arrived early on the Saturday morning, enquired where the nearest bus garage was and promptly made our way there. Before leaving Leeds a two-sided A4 *Newsletter* 'Bulletin' had been duplicated. The front and half of the back outlined the need for solidarity for the busworkers from the labour movement, with a list of demands directed at all trade union branches with a strong emphasis on branches of the Transport and General Workers Union – the busworkers' union. The bottom half of the back was publicity for the National Industrial Rank-and-File Conference. The previous night, on our Gestetner duplicator (hi-tech stuff this) we produced 1,000 or more copies. We were to sell them at one penny each. By midday Gerry and I had covered every bus garage in Sheffield and had a fantastic reception at every one. We returned to the central garage where the strike committee held their meeting. Hoping to be able to get a statement from them for the next issue of the *Newsletter*, we hung around talking to the busworkers who were waiting for a progress report. At long last the door of the committee room opened and one of the strike leaders came out and asked if those two who had been selling the *Newsletter* 'Bulletin' were in the garage. Gerry and I moved forward. He said, 'Will you come in here? The committee would like to have a word with you.' It all sounded very ominous.

The chair pointed to two seats that had been placed ready for us. We sat down and I for one thought that we were in for a roasting. The chair asked if we were the two responsible for producing the 'Bulletin'. We did not expect what followed. The secretary introduced himself and then said that he had a request to make on behalf of the committee. 'We want your permission to circulate every branch of the Transport and General Workers' Union in Britain with your "Bulletin". We will, with your permission, attach a covering letter explaining that the strike committee fully endorses the contents.' He added that they would not change anything and, naturally, the appeal for the Industrial Rank-and-File Conference would be included.

We looked at each other and conferred for all of a couple of seconds. I said that I could not see any problem with their suggestion. They thanked the two of us for giving our permission. With that we left the room along with the committee, to report to the strikers' meeting in the garage. We were allowed to stay at the meeting. The report included that permission had been given for the strike committee to circularise the *Newsletter* 'Bulletin' to every branch in Britain. Gerry and I decided that we would stay overnight and continue with our work.

A Central Committee meeting was taking place this same weekend so we decided that we would have to notify them of our progress. Jack Gale was brought out of the meeting to the telephone. I explained to him what had happened. He went back into the meeting and I later learned that he interrupted the proceedings to explain. An immediate decision was made to inform all our members that, wherever we had contacts in the Transport and General Workers' Union, they should make them aware that the circular was being sent to every branch. It was now somewhere between 13.00 and 14.00 hours and as we had been on the go since 05.00 hours that morning we took a break and had some lunch.

Back at the garage we discovered that the newspapers had been sniffing around. A reporter of the *Sheffield Evening Star* had a copy of the 'Bulletin' and wanted some comments on it. He was apparently keen to interview Gerry and me, but he and the photographer had been despatched kindly but firmly by the pickets who suggested we stay out of sight until it was confirmed that they had left the area. But it was too late; the damage had been done. The *Sheffield Evening Star* that night had a front-page article with a headline 'Trotskyists Infiltrate Bus Strike' with comments on the *Newsletter* 'Bulletin' and the decision of the strike committee to endorse the contents. We had met our first pickets at about 07.00 hours; ten or eleven hours later our work had led to this. As was to be expected, this had an effect on some of the more reluctant strikers, with the encouragement of a few Communist Party members who had suddenly appeared on the scene. (One of them was a leading AEU member and the father of a future leading Labour Party MP. There was also a CP member from Leeds who, I believe, reported for the *Daily Worker*.) They attempted to get the support for our 'Bulletin' rescinded by the committee. This did not happen, but the real danger was that the following day (Sunday) there was to be a meeting of the strikers in one of the main halls in Sheffield. If Saturday night was anything to go on, the CP and the right wing would be pulling out all the stops to prevent the endorsement and circulation of the *Newsletter* 'Bulletin'. As far as the union bureaucracy was concerned it had to be stopped at all costs. No way did they want any activity that could encourage nationwide support for the Sheffield busworkers.

On the Sunday afternoon Gerry Kitchen and I made our way to the meeting. We were on the steps leading up to entrance when the strike committee made its way into the hall. They assured us that they were not going to back down but were going to recommend that the original decision was to stand. I think it was the secretary who said to me, 'I can't see anything wrong with appealing for support from other garages, I don't understand why anyone can oppose it.' The strike committee won the vote by an overwhelming majority. After only a matter of days the union leadership decided that the strike had to be brought to an end. So a deal was struck with the employers; no doubt the fear of national support scared both employer and the Transport and General Workers' Union. The resulting compromise was accepted by the strikers, but they lived to fight another day. On reflection it is obvious that they were not concerned with the political differences between the Stalinists, the right wing, and us. Working-class solidarity was at the heart of their support for the *Newsletter* 'Bulletin' and that support was our link with this section of workers. If we had approached them as the vanguard party of the working class telling them that the only way forward was to join us we would not have lasted five minutes. We approached the strike in a way that made it possible for the strikers to approach us. A bridge was built between the conscious leadership and the working class.

The highlight of the Leeds Labour Party social calendar was the annual dance at the Town Hall. All members of our group attended and this particular year we took as many Young Socialists as we could. Hugh Gaitskell, the leader of Her Majesty's parliamentary opposition, was there holding court. I asked him if he would be kind enough to meet a group of youths who were anxious to talk to him. He agreed, and the YS members immediately surrounded him. Dougie Thomas, a young miner from the Temple Newsam pit, asked him if he agreed that we should nationalise the coal distribution industry. He said no because at the moment there was a lot of opposition to nationalisation. He added that the reason for this was the high price of coal to the consumer. It was pointed out that the price of pit-top coal per ton was a lot less than what the housewife paid. It was the privately owned coal distribution that was responsible for the high price of coal. I can't remember how it came about, but Gaitskell raised the point that class society was disappearing. As proof of this he said that on the railways there was no longer first, second and third class – there was now only first and second. This man was hoping to be Prime Minister.

A few weeks after the Rank-and-File Conference I was summonsed to appear in front of the Leeds Labour Party executive. The list of prospective candidates for the municipal elections was to be discussed. As I was already on the list it was strange that I was to be interviewed. It became clear when Councillor Gabb warned me of a move being made to throw me off the list. A few of the executive committee members said that they would help all they could. I was called into the room and offered a seat at the table. The first question was whether I attended the *Newsletter* industrial Rank-and-File Conference. 'Yes,' said I. 'Have you ever sold the *Newsletter* 'Bulletin' in public?' 'Yes.' 'You were also seen selling the *Newsletter* at the annual conference, is this true?' 'Well, spotted – yes.'

The chair was a leading Leeds solicitor, Councillor Waterman. He rose to his feet and asked, 'How did you get to know about this conference?' I replied that I had received my invitation through the post. 'Ah, how was it, Comrade Harding, that you received an invitation and I did not?' Councillor Waterman put this question to me in a tone that indicated that he had cracked the case. I explained to the executive that, like many people in the room, I read the *Tribune* every week. No doubt our chair had been known to read it. He said something like 'now and again'. I went on: 'A few weeks ago I spotted an advertisement asking anyone interested in attending the conference to write in with their name and address and the necessary documents would be sent to them. If you, Councillor Waterman, had answered that advertisement, or anyone else in this room had, then you would also have received an invitation.' 'Do you deny that the reason why you were invited was because you are a member of a secret organisation in the Labour Party?' Councillor Dennis Matthews took up the questioning at this point.

Councillor Dennis Matthews. When Jack London wrote 'the definition of a scab' he must have had Matthews in mind. He was a detestable unprincipled individual. He asked me if I was aware that if I ever became a member of the Council I would be bound by the decisions of the Labour group of councillors. He went on to say that as far as he was concerned I would have no loyalty to the Labour group. He then moved that I should leave the meeting so that the executive committee could discuss the issue. After about twenty minutes or so I was called back into the meeting where I was told that I had been removed from the list of prospective candidates, but if I wanted to be considered for the following year all I had to do was to have my name put forward and I would be considered without malice. Or something like that. I was later informed that Matthews had concentrated on the question of loyalty to the Labour group. He had a long list of the resolutions and activities that I had been involved in to back up his theory. A few members of the committee accused Matthews of carrying out a witch-hunt against me. But the end result was victory for Matthews. He was the one who moved the resolution to strike me off the list.

A couple of months later Councillor Arthur Harrison, who worked with my father on the railway, told Dad he wanted me to go and see him to discuss something. I went that same evening. He told me that a struggle was taking place on the Council. The Tories were presenting a motion instructing the Council to make a large increase on the rents of Council houses. The Labour group had met and had decided to oppose the Tories' resolution and had instructed the Labour councillors on the Housing Committee to vote against the proposal. Now Arthur was a friendly sort of chap and had a dislike of careerists in the party. He was present at the executive meeting that moved me off the candidates' list and knew that the driving force had been Councillor Matthews making great play on the question of loyalty to Labour Council group decisions. Arthur told me that Matthews had ignored the Labour group's decision and had voted with the Tories on the Housing Committee to make a substantial increase in rents. It was suggested that I would be doing everyone a favour if I was to expose him at the next City Labour Party meeting. There was a ruling that stopped councillors from divulging the business of the Labour Council group. But once it had been raised at the City Party meeting there was nothing to stop delegates speaking on the issue and there were many councillors who were delegates from their union branches. If I had been a vindictive kind of bloke I would have gone for the proverbial jugular — and that was just what I was planning to do. It felt like being in a quiz and having the answers in front of you.

But first we had to make sure the opportunity to raise the issue would arise. Any mention of local elections or nominations for future candidates would suffice. If this did not happen then we arranged for someone to raise the question of when nominations for the candidates' list had to be in. We need not have worried; the opportunity arose out of the minutes of the last meeting. I attracted the attention of the chair by standing up and asking if I might make an observation on the question of nominations for the list of prospective candidates. I informed the delegates that although I was already on the list I had been invited to appear before the executive committee. As a result of that meeting I had been removed from the list. I went on to tell the delegates that the reason was because Councillor Matthews had convinced the executive committee that I would not uphold the decisions of the Labour Council group and could not be trusted. I think at this point he realised what was coming because he looked very uncomfortable. If you think I was getting any pleasure out of uncovering Matthews you are dead right. I am reliving the moment as I type. I did not blurt out Matthews' disloyalty all at once. I deliberately stalled and let him stew for a few seconds.

After the pause I said: 'I have to inform this meeting that Councillor Matthews, the one who used the question of loyalty to the Labour Council group to get me taken from the candidates' list, that very same Councillor Matthews ignored the decision of the Council group and voted with the Tories on the housing committee.' There was an immediate response from the delegates, councillors, right-wing, left-wing and delegates without any wings at all, with cries of 'Shame!' 'Resign!'

The chair called for order. When he got it he asked me where I had got my information from. I told him that 'my loyalty to the Labour Council group would not let me divulge my source'. There was a wonderful response to that one.

At a Northern aggregate Peter Kerrigan, a leading Liverpool docker, had said that when you get the enemy by the throat and you know you have him, don't let go or he will turn on you. I wanted to throw Matthews to the wolves. I suggested that the chair should ask Matthews to make a statement to the meeting. He asked, but got a refusal. This started another round of heckling. I suspected that the hostility shown at this meeting would not continue in the future. But it was agreed that the executive committee should meet to discuss the issue. I am not clear what happened to him after that.

There were many Labour Party members and councillors in

those days who were on the right wing but had in their past been very devoted to the cause of socialism. One such leading member was George Murray (not the one of the same name who was Hugh Gaitskell's agent). He had been arrested and jailed many times for his activities in the 1930s. He, like many of the others, wanted socialism but differed with us on our approach to getting it. He always showed his admiration for anyone who fought for a principle. He never did the dirty on us. Jack Gale and I were coming through Leeds one Saturday night when we spotted George the worse for drink. We knew that if he was picked up the press the Tories would have a field day. We bundled him into the car and took him home. His life-long partner opened the door; she had the same political history as George. We had a chat and a cup of tea. They thanked us and we went on our way.

But Matthews was of a different breed. There are still more of his kind around today. The Labour Party can't even be mistakenly referred to as a socialist party.

8

CHANGING FACTORIES

In 1963 I had to consider very seriously my position at John Barran's. The Stalinists were putting me under tremendous pressure. Ever since the Yorkshire Area Conference of the CP had passed the resolution blaming me for the collapse of the factory branch and the sales of the *Daily Worker,* the hard-core Stalinists had increased their resolve to attack me politically and personally. At the same time I was penniless. A very low wage and heavy political commitments kept me continuously without money. I discussed the situation with my comrades and then took the decision to find work at another clothing factory.

A clothing worker called Fred Meredith had recently taken on the job as secretary of Leeds CND. He relied heavily on SLL members to rescue many activities that were on the point of collapsing. He couldn't organise a pub-crawl in Otley (where you can turn on a spot and count more than twenty pubs). He was shop steward at Black and Lupers (Executex) in Kirkstall Road. I explained to him that I wanted to change factories and he said that he could get me a job at his factory. The money would be better so I would be able to sell my motorbike and try to run a car. But this decision was taken as a political and not a personal one. I would remain in the same union branch as before. I accepted his offer. An interview was arranged. I got the job and so, after nearly 20 years, I left John Barran's.

I was very grateful to all those at Barran's who in my early years had played a big part in my political education. That, and my ten years in the Group and SLL, prepared me for what turned out to be six very interesting years.

Meredith gave the impression that he was a very militant union member. After only a few months it was obvious that as a militant he was a fraud. He always made sure that he had an escape route. For instance he never did commit himself to unilateral disarmament. He would not oppose it openly in CND, but when he was among the general public and with his Labour Party and union branch committee friends, he would wave the flag with the rest of them. He turned out to be the most impressionist, sectarian, opportunist I had ever known and done battle with. It was easy to work out in advance how he would react in certain circumstances.

As recently as January 2000 (27 years after being made redundant) while out shopping I met a colleague who had worked with me at Executex. He recalled that he had been called into the manager's office and asked if he would take on a job as a charge-hand in the cutting room. During the discussion, trying to convince him he was the best man for the job, the manager told him that Meredith had provided the management with a dossier on everyone working in the cutting room. My colleague asked him how long this had been going on. The manager said Meredith had offered to do these dossiers shortly after Harding started to work there. Not long after, Meredith got the sack. My colleague could not tell me why, as he did not know. He said that I was right to take Meredith on the way I did as it completely separated me from him. It was also pleasing to find out that my workmates at Executex, after I had been made redundant, had said they respected me as much as they mistrusted Meredith. My colleague also added that it was obvious to everyone that if I had not started work there the chances are that Meredith would never have been exposed. This was the first time that I have had this kind of feedback. It did give me a feeling of satisfaction.

On my first day I discovered that there were two or three ex-Barran's workers in the cutting room as well as a few who remembered me from the abortive pay struggle back in 1954. This made me feel a little more welcome. The first few weeks were spent settling in and getting to know as many workers in the factory as possible. After a couple of months I decided to start a cutting-room sick club based on the one that we had at Barran's. It was sixpence per week plus a weekly numbers' draw to boost the funds. Fifteen shillings a week for the first twelve weeks of sickness; after that it went up to £1 per week. This came as a surprise to everyone because it was completely different to every other sick payment they were used to. I used to collect the money every Friday and this gave me the opportunity to move around and come into contact with everyone every week.

One lunchtime I had arranged to go over to George Mann's engineering factory and help Comrade John Walls give out CND leaflets. Two of the men, Ronnie Cust and Bill Jordan, had overheard me telling someone where I was going. They asked me to give them a lift over to St Ann's Cathedral so that they could attend a special mass. I said that I would pick them up on my way back. We got into the car and they immediately expressed surprise that I had agreed to give them a lift to a mass, as I was an atheist. In the short time available I explained as best I could the source of religion. I also said that I was 100-per-cent opposed to all those who said 'get rid of religion and you will get rid of the problems of the world'. I explained that it was the other way round. They already knew that Meredith was an anti-religious bigot. When we arrived back at the factory Meredith ranted on about me giving support to the Catholics, and what kind of an atheist was I? I replied by saying, 'The kind that can discuss evolution with Catholics.' He knew about some of the contradictions that appeared in the Bible, but he did not have a clue about the evolution of humans and society. He was like this on every subject. Without being too unkind this put him in a position of knowing a lot about nothing.

During the latter half of my first year there was general discontent in the factory over wages. Meredith went to the management to ask for a wage increase. He was soon back with the news that the management had said no. 'I did my best,' said the messenger. Following this exhibition of 1 man = 700 votes, I decided that something should be done. It had to be shown that there was a much better and more democratic way of putting forward a 'request' for a wage increase. I thought that the best way would be to have a campaign in the factory to popularise the need for a wage increase, and it would have to be an equal increase for both men and women. The idea was not to rush, but to take it quietly and calmly. Then, when the time was ripe, we would call a meeting of the entire factory and elect a committee representing every department and get the backing of the meeting for an all-round increase. The next step was that the committee would have a meeting with the management. A report-back would be given to another full factory meeting. If the management said no, then we would take it from there.

I had already spoken to a few of those whom I was friendly with; the overall opinion was that to involve everyone in this way would be a lot better than one man being in the office on his own. Ronnie and Bill both thought that to show organisation and strength in this way could mean success without having to strike, but they were also prepared to strike. Both agreed to give me support and were prepared to talk to as many people as they could in the factory. The two of them had worked there a number of years so were quite well known. It was now time to put the idea to Meredith. It was a Monday morning. I asked him if we could have a word in the canteen at lunchtime. After the meal I went over to his table; there were a number of people sitting at the table, so they were able to hear what I was saying. I told Meredith that I thought we should still carry on with our demand for a wage increase. He said that he had been to the management and they had turned it down. I then outlined my plan. To my surprise he let me finish without interruption. I think he was too angry to be able to speak. While I had been talking I was watching him; his face was twitching. I think from that moment he decided that he did not like me. When I had finished I asked if he agreed with the ideas I had put forward. He did not answer; he got up from the table and went downstairs. Not long after this one of the girls from the machine room came into the canteen and told us that Meredith had stormed through the factory and into the manager's office. He was in there for most of the afternoon. When he did come back into the cutting room he did not say a word. We had to wait until the following day, an hour before lunch, before he said anything. He announced that there was to be a meeting of the whole factory in the canteen in fifteen minutes time. When everyone was assembled in the canteen Meredith placed himself at the front of the meeting and without any preamble said that Norman Harding had suggested that we should go on strike for a wage increase. Then without any discussion he had the vote.

Naturally the vote went against a strike by a huge majority. Meredith closed the meeting. He then turned to me and said, 'There will be no committees here.' There was some protest at the way the 'meeting' had been called and handled. Then something happened that could have sparked off strike action. A woman worker shouted from the back of the canteen, 'Meredith, you're Norman Black's lackey.' Norman Black (the owner) must have been listening from the top of the stairs because on hearing this he came into the canteen and verbally abused her. Because of his well-known attitude to the women workers he was greatly disliked. There was a hush at this. I am sure that I did not have to think about it. I stood up and yelled at him: 'What gives you the right to speak to her in that way?'

'I pay your wages and I will speak to these women any way I want.' I told him that he should apologise to her. There was a huge shout of 'Yes, apologise!' With that he left the canteen. A number of the women asked Meredith why he had not supported them on this issue as I had. The look on his face convinced me that he really did not like me. By now it was lunchtime, and there was plenty of discussion over dinner. Meredith for some reason did not eat with his workmates. He spent his lunchtime in the office.

It must have been about 3 pm that afternoon when Norman Black came into the cutting room. Harry Clarke walked past me and said, 'Watch it; it looks as though Black is coming to you.' Sure enough he stopped at the end of my table. I must have referred to him as someone who was backward because he started shouting at me, 'So you think I am backward, do you?' I carried on working and did not even look at him. He asked me this three or four times. Each time I ignored him. I was told afterwards that his face went from pink to red then to purple. I finally turned round while he was in full flow. I put down my shears, waited for him to finish, and then said calmly, 'Go away and get control of yourself. Come back and I might talk to you.' His face went from purple to deep purple.

His brother Ted then came up to him and led him away.

I did not expect to last five minutes after that but I lasted for another four years. That was three-and-a-half years longer than Norman Black; he died of a heart attack six months after our conflict.

Executex advertising, 1962. Styled for men of taste and distinction by Norman Black

At the time of the Cuba Crisis (Bay of Pigs), the Leeds Branch decided that we should have a factory gate meeting at my factory, Black and Lupers (Executex). The factory was leafleted on the morning of the meeting and a lot of interest was shown, but whether or not any one would turn up was a different matter. Our university comrades were asked to come to the meeting to sell papers and help to swell the crowd. I remember it being a nice sunny day, just the type of day you need for a factory gate meeting. The speakers were Cliff Slaughter, Jack Gale and me. I thought we would get a few out to the meeting, but to our great joy we had a meeting of well over 100. During the meeting a lorry that was parked on the waste ground near the factory was being deliberately revved up to try and disrupt the speakers. Jack Kershaw, who by no stretch of the imagination could be said to be a supporter of my politics, went across to the lorry, opened the door and told the driver if he did not turn off his engine he would 'bleep'-well sort him out. Jack, a professional Rugby League player, could and would do just that. The engine was turned off.

I spoke last and just before I was due to speak one of the three police officers, a sergeant, who had turned up to hear what we had to say came up to me and said, 'You blokes are all the same. Why don't you go and speak outside your own factory?' I remember that it was with some pride that I told him, 'I am outside my factory; I work here.' What's more he had given me a great opening for when I made my contribution. I told the meeting what the sergeant had said, and what my reply was. This was well received by the crowd and I well remember the student comrades enjoying the moment. I understand that these comrades got a lot of encouragement and confidence from the activity of that day. I went back into work flushed with success. What a difference from the time, much later, when I stood outside the factory with a loudhailer talking to the walls about the dangers of Barbara Castle's *In Place of Strife*. Even then it wasn't wasted; there were a few who had listened by opening the windows. There was also the usual comment that you get when you are in that kind of situation, 'I'll give him his due, he stands up for what he believes in.' Even that was welcome.

Some time after this I thought that I was going to be able to have a quiet Saturday. No chance. Cliff Slaughter contacted me to tell me that the British National Party and its leader Colin Jordan were in Albion Street selling their paper *Action*. We went down to Leeds centre to see if we could intervene in any way. We began by stopping people as they passed, pointing the BNP out to them and explaining who they were. Slowly we built up a crowd of about 50. Cliff had gone into the Kardomah coffee bar to get support. He then went into the market to contact some of the market lads who came and swelled our numbers. The BNP sellers had positioned themselves at the crossroads in Albion Street and had a group on each corner. We moved round from corner to corner and each time collected two or three. We ended up with quite a crowd on each corner surrounding the BNP. The *Yorkshire Evening Post* appeared on the scene about the same time as the police. By now the crowd had swelled considerably and the police decided to move the BNP on. Gauleiter Jordan brought a truck into Albion Street, loaded his troops into it and they left, flinging up their arms in a fascist salute.

In case the paper forgot to report this story I wrote a letter for publication in the Monday edition of the *Yorkshire Evening Post*. This was published on Monday night and on the Tuesday morning I was surprised by the attitude of some of the workers. It went something like this. Our employer is a Jew so why did I oppose those people when they were against our employer? This was not difficult to answer. I support non-Jewish workers against Jewish employers and Jewish workers against non-Jewish employers. It is a class division and not one of religion or colour. Ted Black came into the cutting room to see me (his brother was dead by this time). In a loud voice he congratulated me on getting rid of the fascists. This had to be answered on the spot. 'The fascists use racism as one of their tactics for weakening the working class by turning worker against worker. We need a strong working class to defeat such as you. That is why I oppose fascism.' Naturally the discussion continued. I am sure it was only a coincidence but not long after that Ted Black died of a heart attack. That same day Meredith, who worked four boards down from me, turned and said in a loud whisper, 'Two of the leaders of his lot are Pakis.' Ken Dawson, who had only recently been employed and was politically close to me, gave him a good old dressing-down. Ken would not join the SLL for domestic reasons but he attended as many of our activities as possible. He also attended the union branch with me.

In 1966 the SLL was committed to sending a delegation of 500 to a demonstration against the Vietnam war that was being held in Liège (Belgium). The Young Socialists did a mass leaflet distribution around the factories, mine included. The leaflet not only explained the political reasons for the demonstration, it also explained how we were going to get there, and this was impressive. A train had been chartered from London Victoria; a channel ferry had been chartered to Ostend, and a number of Belgian members of parliament were to meet us and help to get us through as quickly as possible. We then had our own train from Ostend to Liège. Ken asked Meredith if he was going. He spat back: 'The only ship they will fill will be a rowing boat.' In fact six youngsters from the factory signed up and went. The YS branch had organised a meeting to prepare for the trip and our six were invited. Tremendous pressure was put on these youngsters by the management, using Meredith and a few others as their agents. On the morning of that YS meeting, Barbara, one of the women in the machine room, told me that one of the six had told her that Meredith had arranged for a steward from another factory to get him invited to the meeting as a clothing-worker shop steward. Meredith announced in the cutting room that he was going to speak at one of Harding's YS branches. In a very roundabout way, through others, he was trying to get me to go to the meeting to have a confrontation with him. At this time our leading YS members were still members of the Labour Party. As an expellee if I did go I expect he would have informed the Labour Party and that would cause problems in many ways, perhaps affecting the Leeds delegation to the demonstration.

On some pretext or other I asked the cutting room foreman to let me use his office to make a telephone call. I managed to get hold of Comrade Guyton, the YS branch secretary. I briefly explained the problem and told him to ring the other shop steward, and also to ring Meredith cancelling the invitation. Early in the afternoon there was an announcement over the tannoy informing Meredith that he was wanted on the telephone. When he came back and was faced with, 'What's up Fred? Where is the meeting Fred?' and such-like questions, he lost his temper, came to the end of my work board and screamed at me that I was an 'ugly bastard'. I told him to watch his blood pressure; there were two down and would he be the third? He must have been very sensitive because for some reason he lost his power of speech.

A few days before we were to set off to Liège, my father had a heart attack. I visited him in hospital on the Wednesday and Thursday evening and again on the Friday morning. I was to telephone before we set off for London. It was only when we returned from Liège that I discovered that Dad had had the third of a set of three heart attacks on the Friday afternoon. The first thing I did when I was back in Leeds was to visit him in hospital, where I was told what had happened. He had refused to let anyone tell me of his real condition. He had not wanted me to be disappointed by missing the trip. Two to three weeks and he was home and made a great recovery. And he was soon back with his concert party.

Arriving in London I was given the job of working with one of the railway workers checking tickets and counting everyone who passed through the gates on to the platform. Five minutes before the train was due to leave the railway supervisor came to see how

One of the posters on the side of the campaign car says 'Enjoy Life — Join the Young Socialists!'

things were progressing. The last of the delegation from Scotland had just arrived; they were counted through and it was a total of exactly 500. This was our target and the figure that had been given to British Rail. The supervisor was very impressed and said that he had only come to sort out the expected problems of late arrivals and a late departure. We left dead on time.

The French comrades had matched our 500. With the Belgian contingent and others there must have been 2,000 or more on the demonstration. The only problem that developed was when we unfurled a banner celebrating the tenth anniversary of the Hungarian Revolution of 1956, which raised some problems with the French contingent. At the meeting in the evening it was obvious that Healy was in conflict with the leaders of the French contingent. This was the first time that I had experienced this kind of disagreement. It appeared to be one of personalities rather than a difference of opinion. In later years I was to understand that Healy was scared of not being in control.

We were well fed: plenty of wonderful crusty bread, and a wide variety of ham and cheese. With the inner man satisfied we set off to walk to the station to board our train to the coast, board our boat, train to London, collect our minibuses and back to Leeds. We set off from London with 500 and came back with 500. The success of the trip was soon spread around the Leeds labour movement and, more to the point, my factory contingent was full of it and told everyone who would listen. I felt good about it, but it also meant that I had to watch my step.

The election for the No.2 Branch committee was due and Ken and others were going to nominate me as soon as the nomination papers were circulated round the factories and made available to the members. It soon became obvious something was wrong. Other factories had received the nomination paper but there was no sign of ours. Meredith said that he had not received it. One dinnertime Ken and I went to the union office in Circle House, Lady Lane, and asked why we had not received it. The full-time secretary simply said that as far as he knew it had been sent, and what could he do about it? One of the girls in the office overheard our discussion and informed us that the nomination form had not only been sent but had been returned. She got the file and showed us it had Meredith's name on it, with two of his cronies as mover and seconder. The full-time secretary reluctantly agreed to let us take the nomination form back with us so that the rest of the members could have the opportunity to be nominated. Arriving back, Ken asked if he could confront Meredith with the hard evidence of his deceit. He approached him and when still some distance away he shouted, 'Fred, I have the nomination form, just collected it from the union office.' Meredith held his hand out to get hold of it. 'You don't want it,' said Ken, 'your name is already on it.' It was a very embarrassed Fred who scuttled off to his board to start work and then later, on some pretext or other, to the office.

At this point I considered forcing an election for a new steward. It was clear that this would open a whole new can of snakes. Ken, Bill, Ronnie and others said that it would only end up with me getting sacked. I thought I was in danger of being sacked anyway, but I agreed to wait until after the branch committee elections. My view was that if elected I would have a base to fight on. The voting papers for the No.2 Branch committee duly arrived and every member of the union was given one. Before the voting papers were gathered in Meredith put a bundle of voting papers on my board and told me that I might as well use them to help get myself elected. After bringing this to the attention of those working closest to me, I made sure that I had witnesses to confirm that I made him pick them up and take them away. At lunchtime I went to Circle House to see Harry Yates, the branch secretary, and reported the incident. I accused Meredith of attempting to rig the union branch committee election and informed him that I had witnesses who would verify my accusation. He advised me to forget the incident, as it was difficult to prove one way or the other. He just did not want to know. I gave him a straight choice: he either came to the factory and was seen to reprimand Meredith or I would raise the issue at the next branch meeting. Who knows what he would have done if this had happened; he could even have said that he was asked to fit me up by someone.

Yates came to the factory and spoke to Meredith on one side. He took the bundle of voting papers away with him. To try and save face Meredith let it be known that he was only trying to help me to get elected; I was just ungrateful and should not have shopped him to the union. Meredith was elected to the branch committee, no doubt by votes from the other factories in our branch.

A youth was employed to work in the cloth room. After a few weeks he started to sit with a group of us at lunchtime. One lunchtime we were talking about the incident with the BNP in Albion Street. At this he told us that his mother's boyfriend was secretary of the Leeds branch of the BNP. When we asked him how he knew he said that he left leaflets and books at his house and was always talking about it. I asked his name. Hainsworth, he said. I knew that was true. A number of weeks later the lad brought a leaflet to show me. It was a leaflet that was to be handed out that evening in Leeds City Square. Hainsworth had asked him to help them and he had declined. I felt that this had to be challenged, but I also suspected that it might be a set-up. I decided that there was only one way to find out and that was to arrange a reception for them. I decided that it would be safer to go to Maurice Freeman's office to use the phone. I thought, 'If I'm caught that's my lot.' But I still picked up the phone and by a stroke of luck got in touch with Cliff Slaughter in his office at Leeds university. We agreed that he would round up as many anti-fascists as possible and meet at 7 pm outside the News Theatre in City Square.

I turned round and Freeman was standing in the doorway; he had heard everything. He came into the office, closed the door and told me to sit down. Freeman was Jewish and he said that because of the content of my telephone conversation he was prepared to overlook my indiscretion. I decided not to go over the political points regarding my opposition to Jewish employers. I did not want to push my luck. So I made a compromise with myself, and kept my mouth shut. I spent the rest of the day clock-watching: 5.30 pm could not come quick enough. I asked around to see if anyone was willing to take part, but only Ken Dawson was prepared to come back into Leeds. I did not bother going home; I spent my time instead at the university seeking out our members. Cliff had already passed the word around. We had made many contacts from our Albion Street experience. With this, the uni, and other avenues we could expect a good turn out.

I was at the meeting point about 7 pm and by 7.30 pm we had about 30 to 35 people. About ten minutes later a group of roughly ten assembled outside the post office in City Square. Hainsworth was there and distributed a bundle of leaflets to each one. We immediately made our way towards them. Before we could confront them, they spotted us and took off. We wandered around for half an hour or so but there was no sign of them. That was all that happened, no more, no less. I say this because the following morning the *News Chronicle* published an amazing front page. The main front-page story was a report of fascists being chased out of Leeds. It referred to a well-organised group of anti-fascists forcing the BNP to leave City Square by sheer weight of numbers. According to the report we followed them in cars to make sure that they left Leeds. This activity was supposed to have been directed by two or three leaders of the Leeds Socialist Labour League from the back room of a local pub.

I was given a copy of the paper as soon as I walked through the factory door. This rag of a paper was well known for its anti-working class slant, which made it more amazing that it should not only publish such a story but also put it on the front page. It can't have been much later than nine o'clock when the girl in the office who acted as the management secretary got a message to me that she had been sent out to buy a number of the papers. Luper of Black (deceased) and Luper had called a meeting of the management to take place that morning. About thirty minutes before lunchtime a girl came to me for some trouser fittings that had been damaged. She also had a message for me asking me to meet the girl in the office at the entrance to Leeds Market Hall on the corner of Vicar Lane and Kirkgate. We went into a nearby café where she told me that a copy of the *News Chronicle* had been given to all the senior managers present. They were told to read the front-page article. Maurice Freeman, the manager who had caught me red-handed in the office making the phone call to Cliff, informed the assembled that what they had read was the result of one phone call. He explained to them that he had caught me making that phone call. Because it was directed at the BNP he had let me off, but now thought of me as a dangerous communist militant. It was agreed that I would have to go. A reason for sacking me had to be found. First they would check on my attendance record and take it from there. If that failed it was just a case of watching my back.

The other thing that I learned was that the management knew about the incident with the voting papers. Meredith had told them what he was going to do. She told me also that he used to laugh when Black came out with his male chauvinist comments, especially when women were present. I had not thought that I could despise him any more than I already did. What was a man like that doing in the labour movement anyway? I asked her why she was helping me in this way; after all, she was putting her job on the line. Apparently she was pleased at the way I had opposed Norman Black's backward attitude to the women workers. Margaret confirmed what was already suspected: that he was in the habit, from time to time, of inviting some of the women workers into his well-furnished office. He had tried it on with her; she had not been sorry when he died. Things were easier now that the harassment had stopped but the rest of them were just as corrupt. Margaret had only stuck it out because she needed the money. Her husband was on a low income and they had two young children.

The investigation into my time-keeping and attendance record did not get them very far. In fact I had a letter from the management received by all those who had made it to work during a week of appalling conditions of snow and ice thanking them for their loyalty. That particular week I was getting up an hour earlier to make sure that I would not be late. I had this letter ready in case I needed it. The weeks went by and no doubt my file was getting thicker. One day Harry Clark, Ken Dawson and I decided we would not go into the canteen for our lunch. We got ourselves a sandwich and sat down on the lower shelf of Ken's cutting board. This meant that we were out of sight. What a stroke of good fortune this was, because we heard the door of the cloth-room open and then the sound of footsteps coming down the main alleyway between the rows of work boards. We could see the legs approaching. They stopped at the end of my alley and one of them put a length of cloth on to the bottom shelf of my cutting board. It was the cloth-room manager and Maurice Freeman, the factory manager.

During the lunch break I wrote a statement saying that at such and such a time the cloth-room manager and Freeman were seen putting a piece of cloth under my board. Ken, Harry and I signed it. Underneath we wrote, 'The undersigned were shown this note before we started work.' Ronnie, Bill, and Big Eric, along with two or three more signed, showing that they knew what was going on before the search began. We did not move from where we were until people started to come down from the canteen. The plan was that I would stand halfway down my alley a few yards from where the cloth had been planted. Ken and Harry were to tell those whom we could trust. We had to make sure that Meredith did not know that we had seen the cloth planted, as he would have warned the management. As soon as work restarted the cloth-room manager and Freeman came into the cutting room, went into the office of Harry Barr, the foreman, and had a brief conversation with him. The three of them walked down the main alley looking under the tables as they passed.

When they stopped opposite me, I intervened and said, 'Before you look under my board I want Harry Barr to read this.' I gave him the statement. He read it, turned to Freeman and said, 'I don't want to be any part of this.' He gave him the statement and walked away. Freeman read it. His eyes were blazing; I fully expected rays to shoot out and disintegrate me. The pair of them were about to turn round and do a retreat. I told them to hang on and said that as the cloth-room manager had put the cloth there he should take it away. My parting shot was to say all they had succeeded in doing was to show themselves up for the little people that they were. They would be a laughing stock and I would make sure that the whole factory got to know what they had tried to do. I told them that I suspected that I would not only have been sacked, but also fitted up and charged with theft. Freeman turned round to say something, but thought better of it. I knew I was in my twilight working there so I was not sorry for freely expressing myself. Later in the afternoon Harry Barr came to me and said that he disassociated himself from what they had tried to do.

For the previous year or two Meredith had been closely collaborating with Jim Roche who had left the Communist Party in 1957 while he was Yorkshire Area secretary. Roche always fancied himself as the guru of the gurus. These two formed a prop-and-cop relationship when they came together in CND. Jim was so full of himself that when CND was having a demonstration in the Goole area of Yorkshire he appointed himself to walk in front of the demonstration as the leader. The Leeds Executive Committee had already decided that the CND members from the Goole area, with their banner, would lead the demo. He was told to fall in behind the Goole contingent. Instead, he went to the back of the demo and walked on his own. He obviously thought that this was the second most important position to take up.

Jim Roche distributed a 'Dear friend' letter, announcing that a new journal was to be published in the Leeds labour movement called 'Searchlight' or maybe 'Torchlight'. Its aim was to encourage discussion on 'Historical Truth'. The joint editors were to be Roche and Meredith. The first edition was to contain 'Is there such a thing as absolute truth?' by Jim Roche. Meredith would write about the relationship between Plato and Karl Marx. Contributions for the first edition were to be sent to the editors. After an anxious few weeks the great moment arrived. It was a Monday morning. Meredith came in full of bounce, opened up a parcel and distributed copies around. As he gave them out he told everyone that this was going to put the *Newsletter* out of business. I was privileged to receive one. It was sixteen pages, shared between the introduction, the absolute truth, Plato and Karl Marx. The front cover was black with a beam of light from bottom right to top left. There was a round circle of light on a wall and projected on to the wall were the words 'The Truth'. Ken, Bill, Ronnie and I had a crack at reading it and we all found it difficult. Plato to Marx was nonsense. It had been written just to show that Meredith had a dictionary. Before work started he asked, 'Well what do you think of it?' No one answered. Then, for the first time for many weeks, Meredith spoke directly to me, 'What did you think of it?'

'If you want the absolute truth, I think it's a load of nonsense.'

How is it whenever I tell the truth I seem to get myself in trouble? He got very angry saying things like: 'You're a fool. The *Newsletter* is run by Communists. Your national secretary [meaning Mike Banda, who is from Sri Lanka] is a bloody Paki.' I raised this racist comment in the union and in the CND. The executive committee told him that he would have to apologise. He refused and walked out of the meeting. The union branch committee took no action saying that it was a 'difference of opinion' between two individuals.

That was the first and last publication, as I understand there had been a power struggle between the two editors for overall control. Then something strange happened. Jim Roche was employed at the factory as a manager in one of the manufacturing departments. Meredith accused him of being a renegade and a traitor. Jim Roche had only been at the factory a few weeks when one of the girls came into the cutting room in tears and told Meredith that Roche had threatened her with the sack for, I think, incompetence. Meredith asked me if I would support him in a demand for a vote on strike action if Roche did not withdraw the threat. I said that I would. A meeting was called and the resolution was passed. Meredith went off to see the management. Ten minutes later he came back and reported that the management had instructed Roche to withdraw his threat and apologise to the girl. A few weeks later Roche was sacked. He must have thought that he was still an organiser in the working class because he said in public that I had played a part in getting him the sack, and that made me a scab. I raised this at the union branch meeting, knowing that the officials would not act, and I also had to raise the issue on the CND executive committee. I explained what had happened and Roche made some comment or other. The committee agreed that such a statement was an insult. To be called a scab could damage my reputation in the labour movement. He was asked to apologise; if he refused he would have to leave the meeting and his position as an executive committee member would have to be discussed. He refused and resigned. The action of the committee indicated the respect we had in CND.

After 1956 many ex-Communist Party members and their fellow travellers in the Labour Party had embraced social democracy with a great enthusiasm. They had become part of the establishment in the party. Some of them reached the dizzy heights of becoming councillors, in some cases even Members of Parliament. Jim Roche was one of those who became a councillor. To do this (as I knew from experience) you had to be someone who could be 'trusted'. Roche had been making his bid for a long time — a long time before he appeared at Executex. My first glimpse of this was during a debate at the Leeds Trades Council on a resolution supporting a joint Trades Council and Labour Party May Day march.

I can see very clearly in my mind's eye Roche getting up to speak. He half turned, pushed his chair back, rubbing his left ear with his right hand. He always did this when he was wanting to create an atmosphere of 'what I am about to say is very serious'. 'Brother Chairman,' he said, 'from my past experiences as a communist I have to warn you that the Communist Party can only disrupt the May Day March.' He went on to recommend that the Communist Party should not be allowed to join the May Day March. Nor should any CP member be allowed to sit on the organising committee. The way he spoke the word communist and linked it with the word past made me very angry. I have always been a firm believer in squeezing every ounce out of everything that comes your way. I raised my hand, and managed to catch the eye of Malwyn Jones in the chair. As soon as Roche had finished he called on me to speak. 'Brother Chairman: this question of Communist Party members sitting on the organising committee,' I said. 'They have as much right as any other delegate to be on it. If this Trades Council is involved in an activity then every union delegate, including Communist Party members, is constitutionally allowed to take part in that activity. If not it would be a nonsense to allow Communist Party members to be accepted as delegates in the first place.' I also said that his reference to his past communist experience was in my opinion a clear message to the Labour Party, informing them that he no longer considered himself a communist. 'You're not a Trotskyist or a member of any other political group. So you can only be a loyal member of the Labour Party. You once told me that the art of politics was the art of making friends. You seem to have lost your skill in that direction. You have changed your politics and have made new friends.'

About this time the Conservative-run Leeds City Council called a Town Meeting. I don't remember if it was to discuss any particular policy question or to give the citizens of Leeds an opportunity to raise any issues, but I do remember that the question of housing dominated the meeting. The Labour Party had encouraged shop stewards to get as many people to attend as possible. Meredith organised a number of people to attend on the grounds that we had to have a go at the Tories. It was very dull until a lady at the back managed to get in with a question regarding the condition of the old house she was living in. She asked what the council was going to do about either knocking it down or making it habitable. The chair of the meeting handed the question over to someone on the housing committee. He started off by saying that he sympathised with the questioner; he understood her problems as he also lived in old property, and the council was doing its best to eliminate this kind of problem. He sat down; nobody moved a muscle. A large number of Labour councillors was present but not one made any attempt to answer this Tory who obviously had no idea of the real world that this lady was talking about.

I decided that, if no one else was prepared to support her, before the chair could call for any other question then I would do it. I did not wait for the chair's permission to speak; I just dived in without a clue what I was going to say. To collect my thoughts I asked the Tory councillor to apologise to the lady who had asked the question. He was taken by surprise at this. When he asked 'Why?' it seemed to kick start me. I asked him if he had any idea what kind of old house she was talking about, and how dare he insult everyone here by comparing her one-up and one-down with his many-roomed comfortable old house. 'In case you do not know what a one-up, one-down is I will explain it to you.' This went down very well. The only other points I remember making were that more council houses had to be built and the old slum houses knocked down. Imagine my surprise when the next issue of the *Leeds Weekly Citizen* (Leeds Labour Party paper) had a full report of my intervention in Nemo's column. It also asked why someone who had been expelled from the Labour Party had to reply to the chair of the Conservative housing committee. Why did the Labour councillors present keep quiet? This became quite a serious issue as far as the rank-and-file members of the Labour Party were concerned and was raised very forcibly at the ward and constituency level. It culminated in a resolution at the next City Party delegate meeting condemning the Labour councillors who were present at the Town Meeting for not intervening on such an important issue.

One important thing in this was that we did not have to organise the protest. The Labour Party councillors did not intervene. The Labour Party members did it for us. The right wing was embarrassed, and the left wing used it to have a go at the right wing. In the weeks following I was asked on a number of occasions if I would consider re-applying for membership of the Labour Party. It was made very clear that I would automatically be but back on the prospective candidates' list. Naturally I declined this offer of corruption. On behalf of the Conservative Party the *Yorkshire Evening Post* tried to make some mileage out of the discussion taking place in the Labour Party. One of the girls put the article from the *Citizen* reporting the Town Meeting on the noticeboard in the factory (manufacturing department) and a copy was passed around; the same happened in the cutting room (Ken was responsible). When it arrived at Meredith he tore it up, and once again my countenance came in for some criticism. Ken immediately produced another and passed it on.

The SLL and earlier the Group organised a two-week education camp every year. One year it was to be an international camp, with contingents coming from Europe (mainly France) and the USA. Everyone was encouraged to attend the full two weeks. For me this meant that I would have to take three weeks off work. I applied to have the week before our official two weeks' holiday and to my surprise received permission without having to argue for it. I remember hoping pressure from the Centre to make up numbers at the last minute would not happen because the large attendance by the international contingents would swell the numbers.

Normally I could only attend the second week of camp, so I always had the job of making sure that the second weekers' travel arrangements were organised. On the Thursday night before leaving on the Saturday, I would always have to be by a telephone and wait for someone to ring from the camp so that I could tell the caller how many would be travelling down from Yorkshire. Bill Hunter telephoned. He asked me how many; I told him. Not enough, he said, you will have to get more. Jean Kerrigan, who was already at camp, was based in Sheffield at this time and was the Yorkshire Area Secretary. Jean had told Bill that a lot of youth gathered at a certain place on one of the estates in Sheffield. I was instructed to go immediately to Sheffield, find these youth and convince as many as possible to go to the camp. Then I had to arrange transport and get the money off them. Bill would be ringing back at 19.00 hours the next day, Friday, for me to tell him how many extra would be going to camp. This was seven o'clock Thursday evening.

I did go to Sheffield. I remember feeling very uneasy about the whole affair. I found my way to the estate, got out of the car and said to myself something like, 'What the hell am I doing here?' No doubt just what I would have said if I had found myself standing outside the cage at the top of Blackpool Tower in a roaring gale. I would certainly have questioned my sanity. I got back into the car and went back to Leeds to start preparing the transport for those who were going. Bill rang on the Friday evening. I told him there was no change. No good, he said, I would have to do something about it. I asked if he could recommend a way of doing this without having to lasso youth on the streets. I was told that this was my problem. If when I arrived at camp there had been no change I would have to explain it to the camp committee. We were setting off at 08.00 hours the following morning. It would be true to say that for the first time since I became a member I had a feeling of hopelessness. I was in a situation I felt I could do nothing about; it was all so unreal. At camp, I and others were told that we had shown that we lacked determination and had simply accepted the situation. We were weak, and social democrats. I admit it made me feel inadequate to the task. Later in the week Healy spoke to me and said that he said those things to bring home the lessons of what had happened. If I was to be a revolutionary then I would have to understand this. So I went away, had lunch and felt a lot better.

The idea was that if you had the will and concentrated on the necessity of carrying out a decision within the context of building the revolutionary party then the problems would be overcome. Those of us subjected to this criticism had not failed to increase our numbers because we lacked determination, but because the decision and the way we were told to do it had been wrong in the first place.

Another example of this 'revolutionary determination' was thrown at the areas for a few years when the figures were always lower than expected for the annual *Keep Left* conference. One particular year all areas were down on their estimated contingents, especially Scotland and the north of England. Scotland and the north-east came in for a right old dose of 'lack of revolutionary determination'. My friend and comrade, Dave Temple, will no doubt still have it imprinted on his mind. As far as Leeds was concerned, we had one hell of a job trying to get everyone to stay under one or two roofs. We were to start off early on the Saturday morning, I think at 06.00 hours. Jack and I started rounding up the youth about three o'clock to get them to the two hired minibuses. Trevor Parsons and I drove one of them. We literally had to peel them off the carpet, drag them out of chairs, hunt for them in different corners of the houses they were in. They were all at parties — it was New Year's Eve! The decision to hold the *Keep Left* conference on News Year's Day was made without taking into account just what this meant. There was no relationship with the working class; it was all 'build the leadership!' This was looked on as revolutionary training, but such decisions only sabotaged the event we were trying to make a success, in this case the *Keep Left* conference.

But back to the international camp, which was a success. I played no part in the daytime activities as I was put on the night shift preparing food for the following day and cooking the breakfasts, all 500 of them. When the camp was over I did my usual trip to Glasgow taking comrades home, then back to Leeds. The camps were always on or close to the south coast so it was quite a trip. This particular time I got a few miles from camp when I had to stop and sleep for two hours. Yes, I know I should have rested at the camp properly. But the whole pressure was to get them off camp to their areas as quickly as possible. We arrived safe, but I had to stop for coffee and rest more often than usual.

Arriving home I found a bulky envelope waiting for me. It contained my cards, £150 redundancy money and a letter telling me that my services were no longer required. No wonder they had let me have the extra week's holiday; they were planning on giving me a permanent holiday. I used the money to buy a new modern loud hailer for the Leeds branch. I gave Mum and Dad some money to boost their pocket money, as they were soon to go on holiday. Then I bought myself a pair of shoes and two new pairs of trousers.

There was a time when I had precious little left on payday after I had put money into different envelopes, each representing one of my commitments. This went on for a very long time. My trousers became so thin that I had to wear pyjama trousers underneath to try and keep warm. And here I was working in a clothing factory. At a Central Committee meeting Party leader Gerry Healy asked me if I could get him a suit length. I agreed to do this even though I could not do so for myself. (Later I found out that at the time when I risked everything — my job and my political work — he had a wardrobe full of clothes.) I explained my situation to Cliff Slaughter. A few days later he gave me some money that he had collected from some of his contacts which enabled me to buy some clothes. I am relating this not to get sympathy, but to show the level of commitment of party members.

9

LOSCOE AND THE NORMANTON RENT STRIKE

I was called over to a table one evening in 1964 on a paper sale in a pub in the Yorkshire coalmining area. I sat down (and tried not to refuse a pint). A group of lads told me about the conditions in a little mining village called Loscoe. What they explained was horrendous. They had relatives living in Loscoe who had asked if I would go and talk to them with a view to helping them organise against the landlords who were subjecting them to these conditions. These lads said that if I agreed they would take me the following Sunday morning, introduce me to their relatives and take me round the village.

This was to be an occasion when I would have my eyes opened. It was like walking into a Victorian slum.

I met the lads as arranged outside the Union pub on the corner of Normanton Road and the lane leading to Loscoe. We walked for about half a mile until we came to a stone wall; about 50 yards further on there was an opening. We turned in through this opening and in front of us there was a patch of wasteland with stubble grass growing on it. Beyond that there were six rows of back-to-back houses. The front doors in each case led straight on to the pavement. From where we were standing we could see down the streets.

We turned into one of the streets and knocked on one lad's uncle's door. We were obviously expected; tea and biscuits were laid out. This house was a two-up, two-down, that is two bedrooms, a 'kitchen' and a room that passed as a sitting room-cum-dining room. In their case it was used as a bedroom as well. I was taken upstairs to be shown the reason why. The walls were not just damp; they were soaking wet and had big green patches with fungi growing along the wall. I was told that almost every house was in a similar condition. I asked if I could go and see some other houses. I was shown some of the worst housing conditions that I had ever seen.

Crumbling, damp houses in pit village

LIVING in houses with roofs that let the rain in and walls that are crumbling from damp, many miners and their families at Loscoe, Yorkshire, eat and sleep in conditions which are a great danger to their health.

In one house a 19-year-old youth has had to sleep for nine weeks on a settee in the kitchen because water was pouring in through the bedroom ceiling. His two sisters slept with their parents on the living room floor.

A bath was put under the main leak and ten to 12 buckets of sludge were emptied out of it at the end of the day.

Toilets are at the end of the street. Tenants claim that these have not flushed for two consecutive months in the past two years.

HEALTH

Sewage is so bad that most parents are sure that it is endangering the health of their children.

A housewife who pays £1 3s. 6d. per week rent told a Newsletter reporter that the only time repairs were done was when relatives gave her help.

Another tenant had to move out of one of his bedrooms because the ceiling was coming in. Now all the family sleep in one room where the walls let the rain in. It is not surprising that both the father and his six-year-old daughter suffer from bronchitis.

Tenants pay 16s. 10½d. rent for the 104-year-old houses while rats live for free around the dustbins in the back yards.

An 82-year-old man and his wife moved from their home because one of them suffered with rheumatism. Their rent was 16s. 10d. Now they are having to pay 25s.

Tenants maintain that the landlords are only too pleased when people leave because that means they can put the rent up again for the next family.

ANGRY

Many of the Loscoe people are angry at the amount of attention they have received from the local Labour council.

'The only time we ever see them is when they want us to vote at election time,' was the comment of one tenant.

But it is the duty of all Labour councils and the whole of the labour movement to take up the struggles of the tenants in their fight against the rent racketeering landlords.

Tenants vote Labour hoping that Harold Wilson or his equivalent on the local council will do something about getting new houses and bringing down the rents.

Newsletter *report about Loscoe on 18 April 1964 (above) was followed by another on 25April (right)*

A young couple with two small children lived in a one-up and one-down. The house was damp but in spite of the terrible conditions it was obvious that a tremendous effort was being made to keep the place clean, as was the case in all the houses I was taken to. I don't think any of the houses had carpets on the floor; they had rotted long ago. There were families where illness caused by the conditions was rife.

I was shown where raw sewage was seeping through the cracks in the practically non-existent pavements. When it rained the sewage flooded out. The household rubbish was tipped into the midden, a

Who's in charge of Loscoe?

TENANTS IN Loscoe, Yorkshire, gave a big reception to last week's Newsletter, which contained an article describing the appalling conditions in which these people live.

As Newsletter reporters went from house to house many of the tenants added more information to that which we published last week.

One man, totally disabled by pneumoconiosis—a disease very common among miners—complained that both his bedroom ceilings let in water.

Lighting

Street lighting does not always work and at night serious accidents could occur in the pitch dark streets which are riddled with holes.

Reporters were told that a Sanitary Inspector had been informed of the bad conditions in Loscoe but nothing had yet been done.

'We would like to know exactly where is the Sanitary Inspector?' said one tenant.

Many of the people in Loscoe told how they had not seen their landlord for a long time. 'I don't think our landlord even knows where Loscoe is,' was the comment of one person.

Rates

Tenants say they have been told that the rates are paid in the nearby town of Featherstone and all sewage responsibilities belong to Normanton, whilst water supplies come from Wakefield.

There is a great deal of confusion as to who is actually in charge of things like lighting, and dustbins.

So far the tenants have heard nothing from the local Labour council which must take some responsibility for such poor housing.

Tenant after tenant has threatened that he will not vote Labour at the next general election unless something is done about their homes.

kind of bunker situated every so far between the houses. This was a great breeding place for rats. Running along the far end of the houses was a beck, or stream — or open sewer. The latter is the best way to describe it. The sewage from the broken pipes ran into it. 'In summer it stinks and it's a full-time job stopping the children from playing there,' one young mother told me.

Over the previous two summers many children had been taken very ill. One child had died. The mother said that she blamed the beck. 'It poisoned him.' The favourite game in Loscoe was to see who had the best dog, judged on how many rats it could kill. I was shown where the rats had their holes in the side of the banking leading down to the beck.

No one knew who the landlords were. The rent collectors did not even know; they were just working for an agent. We were to be up against racketeers of the worst possible kind. To get things started, two or three people from each street were asked to meet in one of the houses that evening. It was agreed that each household would write a letter complaining about the conditions and give it to the rent collectors who in turn would give it to the landlords.

While waiting for the not-expected reply I moved around the village getting to know people. I was soon a welcome visitor to their homes. I asked Celia Gale to help me with the work and she readily agreed. At times, Celia put the two girls, Ruth and Jill, in the pushchair and took them with us to Loscoe.

Two weeks passed and there was no reply to the letters. By this time it was clear what had to be done. Everyone had to be united behind a campaign to publicise the plight of the tenants. Celia and I took statements from about twenty households describing the condition of their homes and of the village itself, and about the state of the health of those living in the houses. Every one of them agreed to sign their statements. We discovered many things doing this. A large proportion of homes was so bad that the upstairs room or rooms could not be used because of the extreme damp. The worst thing was that the children were in constant danger healthwise: in winter from the constant dampness; in summer from infection and disease from the outside conditions as well as in the home. In some cases there had been an attempt to fasten tarpaulin sheets across the roofs of the houses.

We took the residents through every step that we took. All the statements were typed on to stencils and then run off on a Gestetner that we had in the Gales' basement. We made trips over to Loscoe and all those who had written the statements proofread them and signed them.

We then produced a sample copy of an eight-by-ten inch document. It had an introduction explaining some of the history of Loscoe and that the aim of the campaign was to expose who the landlords were and to demand that everyone should be re-housed. Copies of this document were sent to all sections of the media and to the local council. A copy was also left in each pub and club in the area. During the next weeks the *Newsletter* became very popular and accepted wherever we went. The comrades who took part in these sales had a very pleasant reception. I can also say that this was one of the peaks in my political activity. I remember being full of energy and confidence. More than one person said that if I was to stand for the council I would get in; well, maybe, maybe not.

After about two weeks we finally received feedback from the document. I received a telephone call from the presenter of *Look North*, a popular television programme. He asked if I was prepared to appear on the programme. I said that I would. He reminded me that it was a live programme and asked how I felt about that. I said OK. He went on to say that from his experience to get the kind of signed statements that were in the document could only mean that there must have been more than just a one-off visit to Loscoe. He thought that to get this kind of result you would have to win their confidence. There was already a councillor lined up and steps were being taken to get the landlords to attend. I was to arrange for one

Loscoe housing destroying health

SINCE Mrs. Jackson of Loscoe (see picture of village above) refused to pay rent until repairs were done to her home, a man has come and put a couple of slates on a few roofs.

The family told The Newsletter that he was not on any roof for more than ten minutes.

The pavements are now littered with slates again after last week-end's wind.

Another youngster, the 4-year-old son of Marie Smith in Albion Street, is in hospital with pneumonia.

In the back bedroom, half the ceiling is down.

Marie Smith and her three children sleep in the front bedroom. Her son had always been the healthiest one of the family, but his bed always got wet when it rained.

Marie, 6-year-old Bernadette and the baby share a little bed under the window, which has been broken for weeks.

They are unable to repair it themselves because, after paying for coal, rent and diet, they have £4 7s. to live on. The landlord has done nothing.

The council have promised them a re-let house. Four have recently been handed out, but not to them.

The ceiling below their bedroom is coming down from the damp in two places. Bernadette is in and out of hospital, and Marie has chronic bronchitis and chronic asthma.

Loscoe housing is destroying the health of its people. But the landlord does token repairs and re-lets the houses as fast as they become vacant. Featherstone housing committee promised to stop this. So far they have done nothing.

Newsletter *report, 20 February 1965*

of the Loscoe people to go with me. I would be contacted about the date and a car would be sent to pick us both up. I received that phone call on one of the rare occasions that I had gone home straight from work. There was a period when I did not see my mother or father for about two weeks — and we lived in the same house. We used to leave notes for each other. An hour after that telephone call there was another one, this time from the *Yorkshire Evening Post*, asking If I could meet a reporter and a photographer in Loscoe as they wanted to run a feature article based on the document. This was to take place the next morning; it must have been on a Saturday. The newspapermen were very sickened at what they saw and spent longer than I thought they would getting statements and taking photographs. The article was due to appear the following Thursday night. Then we had a stroke of luck; I received a phone call at work on the Wednesday asking if I could be ready at twelve o'clock the next day (Thursday) to pick up the Loscoe representative and be at the Manchester TV Studios by 14.00 hours. So the TV programme and newspaper article were to happen on the same day.

I got in touch with Celia so that we could both go over to Loscoe and give them the news. Jack was out of Leeds at a meeting so we had to wait until he arrived home. We arrived in Loscoe at about 23.30 hours and called at the house of the person who was to go with me. We gave him the news and by midnight there were ten or twelve people in his house. We arrived back in Cross Gates about 1.30 am.

The arrangement was to pick me up at work at midday. At about 11 am I was called to the telephone. It was a call from the presenter telling me that everything had been cancelled. I asked if he meant postponed, but he said, 'Cancelled.' You can imagine I was a bit shaken by this and asked him why. He just said, 'I am very sorry, Norman, I have just been instructed by the producer to cancel.' He finally told me he understood from the producer that 'a legal problem' had developed. I said the landlords must have turned out to be powerful people and to avoid being exposed had put pressure on the producer to cancel. He replied that calling it a legal problem could be a way of getting it cancelled. He said sorry, and rang off.

As I had arranged to have the afternoon off, I left work and drove to Loscoe as fast as I could to explain what had happened. Like me they were devastated; in fact there were a few tears. All the way to Loscoe I had this nagging thought that the feature in that night's paper would have received the same treatment. The only telephone was in the one shop-cum-off-licence. We asked to use the phone to ring the paper. I spoke to the journalist who had visited Loscoe and he told me that the feature had been cancelled. I asked him why; he told me the legal department had recommended it be cancelled. I asked him if they had traced the landlords and whether pressure had been put on the editor to avoid embarrassment. All he would or could say was that he and his colleagues were of that opinion. I asked him if we could have the photographs but he said, 'Sorry, the negatives and prints have been sent to the legal department for safekeeping.'

I went to Loscoe on the Friday night to have a chat about things. When I arrived I was shown a note that had been delivered by the rent collectors warning them that legal action would be taken against anyone who had taken part in the slanders being published in the *Newsletter*. I took a copy to send to the London office. After arranging to meet them the following morning (Saturday), I left to tell Jack and Celia the latest news. The next morning when we arrived at the Union pub about twelve or so were already there. I sat down with my pint and then half a brick and a note was produced. The pillion rider of a motorbike had thrown this through one of the house windows. Those who saw it happen said that they were shouting, 'If he doesn't keep out of here we will get him.' The note simply said, 'Tell Harding that if he knows what's good for him he will give up.'

All this was reported to London. The next step was to begin the fight to get the tenants re-housed and Loscoe demolished. The tenants promised that when demolition started I would knock out the first brick. The next few weeks were taken up by organising ways and means of putting pressure on the council to re-house. The families' doctors were approached for letters to give strength to the claims of the constant fear of illness due to the conditions. We even arranged for a skin disease specialist and Dr Herman

Grunwaldt from the Leeds chest clinic to visit. Letters were then sent to the to the council and the local papers. These were not printed. Dr Grunwaldt was a delegate to the Leeds Trades Council and a member of the Communist Party. I believe that he was Austrian and had fought on the barricades against the fascists. He had also voted for our resolution supporting the Hungarian workers in 1956. I had got to know him because when the clinic received a list of new TB patients he recognised my name as a delegate, and made sure that I was put on his list. This was as early as 1954-55.

We kept up the pressure constantly on the council and the Labour Party. Labour Party members were by now raising the issue of re-housing and demolishing Loscoe. I can't remember the date but I remember one of my visits to Loscoe with Celia to deliver the *Newsletter* to the regular readers. Every house in Loscoe had received a letter from the council telling them that plans were now being laid to knock down the houses and re-house everyone. It was like V Day and VE Day rolled into one. I have to say that the reception we got was very touching.

The promise that I would be the one to knock down the first brick was reiterated. But this was not to be; I wasn't around when it all started to happen. G Healy had moved me to London to work full-time in the Party's print shop, work that I was not cut out to do. Machines and I don't get on well together. But it was pointed out to me that it was my 'revolutionary' duty to overcome this. While I was very proud to work full-time for the party it was obviously a great mistake for me to go. It is now very clear that Healy just wanted me out of the area, to train me as one of his circle where he would have control over me.

We were having a branch meeting one Sunday Morning in 1966 when Jack Gale raised that he had read a letter in the Saturday issue of the *Yorkshire Evening Post* from a housewife on an estate in Normanton complaining about the Normanton Council increasing the rent. The letter told us that the protest was already under way and urged others on the estate to support them by refusing to pay their rent. The branch decided that immediately the meeting finished

I should go to Normanton, find this woman and then play it by ear. I don't remember her name, so we shall refer to her as Mrs Normanton.

After the meeting I went on to the estate in search of Mrs Normanton. I started to do a door-knock asking if anyone knew her. It took no more than half an hour to find out where she lived. I had already worked out my opening words so, as I remember it, I went straight up to the front door and knocked. Mrs Normanton was in; I introduced myself as secretary of the Leeds Tenants' Association. I explained that I had seen her letter in the paper regarding her protest at the rent increase put on them by the Normanton Council. She was eager to find ways of spreading the dispute. I asked her if she had anyone who would actively support her. She told me that two of her neighbours were keen to do something. 'The problem is, what can we do?' She suggested that she should go for them so that they could be part of this discussion. I readily agreed. She was out for ten minutes and returned with five or six other women, obviously ready to do battle. We discussed the way the rent increase was foisted on to them and the effect it was having on the estate. I was also told that about twenty households were already withholding their rent.

I suggested that we should organise a meeting for the following Sunday to discuss how to proceed. At this they asked me if I could wait for a short while as their husbands would be back soon from work. I think it was about 6 pm when Mr Normanton arrived home. His wife explained what was happening and he promptly went back out to get the others. By about 6.30 there were twelve or more in the front room. As soon as I repeated the idea that we should have another meeting the following Sunday to plan what to do next, there was an immediate positive response. One of them suggested the meeting could take place in the committee room at the Miners' Welfare Club. From past experience I knew that it could be difficult to get such a venue at short notice, so I asked if we could get in touch with the secretary of the club. In no uncertain tone they let me know that as far as they were concerned it had just been booked. The men at this first meeting were all mineworkers, as were the vast majority of men in the area. Before we broke up one of the men asked if I would come along on the Wednesday night so that we could discuss the agenda and have some suggestions to take to the Sunday morning meeting. I think I realised then that I was going to learn a thing or two over the next period.

I went to the Wednesday meeting as arranged. My main proposal was for a public meeting in the very near future. There was a general discussion around this suggestion. It was proposed that we should put this to the meeting on the following Sunday morning, and get as many others to attend as possible.

Sunday morning arrived and I was sitting on the doorstep 45 minutes early waiting for the Miners' Club to open. At 11 am sharp the club was opened and I made my way along with a few others to the committee room. Five minutes later there were at least twenty at the start of the meeting. The women had brought their husbands, all of whom were miners. At least two of them were active NUM branch members. One of these was elected chair. You had to be there to appreciate fully what followed. He called the meeting to order and in a no-nonsense manner asked me to put my suggestion for a public meeting. He then called for suggestions. 'Let's have a meeting next Sunday morning on the field.' Now all along I had been thinking in terms of a meeting taking place in something like the concert room at the club, so I was a little taken aback by this. There was a field in the middle of the estate surrounded by houses with a road round the perimeter; only one part of the field wasn't overlooked by houses and that area was covered by the pub. The chair told Joe to tell the landlord what was happening. So the venue was sorted.

On the agenda I had listed all the things we would need for an indoor meeting so I had to quickly adjust this list to the needs of an outdoor meeting. Publicity was the next item. First in my mind was a leaflet distribution round the estate. Chair: 'Bill, get a thousand run off in the branch office. As for the wording we will work that out over a pint.' He turned to me and said, 'Will you stay and help?' 'Er, er, yes,' I replied. 'George, can you cover the Working Men's Club? Use leaflets and get it announced from the stage before and after the turns.' The Liberal Club, The Miners' Welfare Club, and all the pubs in Normanton were to be covered in a similar way.

Any leaflets left over were to be distributed to the far edges of the estate by the 'young uns'. Next item: a platform. I explained that a platform would be better than just standing on a few beer crates.

Chair: 'Any ideas?'

Harry: 'I will ask Jim to let us use his flat back lorry.'

Next item: sound system. I volunteered to get the sound organised. I raised the question of power in case I could get a mains system. Chair: 'No problem. We can park the lorry on the concrete between the pub and the field and run a cable into the pub. Joe, let Toby [the landlord] know what we will be wanting to do.' Failing a mains system I was to hire a couple of batteries.

Next Item: speakers. I was asked to be the main speaker. Then there was to be one of the women who had started the rent strike. The NUM committee at the local pit was to have a speaker. Two of the committee were already involved; one was to chair the meeting and the other would be the speaker. Before leaving Leeds for the meeting I had been told that I had to get Dave Ashby, the National Secretary of the Young Socialists (one of our members), on to the platform. As London had been informed of what was happening I suspected that this instruction had come from there. As I remember, no one in Leeds had intended to try and do this. I remember feeling uneasy when I made the suggestion that Dave should be invited to speak, but I did loyally carry out the instruction. It was agreed. Looking back, it was a mistake because it gave the right wing and Communist Party the one and only opening to try and create an atmosphere of mistrust among a few of the activists, although not enough to sabotage the public meeting.

Any other business: I had two points to raise. 1. Immediately after the public meeting we should have a demonstration around the estate, mainly to give publicity to the rent strike and publicity for my second suggestion. 2. To have a mass picket outside Normanton Town Hall on the Wednesday following the public meeting as the Town Council would be in session, no doubt discussing the rents. I thought it would be a good idea to give them some help with their deliberations.

I remember clearly just how this struck their imagination. There were grins and a rubbing of hands as they responded with a unanimous 'Yes!' So it was agreed that the public meeting would end with an appeal for the biggest possible picket at Normanton Town Hall on the Wednesday following the rally. I felt that any doubts that they might have had about Dave Ashby speaking, somebody pushed on to them from the outside, were now at the back of their minds.

There was one other thing that I thought should be done: this meeting should elect a deputation and demand the right to go in front of the council and fight our corner. I was nominated but I declined saying that it should be made up of tenants from the estate. Five or six were elected for this job. As far as I can remember this Sunday morning planning meeting took no more than two hours. I had a drink in the club afterwards where naturally the discussion that was taking place around the club was the rent campaign. Mrs Normanton had certainly started something when she decided to send that letter to the *Yorkshire Evening Post*. Before I left I told her that she was to blame for all this activity. She had a big smile on her face as she said, 'I suppose I am'.

My mind was in turmoil as I drove home (no, not from the beer). Things had happened so quickly. I simply had to make my way to see Jack and Celia so that I could empty my head and then reassemble all that had happened over the last week. I remember while doing this I said, 'Oh hell, posters for the demo and picket.' The Leeds branch of the SLL managed somehow to get about 50 posters made. I think we had two slogans: 'Support the Rent Strike', and 'Not a Penny on the Rents'.

The SLL got as many members as we could to Normanton on the Sunday to sell the *Newsletter*, our weekly paper. The members and the posters were transported over to Normanton. I remember that the younger members of SLL and the Young Socialists were fired up and full of confidence. The events of the last week had been widely discussed in the Leeds branch and I think there was a 'feel good factor' around. Looking back on it, we all acted in quite the opposite way to what I suspect would have happened had we been in London. The success of the campaign was not going to be judged on how many signed our membership forms.

We arrived at the field in good time. The lorry was already in place and the tannoy system that I had taken over during the week was already set up and connected to the battery. There were two big horns on poles at each front corner of the lorry and the microphone and stand was nicely placed in the centre at the front of our platform. The women and the miners who were in the leadership were obviously nervous, in contrast to the extreme confidence that they had shown at the previous meetings.

I was nervously excited. This was different to anything that I had been involved in outside of the clothing industry. While we were waiting for the meeting to start Mrs Normanton and the others said that they were anxious about making sure that the picket on the following Wednesday evening was a success. They had discussed this; instead of tagging an announcement on at the end of the meeting would I include it in my contribution? This added to my nervousness because I realised that here we were in the middle of a housing estate, in a coal-mining area. I had known the leadership of this rent protest no more than two weeks, yet I was being asked to make the call for the next very important step in their struggle.

I spoke to someone about how I felt, I think it was Fred Slaughter (Cliff's father). I thought that he was the most likely comrade to have had some experience as until 1956 he had been a long-time member of the Communist Party. The advice that I received was something like, 'Make sure you know what you are going to say, and sound as confident as possible.' He said that to speak confidently in circumstances like this is very important. I also remembered the advice I was once given by the great London dockers' leader, Harry Constable: tell the assembled what you are going to say, then say it, and then tell them what you have said. No doubt he was referring to dock-gate meetings.

We climbed on to the lorry and then I saw the assembled: it was estimated that no less than 1,000 were on the field. Whole families had turned out. Because I was to make the appeal for the picket I was to be the last speaker. The chair opened the meeting, then I think Mrs Normanton spoke, then the other NUM committee member spoke, not only as a tenant but as an NUM member, saying he would fight to get support from the local pits. Dave Ashby was introduced as the National Secretary of the Young Socialists. I

Important youth backing for tenants

Newsletter Reporter

AFTER a mass meeting attended by 1,000 Normanton (Yorks) tenants last Sunday (July 17), over 250 took part in a demonstration all round the town. Well to the fore throughout were the Normanton Young Socialists, many of them from council house homes.

Opening the meeting, held on a plot of land in the middle of a council estate, Mr. T. Brown of the newly-formed tenants' association, said that they were determined to carry the fight through and he thanked the YS for their efforts in the support of the campaign.

The support of the youth was of great importance and the Normanton tenants welcomed it. They had asked Dave Ashby, chairman of the YS National Committee, to speak from the platform.

Ashby said the meeting showed that intense feeling had been aroused by the means test plan and the tenants had rightly replied by organising.

He quoted many examples of bad conditions in council houses.

Was this the result of tenants and workers voting in a Labour government and a Labour council?

Must tenants pay?

Many houses had been paid for several times over. Why?

If the council had run up bad debts, must the tenants pay for council wastage. His speech was loudly cheered.

Mr. Appleyard of the Tenants' Association attacked the so-called socialists who voted for the Prices and Incomes Bill and then put up the cost of living by rent increases.

The rebate scheme would assess people on wages before tax, National Insurance, etc.

'We will be taxed twice,' he said.

Local councillors had said tenants suspected this was a means test. They were right. Tenants knew it was.

Norman Harding of Cross Gates Tenants' Association (Leeds) said the main concerns of workers were houses, food and clothing. Any attack on these hit workers' living standards.

Big step

The foundation of Normanton Tenants' Association was a big step. What was needed now was a fight to change the rotten system.

'We need real socialists representing the workers. We have been told we were through with the means test and the bad old days of unemployment, etc. Now we must fight against a return to the bad old days,' he said.

A vote on a resolution of support for the campaign and the sending of a delegation to the council was carried.

Two letters were read to the meeting. One was from the Labour Party which disagreed with the tenants' views and was unable to be represented due to another meeting. The other was from the Young Socialists who came in support of the tenants.

Over 100 Newsletters and many 'Keep Lefts' were sold.

Police called to council meeting

LOCAL councillors called on police to remove several tenants from a council meeting on Tuesday after a close questioning of the council's rent policy.

Several tenants had been earlier allowed in, leaving 70 waiting outside.

Mr. Brown told the council they should freeze the rents and called on them not to carry forward the rent increases. Councillors said they could not do this.

At a meeting after the police action, tenants' leaders called on the tenants not to pay the increase.

Newsletter, *23 July 1966*

can't remember what he said, in fact this part of the proceedings is very blurred in my memory. The things that I remember about my contribution are the points that I had underlined many times on my notes.

I introduced myself as secretary of the Cross Gates Tenants' Association in Leeds and secretary of the Leeds Tenants' Associations. I congratulated Mrs Normanton and her friends in taking the initiative in getting the protest started and said that Normanton Council would be very worried to know that this meeting had been a huge success. I used this moment to say something like: 'and when they find out what is going to happen on Wednesday night they will have something to worry about'. After a couple more points I said, 'Now for the Normanton Council.' I then invited everyone at the meeting to attend the picket and make their presence felt. 'Anyone who will be taking part in the demonstration after the meeting take the posters and publicise the picket. All those with posters take them with you on Wednesday evening. And let's give the Normanton Councillors the fright of their lives.' I make no apologies for saying that the response and the applause it received gave me a feeling of pride. We had been able to join a section of workers in their struggles.

The Chair closed the meeting and the demonstration took place. Then everyone made their way to one of the clubs or to their local pub. Some just went home. I went with the 'committee' and those who had been elected as a deputation to discuss the picket. We decided that the deputation would be at the front of the crowd and send in a request that they should be heard. The rest would take up the demand of 'Let them in'.

A pint in the club, a natter, and then I departed for Leeds.

The events of that Sunday were reported in the local press. The *Yorkshire Evening Post* deliberately reported that Dave Ashby was the secretary of the National Socialists, instead of National Secretary of the Young Socialists. I had to go over to Normanton in case this deliberate provocation was causing any problems. The only one who raised it with me was one of the NUM members, only because he was of the opinion that it was a deliberate attempt to cause trouble. Two or three days after the picket a couple of members of the Communist Party and the Labour Party tried to take advantage of the report, but the picket was untouched by the attempt to discredit me as the one who had suggested that Dave should speak at the Sunday meeting.

I went straight from work to the picket and by the time I arrived quite a big crowd had gathered. The deputation was there at the front waiting for the written request to go in; I had been asked to prepare it and bring it with me. The police officer on duty told us that the councillors had all been told to be in the town hall before five o'clock in order not to be confronted by the picket. He was a local bobby and sympathetic to the cause. One of the women said that he had to support us or else he wouldn't get any tea – he was her son. Like a dutiful son he took the request into the building and handed it to the council. There was an immediate answer 'No'. The chanting started: 'Let them in'.

The crowd had swelled to a few hundred and more were constantly joining. There was a bit of a push and the door was bolted shut. They must have sent for reinforcements because another two bobbies arrived. One of these apparently was on the same dart team as one of the members of the deputation. These three policemen were in absolutely no position to do anything about the situation. At last a message came out of the besieged town hall saying that they were prepared to meet the deputation. Mrs Normanton led the way with her written speech clutched in her hand. It must have been about half an hour before she came out. She had been sent out to report that if the crowd dispersed the councillors would agree to try and reach a compromise. The deputation wanted those outside to give them a resounding 'No'. I was asked to report this to the crowd; I found myself standing on a wall relaying this message. About 300 (a conservative estimate) gave them one hell of a 'No'. A short time after that one of the policemen stuck his head round the door and said that all hell had broken loose upstairs. Almost immediately one of the deputation came out and said that I was wanted upstairs. I asked who it was that wanted me; he said, 'We do.' Before I went inside he told me that they had been accused of letting a Trotskyite trouble-causer hijack the rents protest. The deputation wanted me inside with them to show that they were on my side. The police were told not to let me in. Those at the front near the door made it very clear that if I did not go in they would, with me in front.

Once in the council chamber I accused them of starting a witch-hunt and said that they were attacking the very people who had put them in power and they were in danger of losing their seats to tenants' candidates. The accusation that I had hijacked the protest was put to me. Before I could reply Mrs Normanton said, 'Don't be daft, we hijacked him.' This caused a burst of laughter from the tenants who by now had the door open and were listening to what was being said and passing it down the stairs.

The confrontation ended with the NUM members on the deputation making a demand on the council. End the rent increase and pay back the increase to those who had already paid it, or we will take the protest to the local pits and the NUM. With that we turned round and made our way outside. I was asked to tell the crowd what had happened. I stood on the wall and reported what had transpired. There were approving sounds. Then I was asked, 'What next?' I answered by saying some meat would have to be put round the threat to involve the pits and the NUM. This suggestion was acceptable to the two local NUM committee members. We agreed that the sooner it could be announced that the pits were in solidarity with tenants and were going to call solidarity action, the sooner a bomb would be lit under Normanton Council. They agreed to get it started at the next shift.

Running parallel with this I had to visit a number of people regarding the press report on Dave Ashby. I discovered that the only ones who queried it with me wanted to believe it any way and had kept the protest at arms length.

The following Wednesday the Council caved in; the thought of the miners going on strike had scared them rotten. The rent increase was ended and all those who had paid the increase got a refund. A victory, and what a victory!

We had been doing *Newsletter* sales in the Normanton area for a long time. The reception we got in the pubs and clubs following this victory was tremendous. I used to drive the sales team but now someone else had to drive; there was a pint in every pub and club.

I am very proud that I was able to take such a leading role in this struggle and proud of the part the part played by the Leeds Socialist Labour League.

Loscoe and Normanton were two places where I experienced the communist, comradely relationship that developed between everyone involved. The spirit, determination and the aspirations for a better quality of life are ingredients that can move mountains. An ounce of leadership is worth a ton of rhetoric.

I did try to find the site of old Loscoe once when I was up from London. Everything had changed. Where I thought Loscoe had been there was a roundabout.

One night in 2000 I was talking to a young man in our one-and-only pub. During the conversation he mentioned that he originated from Normanton. I asked him if he had heard of Loscoe, and explained why I asked. He had never seen Loscoe but his grandfather used to live there. He remembered him talking about the struggle, as he put it, to get it blown up. Then he told me something exciting. Somewhere amongst his granddad's belongings was a pamphlet called 'Loscoe: the Forgotten Village', not properly printed, but copied and stapled down one side. It could be the only one in existence. But to date it has not been found.

10

FROM EXECUTEX TO THE BRITISH MUSEUM

Not only did I have to spend a lot of time in Normanton where I was active in the rent strike on the big housing estate but I now also had to find another job.

This proved to be very difficult. For starters I discovered all the big clothing firms in Leeds blacklisted me. The only ones that would have me were the small ones that you found up rickety stairs in an old warehouse somewhere. I toured the area trying to find work in a suitable factory without any luck. So I went through the papers to see if there was anything on offer. I was always too late. 'Sorry, but the position has been taken,' was the usual reply I would get. Then I struck lucky. I was taken on as a forklift truck driver at Catton's iron foundry. It was very hard work but worst of all the fumes were horrendous, working in a confined space amid a deafening noise of clanging and banging. By the end of the day I was a nervous wreck. My foreman turned out to be the husband of one of the members of the Leeds Federation tenants' committee. He recognised that I had come from a completely different kind of industry, so he was very patient with me.

I had been working there a week when Mum and Dad came back from their holiday. When I told them where I was working Mum got very excited, and said that her dad worked there as a moulder for years. He had been the moulders' steward and secretary of the Leeds moulders' union. After about three weeks of torture I decided that I would tell the foreman that it would be better if I left.

I did this only to find out that he had come to the same decision. He gave me a letter for my next employer explaining why I had left, and a good reference.

I soon got another job, this time at Tapp and Toothill, a very well known colour printer at Stanningley on the west boundary of Leeds. They had a department that produced pattern books for clothing, furniture, curtains, etc. Their big job was to produce the Gratton's mail order catalogue four times a year. To do this they had the biggest battery of Heidelberg flatbed printing presses on one floor in Europe. They also had a very large Martini-Sheridan. This machine had a continuous belt that took sections of books from station to station, placed the sections together on top of each other until complete, and then stitched or glued the sections together, followed with the process of putting on the cover. The catalogue was then trimmed on two automatics and a manual guillotine, stacked on pallets, covered with polythene, strapped to the pallets, fork-lifted down to the loading bay, and away. I landed the job because of my knowledge of cloth, and was employed to help prepare the different materials for the pattern books. This included doing the layout for the pages of the catalogue that featured material.

As soon as the production of the catalogue reached the collating stage I was put to work feeding or taking off and stacking for the manual guillotine operator. After working on two seasons of Gratton's, the imperial FOC (Father of the Chapel) came to see me and told me that the chapel (the union branch of SOGAT, Society of Graphical and Allied Trades) and the management had agreed I should be given a full union card. The chap I worked with said that he had waited five or six years to get his full card, 'and you do it in six months!' Having this card meant that I could operate all printing machines covered by SOGAT. There was one big snag to this — I did not know how to operate them.

A number of weeks later at a national committee meeting of the All Trades Union Alliance in Oxford I showed my SOGAT card to Party leader Gerry Healy. He was impressed and asked how had I managed to get it. I explained. Healy then told me that we had established an NGA chapel at Plough Press (our printshop).

How would I like to work in the printshop and establish a SOGAT chapel? He didn't refer to it again that day.

I was not involved in any political activity at Tapp and Toothill's other than discussing with individuals. I enjoyed my work there and for the first time in my life was on the verge of having a decent wage. The only negative thing about the job was that I had to be up every morning at six to make sure I would get to work on time. It was a round journey of 30 miles. Most nights in the week I would have go straight from work to wherever I had to be. Ever since I joined I seemed to be the last one to bed and the first out of it. Get everyone else home and then go home myself.

The expected message finally arrived. I had to start making preparations to leave Leeds. I could not move directly into Plough Press, as SOGAT wasn't established. The idea was that I was to get a job elsewhere in London through the London Central Branch of SOGAT. The first step was to get a letter of introduction from the Leeds branch, then make an appointment to have an 'audience' with one of the three London full-time secretaries. This took me longer than expected, about three weeks. My trip to London was one of those rare occasions when there was no need for me to go to the Party Centre in Clapham. This was going to be a day out in London.

I went straight from King's Cross Station to the union office just about ten minutes' walk away. I arrived about ten o'clock. I had to wait about an hour before one of the three wise men could see me. At last I was called in to be interviewed. He read my letter of introduction, then said: 'So you want to work in London?' 'Yes,' said I. 'Why?' said he. 'More money,' said I. 'You can forget any idea you may have of getting into Fleet Street. The only job that I can offer you is at the British Museum.' I was a bit taken aback — it was the last place I expected SOGAT to have a chapel.

I went directly over to the British Museum, contacted the FOC and showed him the card that I had been given. He decided I was suitable and signed the card for me to take back to the union office. Before I left he took me on a tour round the departments I was to work in. The job was working on the library catalogue of books. He took me to where the catalogue was kept; it filled as many shelves as you would find in the central library of any major town or city in Britain. I was then shown the labyrinth of passages leading to the rooms and galleries where the museum's massive collection of books was stored. We paused at a spot in one of these galleries, he put his key into a keyhole behind books on a shelf, and opened a door. The other side of the door was an exhibition case. It gave the museum visitors a shock when we stepped out from this 'secret door'.

The next stop was the famous circular Reading Room. This was very impressive. Members of the public could only use the library and the reading room if they had a special reader's ticket issued to those who could show they were involved in serious study and not just casual readers. When I started work not only would I have a key that would open the doors to what I considered to be a wonderland, I would also have the privilege of having access to and use of the reading room. I arranged to start work on the Monday in four weeks' time.

The first thing I did after arriving back at work in Leeds was to inform the FOC that I would be handing in three weeks' notice. The manager reluctantly accepted my notice, and said that he was sorry to lose me and that if things did not work out there would always be a job for me at Tapps.

My departure from Leeds was delayed for two weeks as Dad was taken ill once again: a week in hospital and a week at home and he was back with his concert party. For that two weeks I spent as much time at home as was possible. On one of the visits to the hospital to see him it was obvious that he had been chewing things over in his mind. He talked about chances coming too late in life. He talked about a few years previously when he had been booked to play at a smoker (dinner with entertainment); also booked were the comedy duo Mike and Bernie Winters. At the time they had a television show and each week they introduced someone whom they had met while working away from television and radio. They offered Dad one of these spots. He was to play a Fats Waller number, and sing one of his Richard Tauber favourites, the *Serenade* from *The Student Prince*. This must have been in 1966, when he had a hat trick of heart attacks. He had had to pull out just before the first rehearsal. When he recovered Dad continued on the normal circuit with the concert party, and anything else that came his way.

A few days before I was due to leave Leeds I had a bit of a do in one of the pubs close to the university, organised by my student comrades. It went very well as I remember and all the Leeds comrades seemed to be genuinely sorry to see me go. I still have the book that was presented to me 'as a tribute to my revolutionary work in Leeds': *Revolutionary Silhouettes*.

I am conscious that I may be trying to find other things to write about in order to delay the recording of my next twenty years in London. At the time I was eager to go but what I did not know was that I would be making a complete break with the type of activity that I had been involved in over the previous fifteen years. I made my last trip with Celia to Normanton and in particular to Loscoe so that I could leave in good order. I wished them well in what we hoped would be the closing stages of their campaign. For the last time I turned my back on Loscoe, the rat-infested, disease-ridden, open midden of respiratory-problem-creating habitats.

Arrangements were made for Celia to keep in contact with them. This was very difficult for her with two young daughters, Ruth and Jill, and the problem was compounded by the fact that Jack was constantly on political work not only in Leeds but also in other parts of the country. On these occasions Celia had no transport, making it still more difficult to get to Loscoe. But even with these problems contact was maintained until the end.

My little red Mini with a black roof, KWR 999D, was packed tight with my worldly belongings when I set off that Saturday morning. I would be staying with Katrina Ainsworth and Bernard Franks, sleeping on a fold-up bed in their kitchen on the Caledonian Road near King's Cross Station, not very far from the British Museum. Katrina had been in the Communist Party and Bernard in the YCL. They made me very welcome — even if I did sleep in the kitchen! I will go as far as to say that my stay with them was the best and most comradely time I had in London.

There was a message waiting for me when I arrived telling me to go to Clapham on the Sunday morning to see Healy in his office. The offices were situated over Pearce's butchers shop in Clapham High Street. I was familiar with the location because of my many visits to London to help in the printshop when I was a member of the Control Commission or on the Central Committee.

Sheila Torrance was in the front office. She buzzed Healy to inform him that I had arrived. It turned out to be just a simple welcome to London. But he did say something that locked itself into my memory: 'Stick by me and you will be a power in the land.' He sent me down to the printshop on the continuation of Clapham High Street, The Pavement. I walked past the end of Venn Street past the Plough pub and on past Grafton Square, turned right up the alleyway between what became the greengrocer's shop and the baker's. Next to the baker was the Bull's Head. Fifty yards up the alleyway there were two big iron gates. I rang the bell and was let into the yard. To the left was what became the editorial office and later the Young Socialists' offices. Opposite was what became the photographic dark room and the light tables where Tony Banda worked on the negatives and pasting up. Later this department became the finance office. When I arrived they were still working with hot metal. There were three typesetting machines with compositors setting the type.

To the right of the yard was the 'warehouse'. To get in there you had to pass through two big wooden doors. In here we had the guillotine, the folding machine, a collating and stitching machine (for magazines, journals etc.) and a Heidelberg flatbed printing press. Later we also had a Japanese Komori press. This was where I was to spend most of my waking hours — and that could mean a very large slice of the day. But before that I had to get through my time at the British Museum and work out my tactics for getting into Plough Press.

Next morning I reported for duty at the British Museum. I was sat at a table, given a pile of books and shown how to allocate them a number and stick it on, then put the books on a trolley with a list of titles, authors, subjects and numbers. The books were taken to be put on to the shelves and the list of books would be entered in the catalogue, each book in its appropriate place.

The first two weeks were quiet and passed by very nicely. In fact, during that period I decided to try out the library to trace the swimming journals produced in the 1930s, to see the reports of the achievements of the East Leeds Swimming Club. It was all there, reports of cousins Lily, Alan, and of course Doris. I lost track of time and one of the lads was sent to find me. He found me sat between two rows of books, reading through these magazines. Back at the department, I fully expected to get a roasting. No, all that was said was something like: 'You must have found something interesting; I was worried that you had got lost in the maze.'

Late on the Friday night of my second weekend in London Richard Goldstein called in to tell me to go to the printshop at eight o'clock the following morning. When I arrived, Comrade Larry pointed to a couple of pallets piled high with, if I remember correctly, rule books for ASSET (the Association of Supervisory Staff, Executives and Technicians). I was given about half an hour's tuition on the guillotine and told that they had to be trimmed top, bottom and front, wrapped into neat parcels, then re-stacked on the pallets. The layers had an alternating pattern similar to a bricklayer building a square pillar. This had to be completed by Monday morning, ready for delivery.

I managed the guillotine very well. The clamp, blade and whatever I was cutting only moved when I moved, which couldn't be said of the unpredictable folding machine, which I couldn't handle. The flatbed printing machine produced the necessary quantity of each section of whatever was being published, maybe 32 pages on each large sheet, sixteen on each side. Those sheets would have to be folded to produce 32 pages of a book. You think everything is set up ready, press the button and the blasted folder takes charge! Anything up to four straight folds I could just about handle. Working with one fold on a light card was my idea of a relaxing job.

Anyway I finished my trimming and wrapping and produced two or three very neat pallet boards of parcels. I had to work all day Saturday till about midnight. I had a sleep on a camp bed. The guard woke me at about 6 am. I finished the job early evening. I was about to leave when Comrade Torrance rang me from the front office. Would I cover until the night guard came in so that the day guard could go into his branch? The night guard was going to be late because he had to stay in his branch. I was assured that I would be able to leave in time to catch a tube to King's Cross. I caught the last tube and arrived back at Katrina's well and truly knackered.

I reported for work on time at the British Museum but I had to struggle to stay awake. A pattern of work started to take shape: 8 am to 5.30 pm at the museum, three or four times a week straight over to Clapham to work in the printshop. Sometimes I managed to get home. Other times I ended up having to go to the museum from the printshop. Sometimes I had two or three hours' rest, but mostly I had to work all night. I think it would be true to say that with the odd exception I worked every weekend.

After a couple of months of this it was noticed that I arrived at work looking pretty rough and was falling asleep during the day. The others in the department became very concerned, so much so that one of them spoke to his wife who was a nursing sister. He told me that his wife recommended that I go to a doctor as soon as possible as she was worried that I could have a heart problem. I promised to do this. From then on I always tried to make sure that I had at least one hour before going to work so that I could have a wash, shave and change my shirt. I also had to make a conscious effort to be bright and cheerful first thing in the morning.

Unbeknown to me at the time, being bright and cheerful first thing in a morning was to become a way of life. All will be clear as time goes on. My dual role continued. I was becoming established at the British Museum, and I was being continually called in to Clapham to the printshop.

I had become friendly with a chap called Bill who was responsible for organising the restoration of old books. One of his claims to fame was that he gold-blocked the wedding albums of the Royals. Following the severe floods in Florence he was sent to organise the restoration of the books damaged in the floods. A BBC film recorded the work and it was later shown on TV. One day Bill took me to see one of the restoration workrooms which was a little larger than a living room that you find in one of the older houses in an affluent part of London. A bench went all round the perimeter of the room and a worktable was situated in the centre of the room. Under the table was an assortment of glue, varnish and a large collection of different types of paper, parchment and even papyrus.

The books on the bench to the left as you entered the room were books that he had just started, on the right were books in the final stage of restoration. The man who worked in this room was just what you would expect to see: short, with a stoop, bald in the middle, and longish grey hair on either side. He blinked at you through glasses halfway down his nose. Naturally he was wearing a white coat. Bill had warned me that he was a bit of an eccentric — he certainly looked the part. I asked him how long it took for a book to travel round the room. 'Sometimes quickly, one or two years; others take a little longer, five to ten years. Each day I work on a book that takes my fancy,' he said. When we left him to get on with what was obviously his reason for living, Bill told me that he came in on a morning, hung his coat on the same peg that he had used for the last 40 years or so, put on his white coat and prepared whatever he decided to do. He got so engrossed in his work that someone had to go in to tell him it was lunchtime and again when it was time to go home. Apparently he refused to have a clock in the room and would not wear a watch. Time was his only enemy.

Another time Bill took me into the department of Chinese antiquities. I was allowed to open a box, about ten inches square and the same depth. Inside was a sheet of what I think was copper. It was hanging with leather thongs from a bar across the box. I was allowed to lift it out, and was told that it was a poem in ancient Chinese. Only after I had replaced it that the lady in charge of the department told me that it was estimated to be no less than 8,000 years old. I remember remarking to her that I felt privileged to have been able to see it.

A few days after this Bill said that because I had shown an interest 'in the accumulated knowledge of mankind' he had a treat for me. First we were to go to a room in the basement, which I believe was the department of ancient manuscripts. The door would be locked from the inside. We would knock and wait to be let in and once inside the door would be re-locked. This wasn't because of security, but to prevent anyone unexpectedly opening the door and creating a draught around the room. Six or eight people were standing around a table dressed in white coats and wearing white gloves. The room had controlled temperature and humidity. Each person was working on something using what appeared to be a scalpel. After about five minutes Bill tapped me on the shoulder and indicated that we should leave. The door was opened for us and closed behind us. No one had spoken while we were in there. I could see the intense concentration on those who were facing the door and I felt as though I had held my breath for the whole time. Bill then looked very serious as he told me that I had just seen the Dead Sea Scrolls. Work had been going on for some time, and very few people realised that the scrolls were even in the museum. I felt very fortunate to have spent five minutes in that room.

That wasn't the end. I was shown three important documents. The first was a manuscript of Leonardo da Vinci, the second a letter written by a lady-in-waiting to Mary Queen of Scots, an eye-witness account of her execution. The third document was Lenin's card for the library using the name Karl Richter. At a later date I also managed to get a close view of the Rosetta Stone. Bill told me that it was widely acknowledged that the British Museum had the largest collection of stolen property in the world.

Not long after, the chair of the SOGAT Chapel retired and I was asked to stand for the post, which I got. This was considered quite a privileged job.

Meanwhile, back in Clapham, my other work continued. We had just finished another job for the union ASSET (which later became ASTMS, the Association of Scientific, Technical and Managerial Staffs). It was trimmed and parcelled, waiting to be delivered. I was asked to take the following afternoon off from the museum, as there was a job for me to do.

Arriving at the printshop after making an embarrassing sickness excuse, Larry asked me to bring the transit van into the yard and load it up with the parcels. I had to carry them out, put them on the back of the van, climb in and stack them as high as possible, until finally the van was full. Having done that I was handed a note with directions to get to the union's offices. I reported to reception and was told that I would have to take the parcels to the storeroom, five flights up a narrow staircase. The van was parked in the road opposite the gate and the most I could carry at a time was two parcels. I had to cross over the pavement, go through a yard, down a passage into a courtyard, through a door and then up the five flights. I had to make at least 100 trips.

About halfway through I was at the third or fourth floor when one of the ASSET workers opened a door to see what was going on. I explained. Poor sod, he said. On my next trip I noticed that he had put a chair on the landing so that I could have a rest. Who said that there was no compassion in the trade union bureaucracy? He could at least have left a jug of water by the chair. But what really made me say 'Oh, heck' was when I was called to the phone. It was Larry asking what was keeping me as the van was needed. I told him that I could only get the van as far as the second floor, so things were a little difficult. By the time I had finished the staff had gone home and the caretaker was complaining that I was holding him up.

This level of physical hard work and the pressure of time continued in one form or another for years to come, linked with long hours and lack of sleep. I suppose it could be said that it was character building.

11

WORKING IN LONDON

Before I settle down to go over my work in London I will describe the only times (during more than twenty years) that I was able to have members of my family down for a weekend in London. The first was in 1974 when Mum, Pauline and Debra came down. I arranged for them to stay at Bob and Mickie Shaw's house in Vauxhall as they were out of London. To make things a little easier I was able to borrow Vanessa Redgrave's car and television.

Mum volunteered on the Saturday night to stay in with Debra who was only five. I took Pauline to see the shops in Soho. We had a drink and then made our way back to Vauxhall. We all had a meal at the Standard Indian restaurant in Clapham before they left. Little Debra fell off her chair, much to the amusement of the staff. For years after that the staff always asked about my niece Debra.

The second time, Debra came down on her own at the age of sixteen. She stayed with my comrades Maureen and John Spencer. I met her at King's Cross Station on the Friday evening and only spotted her when everyone else had come off the train. The thought that I had missed her really shook me up. I took her to her digs with her case and then over to the Standard Indian. I had told them that she was coming and they gave her a very friendly welcome. We had a nice meal and shared a bottle of wine. As a treat, we were given a complimentary Indian ice cream dessert. From there we went to the Plough, where she met a number of my friends and comrades. One Young Socialist from the Centre, Frances Goldstein, came so that Debra would have someone her age to talk to. Next morning,

Saturday, I picked her up from Balham and we made our way to Knightsbridge to pop in to Harrods for a 'bit of shopping'. There wasn't much in the jewellery section, nothing worth buying anyway. So we went to the sales section. I managed to buy her a grey skirt for £50 — or was it a fiver? Well, it's the thought that counts. The carrier bags came in very useful for carrying her folders and books to college. For the night's entertainment two comrades, Helen Gill and Sam Cox, gave me very good tickets for the play they were in, *Run for Your Wife* by Ray Clooney at the Criterion Theatre in the West End. Afterwards we had a drink in their dressing room. They took Debra to meet James Bolam and Ian Ogilvy ('the Saint') and showed us the stage area. On Sunday we had lunch in the canteen at the printshop. Then I took Debra to catch her train because she wanted to be back in the evening for her college dance.

On two occasions over the years Malcolm, Graham and Steven enjoyed a fishing and camping holiday in Scotland and a camping holiday in the Lake District with 'Uncle Norman'.

The rest of my time in London was an unremitting routine of party activity. This precluded any kind of a family life, of cultural pursuits such as listening to music, or of simple, normal human relations with other comrades.

The daily *Workers Press* was launched on a Saturday in September 1969. There was great tension all through the Friday right up to the time when the papers started to roll off the press. The three-station web-offset press could print at great speed. The bulk of the papers were half folds but some were 'quarter folds' for the postal subscriptions. The printers were members of the NGA union, non-party members, except Mike Banda, later our General Secretary. The folder was set to kick every 50th paper so that we, the SOGAT union members, could pick them off the fly in 50s, knock them up and put into piles of 50, reversing the crease edge each time. Each night a team of branch members came in to help with the despatch of the paper, on a roster basis. One person had to carry the papers from the press to the despatch, two counted the papers and put in inserts (tickets, leaflets, debt sheets and the like) and one helped me parcel and string. We also had a roster for a team of drivers who delivered the papers to the stations and to the different places in London where the branches collected their papers. The problem with the inserts was that very often, just at the point when we were all ready for the off, Sheila Torrance (leading organiser) would ring from the front office telling us not to start parcelling, as there would be something else to put in the parcels. This risked our time schedules at the different stations. I was the one who had to work out all the schedules and alternative plans when things went wrong.

There were those who thought that doing things at the last minute was good organisation. Sheila Torrance was one of them, not so much a good organiser as someone who was very skilled at covering up. She would do this by losing things in a fog of shouting, blaming everyone but herself, and creating a panic situation that might be mistaken for good organisation.

The parcels were put into separate piles, for a railway station or a London area. Scotland was sent by air; Higgs newspaper delivery service on Grays Inn Road handled this for us. As soon as a station or a London area was complete the driver would load his car and get on his way. These comrades were so well versed with the system that they could be away very quickly and efficiently. The order of delivery could change each night depending on the time the papers came off the press. It could mean a mad dash to the stations with the papers that had to catch the early departure times and then another mad dash with those for the later trains. To a stranger watching the proceedings it might have given the appearance of chaos but it was far from it. It was well organised; everyone involved on any particular night knew just what to do. We really did work as a team. Each night the comrades who were involved in this work would be up well into the early hours breaking down the distribution of the papers: individual papers to readers, or a few to a comrade who would then break down that quota. Papers had to go to a number of shops and newspaper stalls. Then, at night, pub sales. A large number of these comrades were involved in all or anyone of these tasks, every night.

Whole weekends were spent going round the readers collecting the money, taking part in high street sales during the day and pub sales at night. Then, very exhausted, the comrades had to go to work, and try with great difficulty to take part in 'political work' along with the extra effort and energy needed to have a normal relationship within their families.

Many, many times I have seen comrades having to sleep in their cars because they were too tired to go home to bed or had not enough time because they had to go straight into work after the night's party work. This was repeated in every branch in Britain. Yet when branches fell behind with their money (and every branch did) instead of help being offered, they were insulted by the leadership and told that they were not trying hard enough. They were denigrated, vilified as 'social democrats' who did not understand the need for a revolutionary party. Yet these comrades were the very sand and cement of our party. Wherever and whatever these comrades are doing now it was a privilege to be associated with them and have them, in the real meaning of the word, as comrades. I will guarantee that any of these comrades, wherever they might be in the world, will always remember the great tiredness and the great urge for sleep. That was always with them. It proved fatal on at least two occasions when comrades were killed in motorcycle accidents. One was Comrade Peter Archer and the other Comrade George Myers. Party leader Healy said to Bob Myers: 'Your brother conned me; he told me he could ride a motor cycle.' What an insulting thing to say to someone who had just lost his brother and comrade. Some died; many more are lucky to be alive.

Apart from our party printing the most important printing job we did was the journal for ASTMS, the Association of Scientific, Technical and Managerial Staffs. This was printed four times a year with a run of tens of thousands. Each issue would take at least two weeks to print and despatch. The press would be belting them out and we would be at the end of the machine knocking them up and stacking them on pallets. This would only stop each day for our paper to be printed and despatched. The printers would go home and we would carry on with the job of despatching the journals. This could only be done during the night. The London area sent members in each night to help with pasting the wrappers and wrapping the journals into the already addressed wrappers, along with any insert that had to go in. They were elastic banded into bundles of twenties, ten bundles to a mailbag.

At about 06.00 hours at least three mail vans would come and take away the night's work. At 08.00 the printers would come in and prepare to start another day's printing. We were expected to be bright-eyed and bushy-tailed, washed and shaved and ready for off, so that the non-party printers would not suspect that we had worked late through the night. There would be some comment from the non-members about the mystery shift that got rid of the previous day's work.

The summer issues were the worst as we were unable to get out for a bath and a change of clothes. We could go fourteen days and nights without being able to leave the premises. I remember having to wrap clean machine-wiping rags on our feet to try and get some comfort. Others could occasionally get home, but somehow the duties I had always stopped me. Once when a night shift was organised for the printers we of course had to be there. In the morning everyone went home. It was usually late afternoon before I managed to get away, if at all. Between finishing the paper and having to start on the journal we would see the editorial comrades leaving either for home or the Plough.

During one of these daytime runs of the journal I was on the fly of the machine taking off the papers. They were coming at me at a hell of a rate of knots. Sneeze and I could miss one of the kicks of 50. I was on my own. One of the girls from the front office on Clapham High Street came into the warehouse and told me that I had to cut her some paper. She held up two pieces of string, one for the length and one for the width. I told her that she would have to wait until the reel was finished and I would do it before the other reel was fitted in place. I flew up the ladder to where the paper was stored and decided that the unspecified paper was newsprint, and that 'some' = 500 and cut it one string long and one string wide. I got back to the press just as they were starting to print.

Within fifteen minutes she was back. She told me I had given her the wrong paper and she needed 1,000, not 500. The message from Torrance was to do it right this time. The printers had just started a new reel so I told her that she would have to wait about twenty minutes. She shouted above the press that if I did not do it now I would find myself in trouble. Some comrades seemed to be oblivious to what was going on around them. Between reels I cut it for her and off she went. Apparently the job in hand was one that Healy had given Torrance to do at the front office on a little press that they had there. It had to be with Healy that day at noon. At some time in the afternoon the leaflet was delivered to him. There was a minor explosion. The comrade came over and told me that I was wanted in his office. Once again I had to explain that I could only leave between reels. She went back. This time it was Healy's secretary, Aileen Jennings, who came over and said that I would have to come immediately. Torrance was also in the office. Healy said: 'These comrades tell me that it was your fault that this leaflet was delayed.' I told him about the bits of string and the problem I had to keep up with the press. He would not listen, took their side and told me that I had to help these comrades and not create difficulties. I was dismissed and sent back to the press, where I was greeted with a pile of journals, and the printers waiting for me to clear up the press before they could start again.

This was also the week that Old Bill, the chap who used to clean up the kitchen and toilets as well as make the printers their tea, was on holiday. It was down to me to make their tea.

During one of our general election campaigns, posters, manifestos, leaflets, meeting tickets and so on had to be sent around Britain by road. Our vans went to various feeding points where the branches collected their quotas. Sheila Torrance told me not to put the Bristol quota into the Western Region van as a member was coming in to see her and would take them back with her. I knew that this member only had a Mini and that no way could we get the quota into her car. I suggested that we stick to the original plan. As much as I tried to explain the problem Torrance took no notice and told me to get on with it and put them into the Mini. The Mini was filled and the rest piled up by the side of the car. I rang the office and told her that we could not get them all in the car. 'Do I have to do everything myself?' 'In this case, yes,' I replied. 'I am coming down. You are all useless,' she said. Whether she thought it was a case of mind over matter or revolutionary determination I do not know but when she came into the yard and saw the parcels in the Mini she thought we had carried out her wishes. When she was finally convinced that the mountain at the side of the car was the balance she told me in no uncertain terms that I had misled her as to the bulk. The ground was laid for me to get the blame. Healy came out of his office and asked what the shouting was all about. He was told that I had delayed the election material getting to the Western Region. I received the social democrat treatment and was instructed to get everything to the Western Region now. I had already planned this the day before. They were put into the Western Region van and off it went.

I can't ever remember being told that I was to be in charge of the national distribution of the *News Line,* as our daily paper was called from 1976. It appeared to be a natural progression of responsibility from the weekly, the bi-weekly and the daily *Workers Press*.

I started by building up a national system of communication quite separate from the one that Torrance had. Sometimes the *News Line* failed to reach its destination. In this event I had to drop everything and get another parcel sent. In time I was able to build a chain of contacts at all the stations, making it possible for me to get these replacement parcels put directly on to the train, bypassing the railway's parcels office. These contacts also made it possible to collect articles and films that the areas sent down by train. I was able to get directly on to the platform and, more importantly, into the goods van to sort out whatever it was that I had to collect, once again bypassing the Red Star Office. I would take off the ticket and give it to Sinjan, the RSO supervisor, the next time I was in the office. If for some reason I had to collect something from the RSO and there was a big queue, as soon as I was spotted I was given the nod to go round the back to collect whatever it was. If by chance it had not turned up he would send someone down to the platform to wait for the train. All this saved us many hours and quite often made the difference between being able to print the article and pictures or not. This was all very well but, because of the set-up, I was the one who had to drop everything and go. I wish I had a pound for every time Paul Jennings rushed into the warehouse shouting: Norman, package coming on such-and-such a train at one of the London stations.

I usually started preparing for the despatch at about 16.30 hours. From then on I had to be at my sharpest. This was very difficult as it was possible that I had either been working late on a commercial job along with the other comrades or delivering branch papers (or both) and getting to bed between 2 and 4 am. And bed might have been a pile of mailbags.

There were those who thought of the warehouse workers as some kind of 'second class' members. In the main this view was held by those who had joined or come to work on the paper after it had been established – especially those who were recruited and immediately put on to the Editorial Board, the Political Committee, and the Central Committee. Three names spring immediately to mind: Corin Redgrave, Vanessa Redgrave, and Alex Mitchell, a very able newspaperman recruited from Fleet Street. It seemed the only qualification was that Volume 38 of Lenin's *Collected Works* had to fit under their armpits. This is not an attack on Comrade Lenin but an indication of how Healy degraded Lenin. I suppose they were out of their depths in the type of work that they were expected to do. Alex would bluster and bluff his way through. Many times when he gave a report of some meeting or other at which he had been speaking, anyone who had been with him could not be blamed for thinking that they had been at a different meeting. He always reported back the way that Healy wanted it to be.

On one occasion Alex approached me saying that he had a very important letter to be sent to Comrade Slaughter. He told me to put it in the Leeds branch papers and asked if I could guarantee that it would get to him. I said no. If he wanted this guarantee it would be best to send it recorded delivery in the post. He rejected this and told me to put it into the papers. The next morning I received a message telling me that the Leeds papers had not arrived. I left a message on Mitchell's desk informing him of this. I was expected to be in the Centre before Healy arrived so I was certainly there before Mitchell. He stormed into the warehouse looking for me. 'How did you manage it? Did you contact your friends and tell them of the letter?' (implying that I was an agent). I replied that two people knew of the letter, him and me. If the papers had not arrived in Leeds because of the activities of an agent then it must have been him, as it certainly was not me. I was so furious that I ran round to the front office to lodge a complaint with Comrade Torrance. Soon after that I received a mealy-mouthed apology from Mitchell.

A number of incidents pointed to this 'class' division at the Centre. Tony Banda opened the door that separated his part of the printworks from the warehouse and told me that Torrance wanted me urgently at the front office. I made haste down the road to the old Centre and flew up the stairs into the office. 'What's wrong?' Sheila was talking to Paddy O'Regan. She pointed to a window and said that there was a dead pigeon on the windowsill and would I remove it. I said no, let Paddy remove it. She said that Paddy could not be expected to do this. I still said no, and went back to the printshop.

One night I was on guard as well as working, which meant that I had to sweep up, clean the offices, empty wastepaper baskets, answer the phone, and respond to the gate bell. I did not have time to wash down the steps leading up to the Young Socialists' editorial office. Shortly after the YS comrades had arrived the *Keep Left* editor came into the warehouse and asked why the guard had not emptied his wastepaper basket. I told him that I had been on duty. He invited me to go and empty it and I told him to empty it himself. I was pulled in front of Healy who instructed me to wash the stairs leading up the YS office and empty the basket, as we had to encourage the youth to take up positions of leadership. As I washed down the stairs comrades were walking up and down over the cleaning. I felt very humiliated, angry, and tired.

Even the best of comrades could easily be sucked into this two-tier attitude. Before a full-time cook was employed, two or three comrades would take it in turns to prepare the midday meal. One day one such comrade let the departments know that the meal was ready. We went to the canteen and joined the queue but were then told that as there might not be enough food to go round we would have to wait until editorial members had been served, and if there was any left then we could have some. We did raise this as a complaint and were told that some of the newer members on the paper were not fully committed, and so had to be treated differently from us, the committed members.

When we were short of money our wages were drastically cut or we got nothing at all. Sometimes money had been deducted to pay our branch newspaper debts – so that others could be paid their wages in full. Even when we received full wages ours were considerably less than most of the journalists. I did accept that those comrades who had families and mortgages should receive more than I did, but a number of us were paid a pittance and lived in slum conditions. A group of young comrades once asked me what impressionism was. I told them it was to get a wage packet and think that it had wages in it.

I had an accident in one of our vehicles shortly followed by an incident that destroyed a tyre. I had to pay for both. The money was stopped out of my 'wages'. I mention these two particular examples because shortly after Vanessa Redgrave rang to say that she had had an accident and I was despatched to rescue her. The car was damaged and both front tyres were burst. I arranged to have the car towed and I drove her back to the Centre. Healy asked her how she was and told her that of course the party would pay for the damage and replace the tyres for her. I felt very bitter about this. I rationalised the situation away by convincing myself that I had to pay for my repairs because I was a more committed member than she was.

The daily *News Line* had been going for some time and the editorial deadline was becoming later and later. It got to a point where we were in danger of missing our early mainline train times. I spoke to Paul Jennings whom I considered the most experienced editorial member. He recommended that I attend one of the daily Editorial Board meetings with a prepared statement. I did this, explaining the problems we faced and suggesting that the deadlines had to be set in relation to getting the papers to the readers each morning. This did not go down very well. The general consensus of opinion was that the journalists would write, the printers would print and my job was to get the papers distributed. I was told by Comrade Paul Feldman to stop trying to tell them how to do their job; I should go away and drive vans or whatever it was I was supposed to do. It was obvious that many of them were infected by the privileged way that they were being treated. They put in a good day at the office and, with the job done, either went home or to the pub. If anyone stayed back it was Paul Jennings or some of the women typesetters.

To make it easier for the comrades who came in from the branches to clean the premises, and to ensure the security of equipment in the editorial office, it was suggested that the editorial staff should clean up their mess and sweep the floor so that the doors could be locked earlier. Those who had come from other papers as journalists objected most strongly to this. 'We are journalists, not cleaners.' Healy of course supported them.

Many comrades were very skilled in their particular field of work, rarely taken into consideration when they were assimilated into party work – unless they were very high profile or their financial contribution was the deciding factor. Separated from their skills, many were put into positions as full-time organisers. The change from Socialist Labour League to Workers Revolutionary Party in 1973 unleashed a terrific pressure on the membership. Some 80 full-time organising posts were created. Comrades were sent to the four corners of Britain. Comrades were taken out of their work environment to take up these full-time organisers' jobs – or should I say *News Line* sales agents. Healy was creating in his mind this huge network of regional newspapers being produced through some central control. It was like building a pyramid on the legs of *News Line* collecting tins. A tactic of deliberately separating them from their families was also adopted. This led in many instances to breaking up relationships and families. Many years later I was able to see how this had affected my own relationships. We were fed on a diet of 'building the revolutionary leadership' and a very one-sided meaning of communism.

Our comrades from film, theatre and television were, in fact, force fed. I do not mean to isolate these comrades from the rest of the party but this is where Healy's methods showed up the sharpest. One day Kika Markham (Corin Redgrave's wife) came into the printshop and asked if she could have a word with me. Healy was away so I did not have to get permission to leave the premises. We went up the road to the café to have a chat. She told me that she was feeling very depressed, because she could not understand the relationship between being an actress and building the party. I suggested that maybe she was looking at this question in a very one-sided way. I tried to explain in the best way I could that she should develop activity in her field of work that would help to make connections with the working class, maybe by developing a theatre workshop in the style of Joan Littlewood, the Communist Party member. This, as an aim for our members in Equity (the actors' union), would have been tremendous. We had actors, writers, directors, musicians and representatives from every section of the industry. We could have taken theatre to the streets, town squares, and factories. This kind of perspective had obviously never been discussed with these comrades. Kika was very enthusiastic and said that she would go and discuss the ideas with Corin. I had and still have a great respect for Kika and during our discussion I happened to say that I thought that she was a better actress than Vanessa, more sensitive and warm, and that I found Vanessa cold and humourless. Kika said: 'Thank you, but please do not ever say that in front of V.' I had touched on these ideas when talking to Frankie de la Tour, Tom Kempinski, David Calder, Malcolm Tierney, Roger Smith, Roy Battersby and Peter Armitage. I saw most of these comrades when they came in to do guard at the printshop.

I can only presume that Kika reported our discussion to Corin, and then Corin must have passed it on to Vanessa, because a few days later Aileen (Healy's secretary) told me that Healy wanted to see me at his flat. At the allotted hour I went round. I was able to let myself in through the street door. Apart from those who lived there I was the only one allowed to have a key. I went up to his flat, knocked on the door and was let in. He told me to sit down. 'I understand that you have been discussing ideas with the acting fraternity.' What surprised me was that there was no anger in his voice. He asked me to outline my ideas, then told me quite calmly that the ideas were OK but he did not trust and had 'no faith in the acting lot'. There would be a danger that we could lose control over what they did if we introduced these ideas. The best way to avoid this was to continue organising them in the party the way that we were doing: paper sales round the theatres, fundraising. We had to have a tight control over anything outside this activity. Shows and plays had to go no further than being fundraising events. I had fully expected to be given the usual 'anti-party' tirade. Instead I was given a somewhat kid-glove treatment. I wondered why.

Corin Redgrave was elected to the National Executive Committee of Equity, the actors' union. Everyone regarded this as a victory. Not long afterwards I was privy to a discussion where Healy told him not to let this result interfere with his Party work and instructed him to stop going to his Equity branch meetings.

Working in the printshop and doing branch work (selling papers and collecting readers' money) was very difficult. One day Sheila Torrance suddenly told me to help the youth members by doing youth work, including calling on youth to get them to attend functions. As a 40-plus-year-old I got some very funny looks from anxious parents, I can tell you. Each Young Socialist branch was expected to hold a dance at least every two weeks. The success or failure was judged on how many tickets were sold for any particular function, how many *Keep Left*s were sold, and how many membership forms were signed. I was told to go and help the YS members of my branch steward the expected masses at a dance.

Three of our YS members and about a dozen youth were there. I thought OK, let's keep the music going and try and encourage those outside to come in. But our youth members turned off the music, put chairs around tables and shared the youth between them. In a few minutes they were off. No tickets or papers were sold, no one was signed up and there was no dancing – and that's what the youth had paid money for. At the next area meeting we got a roasting.

The three YS members could see nothing wrong with the night except that nothing had been sold. The next 'dance' was arranged for two weeks later and I was instructed to organise it. The first thing I did was to go to see Maurice, who had Moonfleet, a record shop on Clapham High Street near to the flats. Paul and I knew him from our visits to the Plough pub. I explained what I was doing and asked if he could recommend what music I should use. He picked me out three singles and a bang up-to-date long-playing record. Break-dancing was the theme. I got these on a play-now, pay-later basis. Leaflets were distributed on the big housing estate, an area of huge blocks of flats, giving notice of the dance and that there was to be a break-dancing competition. I had been able in a small way to get the trust of a few of the youth on the estate and I went one night with Frances Goldstein to encourage them to come and help run the competition, judging and so on. They promised to help. On the night of the dance I was reminded to collect the records from one of the members. I told them that I already had the records and showed them my bag with the three singles and the long player. Penny Bloor said: 'Run a dance with four records? No way.' We went to the hall and set up the sound system and waited. As soon as a few arrived outside I played a track from the record so that they could hear that we were up to date with our music. I don't know what the record was but Maurice had certainly picked a winner. We told them that the record was to be the break-dance prize. A few came in and the rest went off to tell their mates, especially the break-dancers. We had about 70 at the dance. A good time was had by all in a smashing, friendly atmosphere. They elected three judges. The winner went off happy with his up-to-date long-playing record. Another dance was requested.

The next morning when Janet Banda (our branch secretary) heard of the attendance she dashed into Healy's office to inform him. We were sent for. Torrance was sent for. Healy was pleased. Torrance was pleased. And then she had a sudden attack of revolutionary fervour and asked the dreaded question: how many tickets did you sell, how many members did you sign up? When she was told none on both counts she hit the proverbial roof. We got the 'anti-revolutionary' lecture and were told that we were not here to hold social evenings for the youth. The evening's work had been wasted and turned into a social night out, not party building. I was held responsible for leading the youth comrades astray and they were told not to let me near the YS ever again. So something good came out of it.

I had many things to fit into my 'normal working day'. If for any reason I could not carry out any of these jobs then it was my responsibility to delegate someone else to do them. To have a holiday it would mean that I would have to involve twelve or fourteen comrades spread over the period that I was away to cover the different aspects of my work. It got to the point where Healy controlled every second of my life (I was not alone in this). If he was in his office I had to be in the printshop where I could be contacted. Wherever I was, he had to know. If he was on the premises many of us had to ask permission to leave, for any reason.

Another of the jobs I had to do was to bring the vehicles in to the yard every night and to clear the yard every morning. At whatever time Healy was due to arrive, the yard had to be clear so that Comrade Aileen could drive him into the yard without any delay. The gate had to be opened as soon as the bonnet of the car was seen rounding the corner of the alleyway. Getting the vehicles in and out of the yard was not straightforward. If I was informed that a certain vehicle, be it a car, van or minibus, was to leave in the early hours the order of bringing them in had to be done with this in mind. On many occasions I had to wait for a car coming in from the areas so that the vehicle leaving early could be brought in last. The entrance to the alleyway was tricky; you were in constant danger of being run into by passing vehicles. The entrance through the gate to the yard was narrow and on a bend. Getting all the vehicles into the yard with only inches in between each one was considered a work of art to all except myself and anyone who was standing in for me. To us it was a pain in the butt.

If anyone broke down (vehicle-wise) the policy was to contact me, daytime, night-time, any old time. One Saturday night I had been able to meet Paul at the Plough pub to have a couple of pints and watch *Match of the Day*. We left the pub together and said goodnight. He crossed the road to his flat and I went to get an

Indian take-away. As I passed the front door of the office on my way to Venn Street to the Hilton Hovel (rooms over the old printshop) the door opened and there was my old mate, Tunji Banjo. He was on night duty. 'Hi, Norman. I was just coming to get you. Sylvester has just phoned in. He has broken down and wants you to go and tow him in. The details are at the printshop.' Tunji got the meal. I finished up dashing up the M1.

I had to go on many a bizarre mission. In the early hours one morning I was woken by one of the printshop guards in a right old state. 'Gerry wants some Perrier water. What can we do?' Aileen had rung telling them to take a bottle of Perrier water round for me to deliver to the flats where several of the comrades lived. If none was available then I had to get some. Rudolph had the good sense to come round with transport so I was able to get away quickly. I went to Earl's Court Road where I knew shops were open all night, bought three bottles and drove back to the flats. I let myself in through the street door and through the doors on each of the landings. I scratched on Healy's door. It opened slightly, Aileen's hand appeared, I hooked the bag on to her hand, and it disappeared inside. Then I went back to bed.

One Saturday morning I was working on the guillotine, listening to the radio and thinking pleasant thoughts. Then the guard opened the gate and in came Healy's dreaded Granada. Like every one else around, you immediately tensed up. Shortly after the arrival the hatch to the finance office opened and Dot Gibson, who was in charge of party finance, asked me to come in. Aileen was there and Dot was holding up an empty packet of lump sugar. Healy had developed another fad: he was using a special brand of lump sugar. She had a kind of smile on her face as she said: 'Go, and do not return without a packet of these sugar lumps.' I spent about three hours hunting in the wilds of south-west London trying to hunt down those bloody sugar lumps. I finally had to admit defeat and bought a packet of common Tate and Lyle sugar lumps and returned to the printshop. Aileen had already taken Healy back to the flat and had returned and was waiting with Dot in the finance department for me to return. I declared that there was not a single packet of the special sugar lumps south of the river. Aileen said never mind, and poured the common lumps into the special packet. From then on I collected plastic bags from all the speciality shops and grocers, the kind where the assistants wore special aprons and straw hats and would walk around the shop with you putting whatever you needed into a basket which they carried. If Healy could not go to these shops then Aileen would ask me to go. But now if it wasn't convenient for me to go to Earl's Court I would go to the local shops or superstore and put the cheap food into the appropriate expensive bag.

On the occasions when I had to drive Healy around I experienced some very strange attitudes from him. One time Aileen was in the doghouse and had to ride in the back. We were going to Oxford Street to one of the big stores. I was dreading this because parking was always difficult. If you could not park close then whoever was driving got the blame. On this trip, just as we approached, a nice big car pulled out and left a nice big space. I pulled straight in and parked. Healy turned round and said to Aileen: 'There, that's the way to do it.' The strange thing about this is that he meant it.

He had already convinced himself that we had some kind of special relationship with the railway workers at the stations we dealt with, especially Euston. This was strengthened when a dispute broke out in the parcels office. I just happened to be there at the time, collecting a roll of film. I got this and Healy convinced himself that this was a special dispensation given to us by the NUR rail union. While I was there I got the NUR rep to ring Paul at the paper with the story. This sort of thing was always built up into something that it wasn't.

Another good example of this was much earlier, when a Fleet Street strike was due to start. Ray Efford and I spent some time campaigning in the union (SOGAT) asking for special dispensation for labour-movement papers. As the SOGAT union rep for Plough Press I was invited to a meeting of the Central branch, which looked after Fleet Street. I outlined our case and the branch secretary said that they would look into the matter and get in touch with me on the day the strike was due to start.

It was a Friday. It must have been the last week in July because it was the first week of our annual educational camp. We had two sets of plates ready, one for the paper and another for a broadsheet that was not categorised as a newspaper. I was waiting for a phone call at the printshop and Torrance was waiting in a phone box near the camp. After what seemed like an eternity the anxiously awaited telephone call came. We were told that we could go ahead and print because we came under a category with the union that was not affected by the strike. I shouted into the machine room that it was the paper! The plates were put on and the paper was printed. I explained to the comrades at the print the reason why we were allowed to print. This was relayed to Sheila Torrance. She rang back a little while later to tell me that when the car arrived to pick up the camp papers I had to go back with the car. She also told me that Healy had been told the reason why we were printing the paper. He had called a camp meeting to announce that because of the fight put up by the Plough Press SOGAT chapel we had been given special dispensation to print the paper. On this occasion I was not denounced as a social democrat but I was a well-respected comrade and was setting a good example of leadership for comrades in the party to follow (or words to that effect). I was invited to take tea with him in his tent – a rare honour. I did try to explain the reason for printing but he would have nothing of it. He was enjoying his own reason too much.

I was guilty at least once of encouraging him to think that we had workers' control at Euston Station. Aileen and Healy had gone to Glasgow for a Scottish area meeting. I drove them to Euston and found out that they would be coming back on the overnight sleeper from Glasgow scheduled to arrive at 06.00 hours. The train always arrived on the last platform nearest to Eversholt Street. Between the platform and Eversholt Street was a very big indoor warehouse area. When I went to Euston to pick them up I arranged for one of my friends to open the gates that led into Eversholt Street so that I could park on the platform. I was shown the spot where the sleepers were expected to stop. I parked the car and prearranged for my mate, when he saw me approaching, to press the button to open the great big gates. Aileen and Healy walked down the steps from the sleeper to the car with its doors ready open. I drove slowly towards the big wall of the shed. Then the gates, which were the full height of the warehouse, started to slide open and we sped out into Eversholt Street. We turned right and across Euston Road, up Gower Street and back to Clapham. I don't think he spoke a word all the way back. Aileen told me later that he had said something to the effect that this incident was the party being recognised, and he made sure that everyone heard his version of the incident.

Clearly Healy was living in some kind of parallel universe of his own creation. There are many examples of him needing to be told what he wanted to hear, to read what he wanted to read, and to see what he wanted to see. Reality on many occasions had to be avoided. This does not mean that it was obvious to me at the time. I only had flashes of informed ideas that I soon rationalised away.

This question of reality became part of our lives. The worst example that I experienced was to do with the 'trucks'. We had five of these Ford Cargo trucks. Healy asked me to write a report on their condition and present it to him the following day. My report went something like this: one has just been serviced and the other four are either in need of a service or some repair or other. Aileen came into the warehouse and told me to sit on the bench outside the office and wait to be called in. I was duly summoned into the office. He threw the truck report at me and asked: 'What kind of report is that?' I was told to go away and do another. I was mystified as to what was wrong with it. Was it bad grammar or bad punctuation? In the meantime, Aileen had taken him to his flat for his afternoon nap. On her return she told me that the report was wrong because it did not say what he wanted to hear. So I made another report basically saying that all five trucks were roadworthy. Later that afternoon when I took my report into him he said: 'That's better. Why didn't you do it right the first time?'

The problem in all such occasions was that we were left to deal with the reality. It was the same when Healy wanted to buy another web-offset press. He sent Aileen to get the statement from Dot of the account that he would use for the purchase of the press. When he read it and realised that there were not sufficient funds to purchase the press, all hell was let loose. In situations like this he was like a wild man. He would shout and lash out with his hands and feet. In the end he had to be given the balance he wanted to see.

But to go back to the trucks. Now we had the problem of getting them repaired, without GH knowing. If I had been caught I would have been accused of making a false report or using party funds for repairs that did not need to be done, and being involved in some fiddle or other. My problem was bad enough but Aileen's and Dot's was a massive one when Healy's secret getaway car was damaged. Our Australian comrades had been asked to raise funds for a very important security problem. This they did at great sacrifice. The money either paid for, or went a long way to paying for, a new BMW. The car was hidden away in an indoor parking lot, so that the police would not recognise it when GH had to go into hiding to lead the revolution – no doubt taking his escape fund with him. Aileen or I or both of us were sent to clean the car and turn over the engine at regular intervals.

Around this time at an annual conference Healy moved that as we were now in a pre-revolutionary situation, he was to take total power and be responsible for the leadership of the party. In this situation all leadership had to be centralised through him.

He spent money as though there was no tomorrow. He was convinced that the paper would be taking off at a tremendous rate. With this in mind he bought about 100 mopeds, to be used by the branches to run around delivering papers and organising the distribution. But to be allocated a bike proved very difficult. Any comrade lucky enough to receive one could very easily have it taken away from him or her, usually because the branch was failing to meet its paper debts.

If Healy wanted the circulation to increase Torrance would increase branch orders by as much as 100 per day. One London branch with a membership larger than average did a good job selling its large quota of papers. Over a period members were transferred into other branches until the branch had half its original membership. A request to reduce the paper quota was refused; in fact it was increased. The debt for unsold papers grew astronomically as it did in all the branches. Each week branches would receive a debt slip for the party-building fund, membership subscriptions, and the newspaper sales. Branches were running up debts of hundreds of pounds. Full-time workers would have money taken out of their wage packets to help pay these debts. It reached the point that the main concentration was on paying debts for previous papers and not on actually selling papers. This was crippling to the branches and was largely responsible for destroying many comrades.

To Torrance and Healy, the print run = circulation = money expected in. At a conservative estimate I will say that less than 25 per cent of the run was sold. Unsold papers were becoming a big problem not only financially but storage-space-wise. I was approached by Eric of the Tottenham branch to help him out of a difficult situation at home. The pile of unsold papers was creating a problem between him and his Mum. I arranged to meet Eric at his home with a transit van. The papers were in one of the downstairs rooms. Eric opened the door as far as he could and slipped in. It was wall-to-wall, floor-to-ceiling parcels of *News Line*. It took two or three trips to a dump before the room was clear.

One particular Saturday our comrades really enjoyed themselves. On the Friday night there was due to be a Fleet Street strike. We were not involved so we could print. Torrance was out of London and Healy was out of the country. Dot Gibson and I discussed having an extended run on the Friday night. All the London branches had to ring in their orders by 16.00 hours. The run was finalised and rung through to Runcorn, where the papers were printed and sent to London by train. All London branches were told to meet at 04.00 at Euston Station Red Star loading bay (my 'office' at the station). I had pre-warned the railway staff and two tractors were laid on to bring the papers from the platform. Each tractor had at least three cages full of papers. The whole loading bay was buzzing; even the night staff was excited by it all. Thirty thousand papers were on the loading bay – there was no counting and parcelling individual branch papers that night. The branches rushed the papers into their areas in the bundles of 500 just as they had arrived. The balance was taken back to the printshop. Wherever Torrance was she must have heard how many papers Runcorn had been told to print. She rang and said that she was rather worried.

The first indication that we were to have a good day was when Peter from East London came into the yard and pushed twenty pounds into my hand and went off with papers. He said that a bookie had paid up front to have the papers in his betting shop. We had racing in our sports pages so bookies were a good source of sales. Two of the branches had combined to sell papers at King's Cross Station. They set themselves up at two points with someone taking money, another organising change and someone handing out the papers. There was a constant queue at these points. Others were walking around with bundles of papers with a constant demand from punters. This level of activity was going on all over London. The Clapham branch had arranged to meet at the tube station and set up a stall. Sarah collected the branch papers but never arrived with them because she sold out on her way to the tube. A constant supply of papers was being sent to these comrades. The mopeds really came into their own that day, dashing in from the areas for more papers and when we ran out at the Centre the mopeds were used to transfer papers from areas that had a surplus to areas that were short. At the end of the day all the papers were sold. That evening, the sales money was brought in to the Centre by the bucketfull. No one can be blamed for suggesting that we had taken part in an opportunist binge. I can rationalise it away by saying that everyone enjoyed it and morale was high.

Healy was due back on the Sunday evening. I took the Granada to Heathrow, found a nice convenient parking place in the multi-storey car park, and then simply waited at the arrivals. Aileen took over the driving for the return journey. As soon as we were on our way he asked me to bring him up to date with events. I took a deep breath and told him about the print strike. 'Were we affected?' he snapped. I told him that the only effect was that we were able to increase our Saturday run of the paper. 'How many did we print?' I answered 40,000, with 30,000 sent to London. There was a pause and then he said: 'Do you realise how much newsprint that would have taken?' 'We had enough and another delivery was due,' I replied. He raved on about wasted paper. I assured him there was no waste as we had sold all the papers. 'How much money?' he asked. 'Still being counted,' I replied. I think the thought of the money calmed him down. When we arrived back at the Centre I was told to hang around as he wanted to speak to me. Once again I was in Healy's office. Torrance and Mike Banda were there. I was asked to report how the decision to increase the print run had been made. I explained that Dot and I had discussed it and contacted the London branches, and told them to ring in their orders by 16.00 hours on the Friday. Dot and I took calls and Dot had tallied up the total on the calculating machine, adding extra as a safety margin. The resulting sales had vindicated this decision

No one asked how and where the sales were organised, or how the papers were distributed around London. The prime questions were how much money had we taken, and was it all in the Centre? The atmosphere was quite amenable. Don't ask me why, but I suggested that this could be a good time to cancel all branch debts, give the branches realistic quotas, reduce the run and avoid wasting newsprint. The result was as you would expect. I was immediately ridiculed by Healy and Torrance. It would reduce the sales of our paper and be an abdication of revolutionary leadership. So the equation, print run = sales = money in, continued. The branch debts continued to rise; money was still being spent daily on wasted newsprint – and this was enormous. Once again I was reduced to being a social democrat and was reminded that 'you can't fight the bourgeoisie with bourgeois ideology'.

Heathrow airport has a special file in my memory bank. I had to deal with many awkward situations there and on a number of occasions with Immigration. Once when comrades arrived from Sri Lanka for an international conference in London, Immigration would not let them in. They looked impoverished and carried cardboard suitcases. It took me about eight hours to convince Immigration that they were coming to a conference and would be using the return half of their flight tickets.

One day we received a call from Immigration telling us that two young men from Greece were being detained because they would not tell them why they were coming to Britain. I was told that if they would say why they were coming to London they would be let in. I said they were coming as delegates to the Young Socialists' Annual Conference. The immigration officer said that if they would say this then all would be OK. One of the two young comrades was put on to the phone so that I could explain, but I could not convince him so I was told that they would be sent back on the next plane. It was agreed they would wait until I arrived at Heathrow so that I could have another try. Face to face I did convince them to 'come clean'. I explained to the officer that they were frightened to say that they were coming to a political conference in case they were locked up. I said that they did not realise that all regimes were not like the one that they were used to (creep!). They were allowed in and wished a nice stay.

Another occasion: 'Norman, Alex wants you down in the editorial. It's something to do with Charlie and Immigration. They won't let him in.' This was in the early hours. 'What's up, Alex?' He was in a right old two-and-eight. Charlie, who was responsible for the Centre's security, had rung to say he was being held by Immigration. The problem was that he had been sent to Frankfurt to buy a small but important piece of surveillance equipment. The officer had told him that if he refused to tell them who employed him in Britain he would not be allowed in. 'What can we do?' says our editor-in-chief and member of our Central and Political Committees. 'Best if you go over to Heathrow and get him out of this mess,' says I. 'Best if you go. I have to be here in the morning for the Political Committee,' says he.

On arrival at Heathrow I contacted Immigration and made an appointment to meet the officer dealing with the case. I discussed with him for a while but I realised that nothing I said would be able to help. Charlie had to tell them who employed him. He obviously had a problem with this. The officer said that he would have to be sent back to Frankfurt on the next flight. I asked the officer if it was possible for me to see Charlie. He agreed and took me to a booth. When Charlie came in we exchanged pleasantries and I told him to ring as soon as he arrived in Frankfurt – I was sure something could be worked out. We shook hands and said goodbye. I felt him press a small object into my hand (it was a part for miniature surveillance). I said: 'Goodbye, mate,' left the booth and hoped that I would not be searched. I made a point of knocking on the officer's door to wish him goodnight. I was very relieved to be on my way back to Clapham and waited until I was clear of Heathrow before I stopped to ring in and inform Alex what had happened. I had to leave a message as he had gone home to bed.

I suggested that someone should go out to Frankfurt with a letter confirming who employed Charlie. This task fell to Aileen, who successfully got Charlie back in. Very few knew what went on that night – or any other night, if it came to that.

Another awkward assignment at Heathrow was when I had to meet a group of comrades coming from the USA. They did not turn up in the arrivals terminal. I reported this to the Centre who checked with the comrades in the States to see if they had caught the flight. This was confirmed. I contacted Immigration and asked if they were holding them. I was told to wait at the information desk. After ten or fifteen minutes an officer came up to me, introduced himself, then proceeded to ask me my name, my employer, and my address. I was told to stay in the arrivals area. I sat down to wait and then noticed that one particular person had passed me a number of times in as many minutes. I amused myself watching Immigration watching my every move. After ten hours I was paged and asked to go to the information desk. I waited there until my latest shadow, after a couple of circuits, came up to me and asked if I was Mr Norman Harding. It's at moments like this when I can't resist making some kind of quip. I said: 'If I am not, then you have been watching the wrong man for the last ten hours.' He smiled and invited me to the office. The officer behind the desk informed me that they were now satisfied that the reason given by those held was genuine and if I went back to the information desk they would be escorted to me there.

It became accepted that if anyone was to be taken to the airport I had to do it, especially if it was to get a cheap stand-by ticket to New York. I was supposed to be some kind of expert at this, and knew all the wrinkles and what airlines went at what time.

Healy once sent for me. He said that Aileen had told him that I had a good sense of timing, so he had a special job for me to do. Phil Sandford, an Australian comrade working on the paper, must have upset Healy because he was sending him back to Australia. Or so Phil thought. I was to take him to Heathrow and park on the roof of the terminal car park. At this time we had two-way radios in the cars. At a prearranged time Aileen called me to tell me to bring my passenger back. It was obvious that Phil was more than a little disappointed and would sooner have been punished and sent back home to Sydney.

One unhappy Heathrow pick-up was when I had to tell Aileen, who had been out of the country with Healy, that her father, Comrade Bob Shaw, had died. I said I would drive back to Clapham but Healy would not allow this and I got a torrent of abuse for telling Aileen. I should have told him, so he could tell her.

Jack Gale, my longstanding comrade from Leeds, had been sent to Australia to work with the Editorial Board of the *Bulletin* after a long spell on the *News Line*. Celia had gone with him. Not long after we received the news that Jack had terminal cancer. On a journey back from Heathrow Healy turned round to talk to me. He said: 'You know Gale is only pretending to have cancer so that he will not have to come back and take up his position on the *News Line*.' This really did hurt. I said: 'But John Troy [a doctor comrade in Fremantle, Western Australia] has confirmed the diagnosis.' I caught Aileen's eyes in the rear mirror, telling me to say no more.

Some time later I picked Jack and Celia up at Heathrow when he came home to spend the rest of his time with Celia and his two wonderful daughters, Ruth and Jill (Cathy, as she prefers to be called). I had known the two girls all their lives and they still have a special place in my life. Healy asked me what time Jack would be back in Clapham, not so that he could be there to meet him, but to avoid meeting him. From the day Jack arrived back in London to the day he died in Leeds Healy did not go to see him once. When he died I was sent to see Celia and find out what the arrangements were. Jack had not wanted a funeral as such and he was taken from the hospital to Lawnswood Crematorium, where he was slotted in between funeral ceremonies. When I reported this to Healy he said: 'So Gale is robbing us of a funeral.'

I was to chair the memorial meeting that was organised later. Healy even asked me if I thought he should go. I said he should. But I could not understand why he asked me in the first place. It was a well-attended meeting held in the Great Northern Hotel in Wellington Street, Leeds. Jack was well remembered. But the contributions of Healy and Mitchell should have choked them. They had collaborated to get the Australian comrades to keep their eyes on Jack, to keep him from the membership, and isolate him in the editorial office. Jack's transportation to Australia and the treatment he received from Healy's cohorts strengthened the opinion that an unsigned document strongly criticising Healy found among Healy's papers much later was the work of Jack Gale.

When Vanessa Redgrave was filming *Bear Island* Healy was part of her entourage. He left us to it while he went to Vancouver and then sailed up the coast to the Arctic and into the frozen north (maybe he had been told that there was gold in them there hills). The difference with this trip was that after collecting them at the airport, when we arrived back at the Centre I was presented with a gift. It was a kitbag full of Arctic clothing: a thick zipper jacket with a hood, fully fur-lined. There were trousers, gloves and boots to match. It was suggested that they would keep me warm when working at night at Euston Station distributing the papers. They also came in handy when I was trucking between Runcorn and London. These outfits had been distributed to the cast and crew. VR told me that the one I got was the one worn by Richard Widmark. Thank you, Dicky.

The best Heathrow experiences were when I did not do the picking up but was well involved with the build-up. One evening (it must have been about 23.00 hours) I was sat drinking a pot of tea, minding my own business and at peace with the world. Healy was in Libya so it had been quite calm for a few days. Then the telephone rang. The voice on the other end said: 'Is Norman Harding there?' 'Yes, speaking.' The voice continued: 'Mr Healy and Mrs Jennings will be arriving at Heathrow at about 02.00 hours. Will you please have the car there waiting for them.' I was more than a little suspicious. 'Who is speaking, please?' I asked. 'This is the pilot of Colonel Gaddafi's private jet.' 'Oh yes,' I said. I must have sounded a little apprehensive because the next voice I heard was that of Aileen telling me that everything was OK. The pilot came back on. I asked him where they were. He said 20,000 feet above Nice. He said he would ring back to confirm.

I rang Heathrow and finally was able to speak to someone

connected with air traffic control. I asked him about the plane that was due in at about 02.00. He said: 'Sorry sir, but there are no planes due in at that hour tonight.' I corrected him and told him the passengers were a Mr Healy and his secretary Mrs Jennings. The plane was coming from Libya, it belonged to Colonel Gaddafi, and it was due in at Terminal Two at 02.00 hours. I knew how this must have sounded. Here he was, air traffic control, being told by some wag on the phone that a plane was coming in, giving him the terminal time and names of passengers and who the plane belonged to. 'I will make enquiries and ring you back.' He rang back immediately but he was only checking to see if the telephone number was genuine. Not long after the pilot rang again confirming the time. He told me that Heathrow had tried to divert him to Birmingham. The pilot had rejected this and told them that he was coming to Heathrow. Then Aileen came on and said that Phil Penn and Mitchell had to come to pick them up. Heathrow rang back and said that they had spoken with the pilot. 'And you told him to go to Birmingham,' I said. 'That is no good to us. It will have to be Heathrow.' I knew that it had already been agreed with the pilot that he would come to Heathrow. 'Tell your driver that when he arrives he will be directed on to the apron to make the transfer from plane to car more efficient.'

Phil, who was in charge of party vehicles, and Alex Mitchell were now at the printshop. I gave Phil the message and off they went. I think it then struck me that was it possible that Heathrow thought it was Denis Healey, the Labour MP. Charlie and I went round to the flats and waited for them to get back. Healy was full of it. Apparently it looked as though they did think it was Denis Healey, for security was very tight. Phil and Alex thought that MI5 and MI6 were there in numbers. What a night that was.

Another very interesting telephone story happened one night when I answered the phone and a voice said: 'Is Norman there?' My first thought was that someone had broken down. I said: 'This is Norman.' 'It's Ali here,' said the voice. The only Ali I knew used to work with Tom Scott Robson in the film department and we used to see each other every day. Ali was from Timbuktu in Mali but I thought he was in Lebanon. 'Are you still listening to Mickey

Mouse music?' I then realised that it was him because this is what he used call Western classical music.

I asked how he was and where he was ringing from. Apparently he was in Beirut and had been out and about when bombing and shelling had started. He had dived into an abandoned building and taken refuge in the cellar. The place appeared to be an office and he had picked up a telephone just to see if there was a line. His words were: 'Bloody hell, I am hooked up.' He realised that it was the middle of the night in London but he thought he would try to get through to the Centre. Both of us were surprised. He told me that the explosions were getting louder and he took the phone as near to the door as possible so that I could hear the sound of the bombs. We talked for quite a long time about his friends and comrades in London. Before leaving London Ali had given me a green plastic folder with his personal papers, student pass and documents. He had asked me to keep it safe for him. Ali said that he was not absolutely sure why he had been sent to Lebanon, other than that he had to take steps to open an office there. He told me to destroy the contents of the folder as he would not be needing it in future. We wished each other good luck and he rang off. The only news that I have had of him since is that it was thought that he had made his way to Greece.

The most profitable telephone story I have is when I discovered that a public telephone near the Centre was linking up international calls free of charge. You can imagine just what a hammering we gave it – calls to Australia, New Zealand, USA, Africa, and all corners of the globe. It was like the time when I received a call from a comrade saying that he had come across a petrol pump that would not stop until you put the nozzle back in place. It was one of those that had to be fed with a pound or five-pound note. I got every available driver to the Centre and we filled up every vehicle that we could lay our hands on for a couple of quid. Healy was not sure that we had done the right thing when he was told the next morning. He thought we might have been set up by the police. He was paranoid about this kind of thing.

Just before a petrol drivers' strike was due to start Healy told me to make sure that we had a supply of petrol on the premises.

Before he set off on a journey in the car petrol had to be stored in the boot. Six cans were wrapped in sacking and placed in a cardboard box with a funnel. The cans had screw on caps, and an appropriate spanner was also placed in the box so that Aileen would have no problem opening the cans. This was all under the instruction of Healy. The car was a virtual bomb. It does not bear thinking about what could have happened if they had been involved in an accident.

Healy then extended the petrol policy into insisting that we had petrol on the premises to make sure that we were never stranded. I was instructed to get the petrol. I used one of our Transit vans as a cow. I filled it up and then siphoned the petrol into whatever containers I could get hold of. I managed to get hold of a supply of jerry cans and then later about six barrels. If there was a garage with petrol within ten miles of Clapham I would get to know about it. The branches had petrol diviners on the lookout. About a week into the strike we had at least a thousand gallons of petrol stored around the premises. The comrades were referring to me as Sheikh Harding. I stank of petrol, and because of the siphoning my mouth tasted like petrol, and my stomach thought I was drinking the stuff. This episode, like many others, could have been considered as funny, bizarre, tragic, or downright dangerous, not only to my health but to the lives of everyone working there. But my only consideration was to keep the vehicles moving.

And no doubt I was very pleased when Healy said: 'Well done, Comrade,' especially in front of others. If anyone denies that this is true then I fear that they have missed part of the reason why we had to get rid of him.

A number of houses turned into flats overlooked our yard. Healy noticed that an extractor fan had been installed outside one of the flat windows. We assumed it was the kitchen window. Charlie (head of security) and I had to work out how to get into the flat and inspect the offending object. Healy had convinced himself that it was a directional microphone. Breaking in was out of the question so we went round on the pretext of apologising for any inconvenience caused when we worked nights. The lady of the house offered us a cup of tea, which we accepted. During the small talk that followed Charlie asked to use the toilet. This was his chance to examine the object on the wall near the kitchen window. And, by jingo, it was an extractor fan!

The year that we had enough candidates in the general election for us to be allowed television time, Corin Redgrave gave our election address on TV. I found myself responsible for the continuity and the order of printing of all the election material and had to give a report of progress to the Political Committee every morning. Comrades Dave Bruce and Tony Banda were the ones who dealt with the technicalities of the printing. When everything had been printed and despatched to the areas I was able to report that the job had been completed. Healy told the PC that without the organisation and discipline of the comrades in the warehouse, there would not have been an election campaign. But it was the branches that had to stick up the posters, distribute leaflets, address thousands of envelopes and insert the manifesto. The comrades who deserved an accolade were never mentioned: the ordinary branch members who, on top of the never-ending selling of the paper every day and all that went with it, were working all night and then going to their jobs, sometimes to dangerous work on building sites, driving, etc.

12

THE REDGRAVES

When they were recruited, Corin and Vanessa Redgrave and Alex Mitchell were immediately put on to the Central and Political Committees. This put them into a position of leadership. I felt that not one of them could lead a pussycat across a country lane.

Maria, a young and enthusiastic comrade, came into the Centre one evening. She had been summoned to see WRP Assistant General Secretary Sheila Torrance. Maria stopped at my bench-cum-office at the bottom of the steps leading up to Sheila Torrance's office. Comrades often used to stop for a chat before going upstairs to face ST. The night before, Vanessa Redgrave had called a meeting of one of the West London branches to discuss the branch's paper and fund debts. The meeting was called for 21.00 hours and ST was waiting at the Centre for a phone message to say that the money had been collected, some hundreds of pounds. ST would be at the other end of the phone until midnight or so to hear from all the branches. Maria arrived for the meeting, parked her moped and went in. Vanessa was not there, but arrived shortly after. She stormed into the room, stage left, and told Maria that she was hopeless. 'You have parked your moped in a stupid place,' she said. Maria went outside to see what the problem was and was faced with the sight of her moped under the front of VR's car. The front of the car and the back of the bike were damaged. Maria immediately realised that this was a sit-on-the-bench-outside-Healy's-office job. So she went back into the meeting and took up the offensive, and told VR that she was not going to take the blame.

Vanessa reported to the branch that they had to pay off the debts that night, and should immediately make plans to achieve this. Then her leadership qualities shone through. 'We will go on a pub collection,' she said. Maria pointed out that as it was now 22.00 hours it was too late to raise the money in this way. I can well imagine Vanessa telling her that she was bending to bourgeois ideology. Vanessa led her reluctant troops out on to Kilburn High Street and into the biggest and liveliest pub in Kilburn, some fifteen minutes before last orders. Soon after, Vanessa had to be rescued from a building worker to whom she was explaining the building of the revolutionary leadership. The total collected was 20p.

When Maria came back down, she told me she had been severely dealt with. She was not to appear before the Political Committee the next morning, but in future she had to treat VR with more respect, as she was a very important member. Maria had to pay for her moped repairs while VR's car was paid for by the party. Lower echelons of the party had to pay while the 'important' members would charge it up to the office, under Healy's instructions.

On another occasion I was to take VR and Dot Gibson to Heathrow to catch a plane for the Middle East. I had prepared a car and loaded the luggage, and Dot and I waited for Vanessa to appear from Healy's office where she was receiving her last-minute instructions. They both came out into the yard and VR immediately shouted in a stern voice: 'Who told you to load up that car?' I replied: 'I did.' I was then instructed by Vanessa to take out the luggage and put it into her car (for some reason I was not to be trusted).

On the way to the airport her car started to shake, rattle and roll. 'What's wrong?' she asked. 'Don't know,' said I. 'It's going to break down,' she complained. She then started to slip into the transferring-blame mode. 'Who told you to use this car?' she demanded. 'You did,' was my reply. She had started to lay the basis for transferring blame in case we missed the flight. I was glad that Dot was in the car so she could hear what had been said. I coaxed the car to the airport and back. When they returned Dot told me that she was blamed for everything that went wrong. Vanessa even asked what Dot had done with her glasses when Vanessa could not find them.

Was Vanessa acting out the building of the revolutionary party and simply changing the script when she took on the role of transferring blame? Was this fight for revolutionary change simply the biggest production she had ever appeared in?

When we had candidates standing in a general election, Corin Redgrave was candidate for the Vauxhall constituency. One day he was leading a door-to-door canvassing team, marking his card with the ones who had shown an interest in voting for him. He was particularly interested in a young couple to whom he had talked for some time. On his return to the Centre he gave me their address, and told me to go and recruit them. His words were: 'They are keen and ready to join.' I rang the doorbell, introduced myself, and was asked into the house. Two minutes later I was on my way out. The kettle did not have time to boil. 'Come in, brother,' they said. 'I understand that you both want to take part in the struggle for socialism,' I said. The young woman said: 'The only place we will find peace and socialism is in the Kingdom of Heaven.' 'Hallelujah,' said the couple in unison. They were both Plymouth Brethren. 'Did you recruit them?' asked Corin. No, I replied. 'But they were keen! They called me brother. I spoke to them for about ten minutes.' I told Corin that they were Plymouth Brethren. I asked what he had talked to them about because I was in and out in two minutes.

But his sister was even worse. During a canvass on a big estate consisting mainly of tower blocks, a young woman came to the door, babe in arms, with two more youngsters clinging to her skirts, obviously a woman with a lot of pressure on her. She told us that she was having problems with the council regarding repairs and rent. I asked her if there was a tenants' organisation on the estate that she could approach for advice and help. At this point Vanessa pushed past me, and started to tell her about the need to change the system. 'The WRP candidate represents the fight against capitalism.' The only way to solve her problems, said Vanessa, was to demand a general strike, and so on. Then out came the membership application form. The young mother was left with 'Vote for the WRP!' ringing in her ears. On the way back from the canvass VR told me she severely disagreed with my initial approach and that she was going to raise it at the report-back meeting as an example of how important it was to fight against social democracy in the WRP. That evening I received a great deal of verbal abuse from Healy, Mike Banda, Mitchell and Co.

The reason why I think it is important to describe the relationship between the WRP's members and the Redgraves is because it goes a long way in exposing the corrupt and reactionary relationship between the party and this layer of the 'leadership', on a day-to-day basis.

I once drove Vanessa Redgrave to the BBC Social Club where she was to meet her mother, who was doing a radio play. While we were walking to the car she asked me if I had seen *Playing for Time* which had been shown on TV the evening before. As it happened, Charlie, Rudolph and I had been banished from the premises as punishment for taking a decision (a correct one) without first checking it with Healy. We had to write the necessary confession and report with it the following morning. But it meant that we had been able to watch the film! It was about a Nazi concentration camp. There was an orchestra on camp, and one of its jobs was to play as the victims were herded to the gas chambers. The music was supposed to calm them. The conductor was Mahler's granddaughter. VR's character was one of the musicians. In the scene where the condemned were heading for the death chambers the orchestra was playing and VR was singing an extract from *Madame Butterfly*. I said yes, I had seen it and that in the scene where the men, women and children were being herded to their deaths I thought that the orchestra had played and her character had sung in a way appropriate to such harrowing circumstances. That is, no one would have been able to perform at their best. She looked at me angrily and said that she was doing her best to sing correctly. I responded by saying that I thought that it came over as though she was emotionally upset, as one would expect. As we pulled away in the car she told me to stop trying to be a film critic and get her to the Social Club as quickly as possible.

We parked outside where I was unsociably left outside in the car. About 40 minutes later the doorman came out and told me that I was requested to go in and join them. I found VR and Rachel Kempson (her mother) with a group from the cast of the radio play.

I felt uneasy and must have looked uneasy. They were all talking among themselves and kept breaking out into what I supposed were their characters. I had been bought a drink so at least I was able to hide behind the glass. One young woman from the cast broke away from the rest, pulled her chair closer and started to explain what the play was about. We entered into general chatting. She told me that she thought it bad that I had been left outside so long. Rachel had asked V how she was getting home and the reply was that she had a car and driver waiting for her outside. She let me know that it was Rachel and not V who had suggested I be told to come in.

I said many things in the party which ended up with me being criticised. Once I was at Vanessa's house along with a number of other people when I voiced the opinion that Jane Fonda had shown some courage in her stand against the Vietnam war. Vanessa came straight back. 'She is an opportunist. She never understood the reason for joining the Fourth International.' The gist was that she was frivolous and not serious enough about what she was doing.

No doubt everyone who has come into contact with VR is aware of her sharp wit and acute sense of humour. Once I was in the car with Healy and Vanessa, with Aileen driving, travelling along Goldhawk Road, near Shepherd's Bush. The traffic was very heavy so we were going very slowly. Passing a row of shops, I pointed out one with a notice outside saying, 'Insurance from birth to death.' I said: 'From womb to tomb!' Next door was an undertaker's with a notice: 'Easy payments can be arranged.' In the same breath, I said: 'Die now, pay later.' Even Healy saw the funny side of this, but Vanessa's face never slipped.

ST decided in her wisdom that I should work with VR for the following six weeks or so. One duty was to be her driver. This was about the time comrades had begun secretly to prepare a challenge to Gerry Healy, which culminated in his expulsion.

I had to pick VR up at 07.00 hours every morning and take her wherever she had to go. This was mostly to Clapham to be at the Political Committee meeting for 08.00, but then to continue with whatever plans she may have had. She had the attitude that somehow I should automatically know where she wanted to go. One morning she was not ready to leave for the Political Committee as she had slept in. Her reaction was that I should anticipate situations like this, and arrive earlier. The Political Committee agreed with her, so no matter how long I had worked the night before – usually well after midnight – I had to be banging on her door at 06.45, after coming from Clapham to Hammersmith. One morning she was excused attendance at the PC because she had an appointment for an insurance medical in connection with a film she was making. She did not have to leave the house until 11 am. She did not let me know, so instead of me having a lie-in, I was up at my usual 04.45 hours. I was banging on her door at 06.45. I did point out to her that if I had been told, we both could have had a sleep-in. There were no apologies, although she did say a little later that the reason she had not told me was that she did not want to 'interrupt the continuity of the arrangement'.

Around this time her father, who was a very sick man, was staying at Vanessa's. I used to pass the time of day with him or sit down in his room for a chat. The Redgrave family had its own film archives, added to from time to time. On one occasion a venue was booked and all the family took part: Michael, Rachel, Vanessa, Corin, and Lynn, acting out scenes from King Lear. In one scene, Vanessa was sat at the feet of her father (playing King Lear).

On another occasion film footage was to be taken at Haddon Hall, near Bakewell in Derbyshire. This time it was to be an Elizabethan scene with Vanessa's mother, Rachel Kempson, as Queen Elizabeth I. It was a two-day job with an overnight stay at a hotel near Ashbourne. I was to spend the night at our Education Centre, near Parwich, a few miles away. After the first day's filming I drove them to the hotel and was invited to have a meal with them. During the meal I was shocked by their conversation concerning a very delicate family matter. It was as though I was not at the table, as if I did not exist. You see films featuring an aristocratic family having dinner, the servants standing a few paces from the table, upright and staring into space. They only existed when their 'betters' wanted another potato putting on their plate.

After the meal we retired to the lounge for coffee. I was given my instructions for the next day. I was to pick them up at 07.30 hours. Then, as an afterthought, Vanessa told me to bring a flask of coffee. I asked her for the flask. She said that she did not have one and that I would have to buy one. I reminded her that it was 22.30, the shops were closed and would not be open as early as 7.30 am. She said her mother was tired and they were retiring for the night. As they were walking away she turned round and said: 'Don't forget the coffee.' This was like Healy asking for Perrier water at four o'clock in the morning, knowing full well that there was none at the Centre and not bothering where it came from or how it arrived.

I told myself that this was just another little problem to solve. When Tony Banda broke Healy's china cup during the night, Tony was beside himself worrying about what would happen in the morning when Healy found out. I was able to get one by getting comrades up in the middle of the night. On that occasion Comrade Clare Cowen saved the situation.

I had to I spend some time working out the options. I decided that the only thing to do was to get up early, go into Ashbourne, buy one, and get it filled at the hotel. But how was I going to buy a flask so early in the morning? This would have to be solved the following morning. The Education Centre Security was asked to give me a call at 06.00 hours. I went into Ashbourne and headed for Woolworths, and waited outside for the cleaners. The first to arrive was the cleaning supervisor, who had the key. I managed to talk her into selling me a flask. She was to give the cash to the first checkout point to open.

At the hotel I asked reception to have the flask filled with coffee. I told them who it was for and asked them to put it on Lady Redgrave's bill. (It was a few weeks before I was able to get the money for the flask.) When Vanessa arrived to settle the bill she noticed the item: flask of coffee. 'What is this?' I explained, and we headed off for the wonderful Haddon Hall. Later, I was seated outside the room being used as a dressing room with the flask on the chair next to me. The expected request for the coffee was forthcoming, but no word of thanks. Weekends such as this could have been very interesting and enjoyable if it was not for the overbearing atmosphere.

I suppose Vanessa was herself a victim and no doubt found herself in situations that she could not handle. Once Healy put her in charge of a course at the Parwich Education Centre. I was one of the unfortunate students. The first day of the first week we were instructed to write an essay on why we had joined the Workers Revolutionary Party. I was the only one who had joined before the formation of the WRP, and the previous Socialist Labour League. I had joined the 'Group', from which the two later organisations came. To answer the essay question, I had to go over my activities in the working class since 1950 and earlier, and the forming of my ideas since 1945. I could not put it straight down on paper. I had to plan it out, and then write it down. At the end of the session I still had not finished. I was given extra time. When I had finished I took it to her room. She said that she could not understand why it had taken me so long.

The second session was called and Teacher handed back our books with comments: well done, could have been better, poor, and so on. I got: too long. It was obvious in her summing up that what she was looking for was a simple explanation as to why communism would be a better system than capitalism. I think this was about as much as she could cope with.

13

LONDON AND BAGHDAD

For a little light relief I will now relate an incident which – with the comfort of distance – can be regarded as humorous. Dave Bruce and I were given the job of taking a vanload of rubbish to the dump. Now, even jobs like these were a welcome break from the pressures of the Centre. Among this rubbish was Healy's old kettle that Aileen had decided to get rid of it as it was faulty. On our return Aileen told us that Healy was in a vicious temper because she had thrown out the old kettle. He wanted it back so that it could be repaired. We knew what could develop when he was in one of these tempers, so we went back to the dump and to the skip that we had put the rubbish in. Much to the amusement of the council worker in charge, Dave and I climbed on to the skip and simulated our previous throwing action, and estimated projection using objects of a similar weight. We would throw and then wade up to our shins in rubbish and search the area where the missile landed until we finally found the kettle. We returned having completed another successful mission. A few days later Aileen bought a new kettle anyway.

Whenever things did not appear as Healy thought they should, it would put him into a complete panic and rage. On one of these occasions Comrade Dot was on the receiving end of one of his worst physical attacks. He kicked her so viciously on her legs that ulcers developed on her shins. I had to take her to the hospital to receive treatment over a period of weeks. Dot insisted — and others, including me, agreed — that Healy should not be told of the damage he had done because it would upset him. He had to be protected from this kind of pressure. We had to sneak out secretly to make the trips to the hospital. On another occasion he caused permanent damage when he struck Aileen over the back with a chair. He constantly physically abused comrades and, as I found out later, there were other forms of abuse going on. I will deal with this in a later chapter.

Moving back a few years, a US establishment dissident, disillusioned in some kind of way, decided to expose a number of CIA agents in London. He sent their names and addresses to the London offices of the national dailies, including the *News Line*. A CIA agent called John Ford lived in the Muswell Hill area and worked at the American Embassy. A job was given to longtime party member and journalist Comrade John Spencer and me: John was to be the cameraman and I was to confront Ford. Our plan was to drive over to arrive at 07.00 hours, park a little way down the street, and wait for him to come out. There was quite a long garden path between his front door and the gate, making it easy for us to time our confrontation. Ford came out of the front door with two young children; he was obviously going to drop them off at school. He came through the gate and approached his car. As he put the key into the lock I said: 'Hello, are you John Ford?' His response was to send his children back to the house. He then faced us and said yes. I asked him if he was John Ford, CIA. He asked who we were. I told him that we only wanted to take his photograph. By this time John had taken a number of frames. Our CIA agent then asked if we would like to take a photograph of him with his hat on. He opened the car door and bent inside – at that moment I was convinced that both John and I were about to become tomorrow's front page. He straightened up, holding a black Russian woollen hat which he placed on his head and posed. We were the only paper to succeed in getting a result.

John and I took part in another mission in December 1980. We were sent to Baghdad as guests of the ruling Ba'ath Party in Iraq. The official invitation was to attend a conference held under the auspices of the Ministry of Agriculture. We were to be there for seven days. The first panic was that my passport had expired and I had little time to get it renewed.

I had often had to get passports and visas for comrades under very difficult situations involving shortage of time and security difficulties. On one occasion a comrade had been refused an American entry visa on a technicality. He was out of the country at the time so I had to go to the American Embassy and sort it out. I had to get the visa that afternoon or the trip would have to be cancelled. Another sacking job. Succeeded.

I arranged my passport in record time: I started on the Friday afternoon and by Monday dinnertime I had a new passport (offices were closed Saturday and Sunday) and a visa from the Iraqi Embassy. We were on the plane that evening.

We were met at the airport and all formalities were waived. We found ourselves being ushered into the VIP lounge and introduced to our interpreter, guide and government representative who was to be the key to many a locked door. On at least one occasion we were granted interviews on our own while the rest of the delegations had theirs *en bloc*. For some reason our importance had been exaggerated. Each delegation made a speech of greetings to the first session of the conference. I remember the East German delegate referring to the farming machinery that they had contributed. Other delegations made contributions of a similar ilk. The contribution that John and I had discussed and prepared did not, and could not, have any reference to any material contribution we had made to the people of Iraq. Not even paper clips. John spoke of our support for the struggle of oppressed people all over the world and of our solidarity with all those in struggle against imperialism, and received a good reception. John's contribution was reported on Iraqi TV, so when we returned to the hotel for dinner we were received very warmly and genuinely by the other residents.

I remember that when anyone mentioned Saddam Hussein the conference rose smartly to its feet and applauded with extreme enthusiasm. On one of the evenings all the delegations went to a banquet hosted by the Ministry of Agriculture in a beautiful ancient hall with lots of atmosphere. There was a bottle of whisky for every four people which was immediately replaced when empty. I have to say that both John and I showed great discipline and avoided getting into the state of many of the other delegations.

Next to me was a delegate from East Germany. Before he became a babbling wreck his political contribution to me was to encourage us to support Maggie Thatcher as this was the best way to bring East and West together. I told him that to support Thatcher would be betraying the working class. His reply was: 'You do not understand internationalism. Everyone has to make sacrifices to safeguard the Communist Bloc.' Very soon after that he introduced his head to the tablecloth.

On another occasion we were having a discussion through an interpreter with a Polish trade union delegation. At one stage of the discussion I asked them if they were aware that Stalin had executed the majority of the Central Committee of the Polish Communist Party. The answer was that that they were aware of this. I think it was the Ba'ath Party guide who decided that it was time for the Polish delegation to go elsewhere.

On a trip to an agricultural and farm college we were greeted by the Iraqi equivalent of the Young Pioneers, who lined up and clapped us in. John and I had to look very intelligently at the prize bull and other animals paraded before us. A car took us one evening to the embankment of the river Euphrates in Baghdad where we were shown the famous monument of Scheherezade with her ladies in waiting at her feet. The night scene with the lights of the mosques and buildings reflecting in the river was very impressive.

The highlight of the whole trip was a visit to Babylon, where we were taken round the excavations. We saw the streets and houses, and remains of temples. But the star of the tour was the statue of the Babylonian Lion straddling a human victim, surrounded by an iron fence. As a kind of symbolic insult, a discarded Coca-Cola tin lay inside the fence.

One morning, between breakfast and being picked up by car, a peasant leader at the conference came to see us at the hotel. He wanted to have a chat. I think it was as a result of John's contribution at the conference. The most interesting thing he had to say was that 'one day poor peasant and poor Jew would fight side by side against rich peasant and rich Jew'. He added that he felt we were the only

Archeological digs at Babylon, the highlight of my trip

two he could say this to. He shook our hands and wished us well with a firm, warm handshake. We returned his good wishes. The Polish delegation sought John and me out before leaving and simply said: 'Keep fighting.' It was a very friendly farewell.

Our last activity was a visit with the rest of the delegations to the Palace for a banquet and personal introduction to Saddam Hussein. We were asked to stay for a further two weeks. We both declined the offer, though a chance to see more of this ancient culture was very tempting. But we were needed elsewhere.

The WRP of Healy did some terrible things. One of the worst aspects was its uncritical relationship with some Arab nationalist leaders. Healy wanted photographs taken for Saddam Hussein's regime of demonstrating Iraqi trade unionists in London. An Iraqi trade unionist who appeared on the platform of a national meeting in Sheffield of our All Trades Union Alliance was arrested on return to Iraq, and vanished.

14

RAID ON THE SCHOOL, SATURDAY 27 SEPTEMBER 1975

This Saturday started more or less like any other. I started work in the printshop at about 07.00 hours. Healy was at the Party's Education Centre in Derbyshire so I was able to set my target to finish late afternoon. I went back to my flat, had a bath, and settled down for a couple of hours' sleep. This sort of day was fantastic. At about 18.00 hours I started my weekly tour round Fleet Street to collect the Sunday papers as soon as the presses started running. This meant that we would get a look at the Sunday papers several hours before they reached the streets. This was one of those rare weekends when there was no pressure to rush back to Healy's flat; I was simply to leave the papers at the front office where a member of our Editorial Board would pick them up, scrutinise them and prepare for the Sunday morning Editorial Board meeting.

The great god Linotype was on my side that night. All the Sunday papers got off to a flyer so I was back in the front office by 19.30 hours. I sorted one of each for the editorial staff and put the rest on a pile for me to take into the Plough pub in Clapham where I would sell them to the eagerly waiting punters (I had to finance a few pints and an Indian take-away somehow) and watch the Saturday night special football with Paul Jennings.

Before going to the pub I decided to flip through the papers myself. I quickly spotted an article in the *Observer* referring to a police raid on our Education Centre. Now if there had already been a police raid on our Education Centre I would certainly have known.

The article was based on an interview given by Irene Gorst, an actress and a member of the Kilburn branch of the WRP. It went on to make a very specific claim: that over 100 police from the Derbyshire police force had made the raid and had discovered an arms cache buried in the grounds. When I read this I couldn't believe it. Initially I thought that maybe there was another education centre in Derbyshire, but the article's mention of the Centre's name, White Meadows, also known as the Red House, soon made it obvious.

I immediately rang the school and spoke to Liz Leicester and Alex Mitchell. I informed them that I suspected that there was to be a police raid that night. I read out the important passages from the paper. Shortly after, Mitchell rang back to double check I had got it right – he must have spoken to Healy in the interim. I was told that they would ring back later. When they did ring, Mitchell had to cut short the call. He had just enough time to tell me that a number of police vehicles had driven into the grounds and had turned on their headlights. 'The police are in; will ring back.'

About 30 minutes later actor and Party member David Hargreaves rang and told me that on his way to the school he had been caught behind a convoy of police vehicles and they had turned up the lane leading to the school. 'What shall I do?' he asked. I told him to park the car and give himself up, and to tell the school comrades that I was anxious to get news.

Liz, the comrade who had answered the phone when I first rang with the warning, was originally from the USA, but had been a member for several years in Britain and was married to another leading member, film director Roy Battersby. Her description of both the raid and the domestic arrangements forced upon her by Party life are very illuminating.

AN EYE WITNESS ACCOUNT OF THE POLICE RAID

My memories of the raid on the Derbyshire College of Marxist Education are punctuated with faces, images, sounds. So much was tied up in the event for me – family, history, politics. My road to those events was unusual. But perhaps everyone could say that. Roy and I had moved into a beautiful flat in Maida Vale in 1968 after living in one of the psychiatrist R D Laing's communities in North Finchley for a couple of years. (That is another story and part of our road to the Derbyshire Peak District!) For some time we had been hosting what were known as the 'Friday classes' in our spacious front room. These were mostly attended by actors, some writers, some musicians. Gerry Healy usually led the discussion because he considered this such an important group of people, but sometimes it was other leading Party members, Cliff Slaughter, Cyril Smith, Geoff Pilling.

I remember one debate in particular between Healy and Laing which I found very painful and difficult. I felt we had to make a choice between what seemed at the time to be opposing ideologies – something I didn't want to do. But that debate was in Michael Henshaw's Regent's Park flat which was several times more spacious and posh than ours. I remember Alex Mitchell at that particular event. He was new to the movement then and got involved because of his relationship with Joy, who worked with Roy at the BBC.

Roy was asked to go to Derbyshire to oversee the extensive building work when White Meadows – or the Red House as it was known locally – was purchased. He had also been instrumental in recruiting the architect for the project, Bill (?), whom he had worked with in films. And off he went leaving me with Tom and Will – then just under four and two respectively. He never came back to that flat. He wasn't ever given any time off the building project. That was horrible for both of us and of course for the boys as well. Roy was probably asked to run the Derbyshire school before he went to oversee the building work but I don't remember. I just know that he agreed to give up film-making and move and that I supported his decision. I think I was allowed to visit Derbyshire once during these months and can remember being accused of distracting Roy and have a vague and horrible image of a London District Committee in the old offices over the butcher (always associated with the smell of raw meat) at which I was lambasted for a variety of misdemeanours. But that may well have been for some other event/mistake/counter-revolutionary action on my part.

I wasn't allowed to go to Derbyshire for the first school – the actors' school attended by the infamous Irene Gorst at which she

White Meadows, Parwich, Derbyshire: our College of Marxist Education

allegedly found out about guns hidden in the garden. Healy wanted everything to settle in before I arrived with the boys as undoubtedly our presence would take Roy's mind off the main task of running the school. So back in Maida Vale Party members Geoff Pilling and Sean Hudson helped me pack up and take apart a life of seven years. They were wonderful. I remember Geoff, who was not exactly handy, helping me take down shelves and both of us laughing and laughing until we cried because we were equally useless. Sean packed and drove the lorry with all our belongings to Derbyshire. I drove our Renault estate with the boys, our plants and our cat Fritz who had been with us for years. It was very emotional for me. Both boys had been born while we lived in Maida Vale, I was part of a close network of women with small children with whom I had shared birth, childcare and friendship. It was a wonderful situation for the boys with a big, enclosed and safe communal garden behind our flats. It was hard to go.

When I arrived I think it was the second intake of students at the school. It was what we called an 'international' school, attended by people from a variety of countries.

At this point, the local community thought White Meadows was a cultural/theatrical/arts centre. They were aware of the involvement of a variety of film and theatre people such as the Redgraves and Roy in the project. No one knew that in fact what had been set up was a College of Marxist Education.

Not long after I arrived in Derbyshire my parents came to visit. They were living in Montreal at that time and travelled to England by freighter, arriving in Felixstowe. I drove down to meet them with the boys. One of my main memories of that trip was that the dipped headlights on the car didn't work and I drove back through the night with irate drivers flashing their lights and honking as I blinded them with my brights. That was the first of many vehicle dramas for me, a direct result of having no time and no money to ensure what you were driving was safe.

I think it was the day after my parents arrived that all hell broke loose. I have a memory of taking a phone call on the school pay phone in the office, from Norman in London. It was a Saturday night and the Sunday papers were already out in London. Norman said that there was a big spread in the *Observer* based on a story by Irene Gorst – who it turned out had not been a genuine student at the first actors' school. As a result of her story, there were allegations that we were plotting and planning against civil society and had weapons buried in the garden. I just remember Norman reporting this briefly and asking me to tell Healy.

(On reflection, I am not one hundred per cent sure that it was me who took Norman's call. But it seems likely as there was a meeting going on in Healy's flat at the time which involved everyone else who was allowed to answer the phone.)

I think I knocked on Healy's door, gave Aileen the message and went back upstairs. Not long afterwards, my mother and I were standing at the bedroom window of our flat upstairs measuring for curtains. I looked out and saw a dark blue transit van driving up the road. Corinna Lotz had been out in the van and I remember thinking that it was Corinna returning. Then I saw that there were lots of dark blue transit vans on the road and almost in the same instant the lights were turned on in them and I saw they were full of police all getting ready to jump out.

This time I am very sure what happened. I ran down the back stairs, through the kitchen and dining room where people were sitting reading and studying. As I ran, the police started coming in through every door, window and possible opening. I just had time to knock again on Healy's door which was again answered by Aileen Jennings. I think I probably said something like 'there are police everywhere', she thanked me and shut the door. I think Alex Mitchell, Roy, Healy, Aileen and Cliff Slaughter were all in Healy's flat. There may have been others.

I ran back up the stairs – I can't remember how I managed that but I guess there was a great deal of chaos. The boys were upstairs asleep and they were my first concern. I don't know what happened to my mother, how she got taken downstairs and I can't remember where my father was. He was probably upstairs with us and I guess the police must have made them go downstairs with everyone else. Because of the boys I was allowed to sit upstairs.

As well as concern for them, I felt I was doing something very important because I had the register of students upstairs with me. It showed that we had people attending the school who came from countries with fascist governments such as Greece, Spain and Portugal and I was very aware of the danger they would be in if they were identified and possibly deported. So throughout the night I sat on the light blue, hardback A4 book which contained everyone's names and countries of origin. I took it with me when I went to the toilet, scared to death that the policewoman who sat upstairs with me would notice and take it away.

And that was by and large my night. My parents were downstairs with everyone else; I had no idea what was happening to them and everyone else. I was desperately worried about everything and told nothing by the police. My younger son Will woke up at some point. Rather than try to get him to go back to sleep, I got out some toys and he sat on the round rug we had in the living room happily playing. The policewoman was being very friendly to him, which annoyed me.

Eventually a group of trenchcoated policemen came into the flat accompanied by Roy and Cliff. I didn't know at the time about the spontaneous and courageous act by all the students who pretended not to know any English and couldn't therefore answer the police questions. I didn't know about the negotiations that had gone on so that Roy and Cliff could accompany the police on their search. I didn't know anything about anything at this point. When the police, Roy and Cliff appeared in our hallway I remember getting very angry and saying to the police that they should let my parents come upstairs, that they had only just arrived in this country and that they were older people who would be suffering a great deal as a result of all this. I will never forget one of the trenchcoats saying to me in the most smarmy, sarcastic way: 'Of course, Mrs Battersby, we are very reasonable people.' I also remember clearly being very angry when they turned on the lights in the bedroom where my older son Tom was sleeping and tipped all his toys out on the floor. I was pleased when they came upon a dead mouse behind the wardrobe. And, needless to say, nothing else.

I only found out later that I had escaped being strip-searched by being held upstairs on my own. All the other women had to go through this, including my mother, who objected and asked the police what they would do if she refused. I'm not sure what they said but it was not pleasant, so she complied. Because of my parents' own political history in the Communist Party in the United States in the 1930s, 1940s and 1950s I knew they would handle this OK. But they were amazed by the actions of the Labour government and police in what they still assumed was a very civilised country in comparison with the witch-hunting USA. My father took great delight in saying a hearty hello to the local Ashbourne police whenever he saw them in the following weeks. They were among the police from five different forces who raided the school that night.

Others can write more effectively and no doubt remember more clearly the campaign that was launched immediately after the raid and the libel trial against the *Observer* newspaper that followed.

For me, one of the sharpest memories is of the following day. I was sent with my parents and sons down to the local pub in Parwich to introduce myself to the pub landlord, Alan Wood. He had got to know the guys doing the building work on the school but, like all the other local people, thought they were working on an arts and cultural centre. It must have been a helluva Sunday morning for all the people in Parwich who opened their newspapers to find they had the College of Marxist Education just down the road and that we (allegedly) had guns buried in the garden!

So I was despatched with my family as the acceptable, family face of Marxism to say hello to Alan and the rest of the Parwich community. My mother and father agreed to come with me and sat with the boys at a table outside the pub. I fought my way in – it was packed with journalists and others no doubt wanting to hear the story and talk about the exciting events of the previous night. I went up to the bar, put out my hand to Alan Wood and said something like: 'Hi, nice to meet you, I'm Liz Battersby, Roy's wife.'

Well, the whole place went quiet. I don't think I've ever had such an impact on a crowd.

That was the beginning of what became a very friendly, if always slightly edgy, relationship between us and the people of Parwich. Some of them were extraordinarily helpful and kind. I remember particularly the farm family down the road, the milkman and the teacher in the two-room school house where Tom started primary school.

And the rest is history.

It was another five to six hours before the school was able to get back to me. I was told that the police had searched the place thoroughly. All they claimed to have found were three 202 bullets in a cupboard at the top of some narrow stairs. The circumstances of this 'find' were suspicious. The couple of hours' warning that I had given our comrades by spotting the danger enabled them to focus their minds on the impending raid and time to plan how they would insist any search be carried out: that leading comrades went round with any group of police. The overseas comrades had time to consider how they would handle any questioning they would be put under.

I learned afterwards that the local farmer and milkman had been out for their Saturday night drink. When approaching the school they had seen the police activity. Not daring to drive past they pulled up a side lane and spent the night in the car. The farmer asked what it was all about. When he was told that they had been looking for arms and had not found any he said that they would have had a better chance at his place!

By now the Plough pub was closed, even the lock-in, and so was the Indian take-away. To quote a phrase: 'Things are constantly changing.' It sure did for me that night.

THE ASTOR CONNECTION

Some more background to the raid is given in the following. It is taken from a file that I found when going through my documents. I am not certain who it was written by.

> The *Observer* is the organ of the Rt. Hon. David Astor, heir to the fortunes of the American Astor family. During the 1930s the family's country seat at Cliveden received notoriety as the meeting place of the pro-Nazi elements of the British ruling class. On one occasion Von Ribbontrop spent a weekend there. When Australian Prime Minister Gough Whitlam was in London in 1974 he went to Cliveden to relax for the weekend with Labour politicians, bankers and Whitehall chiefs. David Astor himself has never occupied Cliveden.
>
> Astor keeps a staff of senior writers who work hand in glove with the Foreign Office and the Home Office. At the time of the raid they included political correspondent Nora Belloff, foreign correspondent Gavin Young, and finance correspondent Andrew Wilson.
>
> The 'Observer Foreign News Service', a news agency offshoot run by the paper, has the closest connection with the Foreign Office, particularly in the Middle East and Africa. Astor, Beloff and company acted as unofficial public relations officers for the Jenkins/ Prentice, 'Social Democratic Alliance', wing of the Labour Party.
>
> The provocation [the raid on the school] organised in conjunction with the Home Office and the police followed a witch-hunt against the 'Militant' group. This was as a result of the

successful ousting of Prentice by the Newham North East constituency Labour Party.

Although the *Observer* had the Gorst Affidavit for two weeks the story was not published until September 28th, the day before the 75th annual Labour Party conference. It coincided with the Blackpool speech by Prentice, pre-released to the press, in which he denounced 'extremists' in the Labour Party, and the publication of an SDA document alleging links between Labour MPs and Trade Union Leaders and the Communist Party. These are clear signs that the raid on the WRP formed part of an orchestrated campaign

During the early 1960s Cliveden was once again in the news when it was discovered that Tory War Minister John Profumo met prostitute Christine Keeler at Cliveden. Among the other guests were society doctor Stephen Ward, aristocrats, a junior Russian diplomat, and the Pakistan dictator Ayub Khan. To this day Cliveden remains a seat of conspiratorial gatherings of the ruling class and its time servers.

Arising out of the police raid the WRP took the *Observer* to court and although we won the case, massive costs were awarded against us. The following passage is also taken from a document discovered when going through my files. It was obviously written between the raid and the Observer Court Case.

BACKGROUND TO THE RAID ON THE EDUCATION CENTRE AT PARWICH, DERBYSHIRE, ON SATURDAY 27 SEPTEMBER 1975

It is beyond a shadow of doubt that the pretext for the police raid was provided by an article which appeared in the *Observer* dated Sunday 28 September. Towards the end of the six-hour raid, senior police officers freely admitted that it was the *Observer* article that had prompted the attack. We couldn't just ignore it, one police officer said.

The first edition of the *Observer* came off the presses in London between 18.30 and 19.00 hours on the Saturday evening. But it is certain that from the amount of pre-planning and sheer weight of equipment and forces that the police were ready to move well before the paper was on the streets.

This means that there was direct collusion between the police and the *Observer* newspaper for the purpose of carrying out a provocation on the WRP and its school. The crucial sentence in the *Observer* reads: 'Members have been known to hint at arms caches hidden in the grounds, and to have access to secret cabinet minutes.'

The information for the article was provided by Irene Gorst, a member of Equity, the actors' union. In her article she says that she joined the WRP in March this year, 1975. It has since been established that she wrote in to the party asking to join and she subsequently joined the Kilburn branch, membership card number 5005.

The next document I want to quote is a statement made by Vanessa Redgrave relating to a telephone conversation with someone called Aveline. It is not known who Aveline was, but the conversation took place shortly after midnight on Sunday 13 October 1975:

When I got home I found a message to telephone Aveline. I rang Aveline while Corin was on the line listening. Aveline sounded surprised that I had phoned him. He seemed to be taken off balance and said: 'Oh yes, just a minute, I'll go to the other phone.' He then suggested that I meet him. He said he wanted to talk 'but not on the phone'. He said: 'Irene Gorst is getting the blame. But she is not to blame. She is 100 per cent WRP; the whole thing has been a terrific miscarriage.' He said that I would 'do myself good to know the real story'.

He then asked: 'You know who I am?' I said: 'Yes.' He said: 'I could meet you tomorrow.' He then added: 'I'm not being taped, am I?' I said: 'No.' He said that he could see me tomorrow. 'But I don't know where I'll be,' he said, 'I'll have to let you know. Where can I ring you?' 'My last appointment is a dentist appointment at 3.30,' I said. 'Well, I'll ring you back on this number tomorrow and let you know.'

He added: 'I can't go out now; it would be noticed. If we meet

> tomorrow maybe we could meet in the park. You come in your car and I will come in mine.' Then he added, 'Didn't I see you today? Isn't your car SMP 954?' I said 'I beg your pardon? Where did you see me?' 'Just a second,' he said, 'there was some confusion.' And then the phone rang off and he didn't ring back.

Vanessa Redgrave's description of her telephone conversation with the unidentified Aveline is puzzling. Was the purpose of the telephone call to suggest that Irene Gorst had nothing to do with the raid? Was Aveline just an innocent actor contact? The precise origins of the raid will not be known without an inquiry of some kind.

15

MINERS' STRIKE

The miners' strike of 1984-1985 raised questions in the minds of many comrades, or at least it sowed the seeds of discontent. They started to raise questions with other comrades.

Healy did every thing in his power to stop the WRP from getting involved with the mass rank-and-file movement that was developing in support of the miners' strike. He told the members that we had to build our own support groups in mining villages in opposition to the community support groups that he described as middle-class, opportunist, and anti-revolutionary. At the same time he pronounced that if the miners were defeated then the way would be opened for fascism.

One morning, after the night-drive from Runcorn with the *News Line* and finishing my distribution work, I learned that I was to set off at 06.00 hours with a minibus to take leading members of the Young Socialists to the Kent coalfield to make contact and start building YS branches in Kent. We soon found ourselves in one of the Kent miners' welfare clubs talking to the women's support group members who proudly showed us how they were organising the distribution of food and preparing meals for the miners and their families. This was no soup kitchen! Places at the table were neatly laid out with the necessary cutlery and glasses with jugs of water, all set on gleaming white tablecloths. In one of the rooms shelving had been put up to store all the different items of food. Perishable foods were found places in many freezers in the area, including in shops. One oldish lady said: 'It's like the old Co-op, ain't it mate.'

The discussion in quite a natural way soon got on to the question of how we could help to support the strike. A decision was reached that the support group would bring a van and we would go round Covent Garden vegetable and fruit market with them the following morning. We had some contact with the market. The YS members and I were delighted at being able to show our solidarity with the miners in such a way. Arriving back at Clapham, we soon put Healy in the picture. He was furious and sent for Torrance. He ranted on that Covent Garden was ours (a fantasy) and if anyone was going to collect from the Garden then it would be the WRP, and we would take it to the miners. When Torrance came in she asked why nothing had been done with regard to setting up a branch of the YS. When Healy was informed that the Kent transport had already been arranged for the following morning he went purple. He said that the only thing we could do was to make the best of it, and make sure that it was understood that it was the WRP who was doing the collecting at Covent Garden. The YS leaders and I were accused of abandoning our responsibilities as 'Revolutionary Leaders'. They were dismissed and told to return to the YS office and get on with their work. As for me, he held me responsible for misdirecting these young comrades into middle-class activity. I was sent up to the canteen (as you were) to write a statement explaining why I had succumbed to bourgeois ideology. I had a good idea what words he wanted to read, so I did not bother too much.

The *News Line* was directed to report and support the strike. Our photographers PJ Arkell, Martin Meyer and Ray Rising were producing by far the best coverage of any of the press, and certainly took great pride in their work during the strike. They often came in with a story and pictures to cover.

The state threw everything into the fight against the coal miners. Government D notices were issued to stop media reports of certain incidents. The media coverage of the battle of Orgreave was edited to falsify the truth and give the impression that the miners charged first, but it is now well documented that the police charged first. I believe that British troops disguised as police officers were put into the police lines, especially at the front, to pass on their skills about how to charge the enemy.

On one occasion an expected confrontation did not take place. What followed could not be published as it would have made Maggie look very foolish and a D notice was put into operation. The police had lined themselves up ready for the push when it became obvious that the only opposition waiting for them was an old retired miner and his Jack Russell dog, ready to face the might of Thatcher's state. A wave of the walking stick and a bark from the dog and they were gone. Not one image or word of this appeared on the TV or in the newspapers (not even in the *News Line*). If we had had a photographer there, Healy's fear of the state was such that he would not break a D notice.

At the same time as Healy pursued the National Union of Mineworkers' full-time leadership he opposed strongly any link between the miners' mass support and the WRP.

Support groups that we were not allowed to be part of were formed all over the country. The Reading miners' support group organised to send Christmas presents to one of the mining villages. They contacted the miners and asked them to send the names of all the children, listing who were girls and who were boys, and their ages. Presents were donated by the community, parcelled in bright Xmas paper with the name of each child fastened to the present. This was noted by our Reading branch who informed London. It was decided that the WRP should also send a vanload. This was duly sent – a pile of black plastic bags containing jumble – to our Reading WRP so-called support group. Our comrades had never been so embarrassed.

Our main concern seemed to be to increase the sale of the paper. Those attending the Education Centre went on sales in places where we were able to get through the police barriers surrounding the pit areas in Derbyshire. I took one such team and many different suggestions were made as to how we should handle the first barrier. Going fishing was one, but we had no rods with us, and this ruse had been well used by the miners anyway. Surveillance was set up by the police on bridges close to the county boundaries to spot suspected transport carrying miners or strike supporters. I suggested that it would be better if we just took the police head on. Arriving at 'Checkpoint Charlie', I asked to talk to the officer in charge as this could save everyone valuable time. The inspector came over to the minibus and I told him that we were not going to join the picket line but to sell our paper the *News Line*. Whether or not he was simply taken by surprise, he smiled and waved us through.

We had a good sale. This was the closest I had been to the picket lines. The houses surrounding the area had gardens facing the picket lines and the miners' families were stood at their garden fences, shouting their support and waving banners. For some reason this activity was deemed 'illegal' and the police were trying to get them to go into their houses. Washing baskets appeared, full of washed clothes which were pegged out very slowly every time the police approached the gardens. When a basket was emptied, they would go into reverse, putting the clothing back into the basket. Picketing miners being chased by the police would jump over the nearest fence, run through the back door and out the front door. The women would stop hanging out washing to hinder the progress of the police in any way they could. What we were seeing was going on every day of the strike.

I had been on many demonstrations that had a police presence; I had been in the cells for fly-posting and picketing against apartheid outside South Africa House. I had moved militant resolutions at trade union and Labour Party branches, but this was different: the vote against a militant resolution became the truncheon of the state. I know this has gone on throughout the history of working-class struggle and oppression all over the world, but this was the first time I had seen it close up. I was never able to get close to the big struggles of the 1970s in London because I was always closeted in the printshop.

All through the miners' strike Healy's main concentration was on sales and making contact with the NUM leaders such as Scargill and the Kent miners' leader, Jack Collins. He was more interested in them than he was in WRP members who were miners in positions of leadership in the pits. I remember, following a Central Committee meeting, saying cheerio to my miner comrade Dave Temple, when Sheila Torrance, in a very sarcastic and hostile manner, told him to get back to the North East to his trade union and trades council: 'You're no good to us.'

Above: The 1985 national march to release the jailed miners. Three placards at the front show anti-apartheid victim Steve Biko with Joe Green and David Gareth Jones, two miners who died during the year-long miners' strike.

During the big firefighters' strike taking place during the very cold winter of 1977 (sound your horn if you support us), Healy behaved no differently. He made contact with the union leadership and for a very short period had meetings with some of the leaders of the Fire Brigades' Union in his office. They were all presented with a copy of Lenin's *Volume 38*. Yet 100 yards away from the centre was Clapham fire station – and Healy never went near it.

When the miners' strike ended Healy must have been petrified waiting for fascism. Torrance went into conflict with him over his opposition to the first national march to release the jailed miners that terminated at Alexandra Palace. He said that the march would be attacked by hordes of fascist thugs. The march did go ahead and was very successful.

16

UNCOVERING AND OVERCOMING THE HORROR: 1984 TO 1986

After the miners' strike WRP members discussed and analysed our part in the strike. Was the separation of the WRP from the mass movement simply a bad tactic, or was it more than that? Did we have to study the whole strategy of the WRP? Did we have an opportunist approach to the nationalist leaders, such as Libyan leader Gaddafi, Iraq's Saddam Hussein, and the Palestine Liberation Organisation's Yasser Arafat? The central question of whether or not we were in a revolutionary situation had to be re-examined.

We continued this deep, political analysis of our activities, and a political appraisal of the leadership, over many years. It centred on a critical examination of the role played by Gerry Healy. This task was initially taken up by a group of comrades at the Centre: Dave Bruce, Aileen, Dot, Clare, Robert Harris, and Charlie. We have Dave Bruce to thank for initially taking on the responsibility of the political examination that resulted in the expulsion of Healy. They did not know that it would not be a clean break, but more of a splintering, an explosion, within the WRP and the International. The right issue and timing were key to successfully challenging Healy and his supporters, and it was important not to get provoked into acting prematurely. If Healy had become aware of what was going on he would have created slanders, and accused this small group of 'anti-party activities'. The membership would have been manipulated into supporting Healy, and the dissenters would have been expelled.

It was winter 1984. I delivered the Sunday papers to Healy as usual at about 8.30 pm on Saturday. Dot answered the door; Aileen must have been away. I was asked into the flat. He had two flats, one for sleeping and one for receiving guests and dining. This one was his dining flat. Mitchell must have been away because there was another member of the Editorial Board having a meal. Afterwards they would go through the papers to work out what to discuss at the Sunday morning Editorial Board meeting.

'Harding,' he yelled, 'you're just a social democrat, just like that Croydon housewife,' pointing to Dot. I could feel my social-democratic blood rising. I remember thinking: what the hell are you doing surrounding yourself with social democrats? Dot's eyes said: 'Don't say anything'. I was dismissed. As Dot let me out of the flat she whispered: 'Wait for me down at the car.' A little while later she came down and got into the car. She said that she was going to tell me something and to make it easy for her would I just listen and say nothing. She told me how Healy had sexually abused countless females at the Centre, irrespective of age. This abuse was conducted with women from all over Britain and also from the international sections. It was mainly carried out against the youth. Dot and Aileen at some point previously had compared notes with some of the youth and started to realise that his abuse was widespread. Up to then each individual thought she was the only one. (Much later, at a meeting we had with an organisation called Incest Crisis Line, we heard how when sexual abuse happens in a family, each one thinks that they are the only one being abused, and how the abuser uses fear to bring this about. The pattern of Healy's abuse was the same.)

Dot dropped me off at my half-a-flat. I let what I had been told sink in. I put my hands on the mantelpiece and wept; what I had heard broke my heart. Then another thing struck me. I was the only one apart from Aileen and Healy who was allowed to have keys to the two doors leading up to the flats (except of course for those who lived at the flats). I had been seeing the girls who worked late at the Centre home safe to the flats after work, or taken women for afternoon discussions with Healy. Sometimes I would pick someone up from the station at six o'clock in the morning – or earlier – and let them into the flats, right up to Healy's door. I was the key to the door for everyone, including comrades coming from the international sections. I was especially busy when we were having an International Committee meeting.

Women comrades from time to time would come and see me and say: 'I have to go to see Gerry but I have some time to spare; will you go for a drink with me?' Unbeknown to me then, the absolute dread of going to see Healy must have been heavy on them. This still weighs very, very, heavy on my mind. I am so very, very sorry. I do know that I was not to blame for what happened on the other side of the door. But I feel very bitter at the way dedicated and loyal comrades were treated.

I remember one young comrade being screamed at by Healy in his office. She had been summoned to have a political discussion. She came running out of the office into the yard in a very distressed state. He was still shouting at her in the yard: 'You're hopeless; you will never be trained; you refuse to be trained; you're an opportunist shit.' I wondered what she had done. Had she not understood some aspect of his political lesson? It never entered my head that she was getting this treatment because she had rejected him. I am sure that this 'guilt' played a big part in the build-up to my mental breakdown a number of years later.

The day after I received the information from Dot she arranged to see me again in the evening. She explained there were others involved in the opposition and told me who they were, and asked if I would take part. I said: 'You bet!' – it was like being recruited all over again. The next comrade I spoke to was Dave Bruce, who said: 'I only want you to take part if you are prepared to go all the way and get rid of Healy.' I agreed. From that moment I was no longer in awe of Healy and had no respect for him whatsoever. I just went on with my day-to-day work. I read and discussed events with the other comrades. We continued to examine our past activities. But we were also on our guard not to give ourselves away. In the past whenever Healy was having one of his rages in the office or in the yard we used to keep out of the way so as not to get involved. But now if I heard a row and he was in one of his tempers I would go into the yard and make sure he saw that I was there. I was now prepared to intervene if he started throwing his arms and legs about.

When any of us were at the Education Centre we would encourage discussions that questioned the line being pushed in the *News Line*. Comrade Andy Blunden, who went home to Australia shortly after the split, has sent me an email describing his attendance at the school about this time. Comrade Peter Jones, who was with us in the growing opposition group, was the lecturer and I was one of the students. Andy explained how Peter and I working together helped him and others to see what was wrong with a particular article that had just appeared in the *News Line*. In his email Andy says he suspected ours was a deliberate intervention but at the same time did not know what to make of it. Later, Comrade Richard Goldstein and I waited for Terry Brotherstone, a leading member in Scotland, to come out of the telephone box in Parwich. We walked back to the school with him and put our point of view in opposition to something that we were discussing that day.

On Sunday 23 June 1985 I was sent to Bournemouth to lead a *News Line* sales team at the conference of the Trades Union Congress. Labour Party left activists were also there selling the *Labour Herald,* a paper that we produced and printed in collaboration with Labour lefts Ken Livingstone (leader of the Greater London Council) and Ted Knight (leader of Lambeth Council). A number of our comrades worked with them on its editorial board. This paper began to take off in the labour movement. Healy's main interest was to use the paper as a way of snuggling up to the bureaucratic left leaders, not as a paper for uniting the Labour left in a fight against the right wing.

Sales were going well. Then, on the fourth day, Thursday 27 June, I received a message from Clare Cowen (*News Line* organiser) telling me to return to London immediately. She hurriedly told me that Bob Archer (Party member and son of my comrades from Leeds, John and Mary Archer) had reported me to the Political Committee for criticising the Party when collecting the papers in Runcorn. Robert Harris would meet me at London Bridge Station to fill me in with details. My first thought was had I blown it? Were we being pushed into premature action? In Clapham I was put under 'flat arrest' and told to stay there until sent for. I was duly told to report at Healy's office at 12.30 hours. Healy, Mike Banda, and Mitchell were present.

A letter dated 27 June 1985 had been sent to the Political Committee by Comrade Bob Archer reporting a conversation that had taken place around the beginning of March 1985. I denied the contents of the letter. I was told that in this case I should charge Comrade Archer for saying these things about me. I refused. I said that Comrade Archer had every right to report to the PC anyone he thought was working against the party and he was doing this out of loyalty, so I would not bring charges against him. They took it in turns to tell me to charge Comrade Bob. I said no. Healy got up out of his chair, took a step towards me, and screamed: 'Charge him!' I told him to sit down and listen. He sat down. I said: 'No!' Banda threw his hat at the wall and Mitchell looked a little baffled. I do not remember if I was officially dismissed or if I just walked out. What those three did not know was that the office was bugged and Dave, Charlie and Robert were listening to the whole thing in the guard box at the gate, saying to each other: 'Go on Norman, give it to him!' My refusal was reported to the PC who unanimously passed a resolution that an investigating committee be set up to enquire into the accusations made against me and to invite me to appear in front of them. Healy said something about me organising a coup against him. That really did make me feel good; he very rarely paid me a compliment.

The committee of Healy, Banda, Mitchell and Comrade Dave Bruce saw me at 12.30 on Saturday 29 June 1985. I was handed a letter from the PC signed by Healy instructing me to lay charges against Comrade Bob Archer. I again replied no. I was asked by Comrade Banda to make a statement to the committee. I said: 'To lay charges would be detrimental to this inquiry and would be a diversion from the politics of anything I may have discussed with the comrades in Runcorn.' During the discussion Comrade Banda said that Comrade Gilbert had something on me. I asked what, but Mike Banda was not forthcoming. I gave another 'no' to the PC's instruction. I was provided with facilities to make a written statement before 18.00 hours that same day.

At the second session we were able to discuss the politics behind what I had said. The first point raised against me was that I had discussed in Runcorn that during the recent miners' strike, Arthur Scargill's signed photograph, thanking the WRP for its help, appeared above the platform of a London area aggregate meeting in the place usually reserved for the founders of our movement, Marx, Engels, Lenin, and Trotsky. Scargill was a militant trade union leader who stood by the members of the NUM against attacks from the Thatcher government. I told my inquisitors: 'Maybe the place for it was on a separate table as a tribute to the miners. He is not a political revolutionary leader. We are constantly saying that the TUC and the trade unions cannot produce the necessary leadership to take the working class to power. This will have to be done by the revolutionary party. To have the plaque where it was only strengthened confusion.'

I had also criticised our attitude to Ken Livingstone. Other labour movement papers – but not the *News Line* – criticised Ken Livingstone because they believed he had abandoned the campaign for the GLC and its workers in the face of Thatcher's decision to close it down. After I had stated my position on this, Healy in his quiet mode said: 'Norman, it's a question of understanding dialectics and leadership. Livingstone is, if you like, on a pendulum. He has swung from the left to the right. If we attack him now and knock him off the pendulum, when the pendulum swings back he will not be on it for us to take him off it.' I looked straight at him and replied, 'You must be f****** joking.' That's done it, I thought. I have challenged his 'dialectics'.

I was then questioned about a statement I had made that Healy had lost touch with reality. This arose when British Rail was refusing to accept our parcels of *News Line,* or any of the other stuff that we sent by train. Our contract had been terminated and they would only accept items paid for over the counter. Although there were the odd times when railway workers slipped our stuff through free of charge, the new British Rail policy was causing huge problems for us both in Runcorn and in London. Comrade Bob had discussed this with Comrade Dot and she had told him not to raise it with Healy and 'make waves'. Bob approached me asking me if I knew why she had said not to make waves. I replied that Healy would not understand the reality of the situation. 'Is he ill?' Bob asked. 'I have just told you,' I said and, later that night, I did tell Bob that Healy had lost touch with reality. Much later he accepted this opinion himself and played his part in expelling Healy and his supporters.

I have known Bob from his childhood when he and his brother Peter used to play at 'having meetings'. Even though we now have political differences, I will always have a great respect for Bob. During the inquiry I am sure that neither of us had bad feelings for each other. And, in the real meaning of the words, we remain comrades and friends.

In the middle of all this Comrade Lorenzo reported a discussion with Comrade Les Ford who told him that Healy had destroyed layer after layer of Young Socialist leaders. Later, Les told me that he felt he had better go back to Portsmouth before he spilled the beans altogether. Little did he realise how close the beans were to being spilled and that he would soon be back helping to clear up the mess.

Before Healy brought the meeting to an end he looked straight at me and said: 'Norman, what I would like to know is, where are you getting your strength from?' He didn't know that the 'Clapham Six' had organised so well that Comrade Dave Bruce was on the investigating committee, alongside Healy, Banda and Mitchell. My interrogation was adjourned on the Saturday night, to reassemble at 10 am on Monday, 1 July 1985. We could not meet on the Sunday because the national march of the Young Socialists was due to arrive at Alexandra Palace for a mass rally.

As I was still under flat arrest I went back to have a nice quiet day and to get some more of that strength Healy was on about. I was looking forward to Monday morning. I reported at the Centre at the appointed time. Charlie opened the gate. 'Ah, Norman! There will be no meeting for you this morning. The letter has gone in.'

> June 30th 1985
> To the Political Committee.
> During the course of action on the Manchester Area certain practices have come to light as to the running of Youth Training

Above: Platform at the 30 June 1985 rally in Alexandra Palace after the Young Socialists' national march to release the jailed miners. Left to right: Lambeth Labour Council leader Ted Knight, WRP General Secretary Mike Banda, Gerry Healy, Young Socialist Simon Pirani, and Liz French, whose husband Terry was a jailed miner

by a homosexual and the dangers this holds for the party in relation to police provocation. I believe the Political Committee was correct in stating that a cover-up of such practices endangered the Party from a serious provocation.

Having realised this I must therefore say to the Committee that I can no longer go on covering up a position at both the office and in the flats at 155 Clapham High Street which also opens the Party to police provocation; namely that whilst for 19 years I have been the close personal companion of Comrade Healy I have also covered up a problem which the Political Committee must now deal with because I cannot.

This is that the flats in particular are used in a completely opportunist way for sexual liaisons with female members employed by the Party on *News Line*, female members of the International Committee and others [26 individuals were then named].

On any security basis one of these or more has to be the basis of either blackmail by the police or an actual leak in security to a policewoman. I am asking the Political Committee to take steps to resolve the position for the Party in the present political situation.

In 1964, after the Control Commission of Investigation Comrade Healy gave an undertaking that he would cease these practices, this has not happened and I cannot sit on this volcano any longer.

Yours fraternally
Aileen Jennings

The PC decided the letter was nothing else but a provocation and many, including me, were asked if we knew where Aileen was. While her disappearance had been planned before the letter went to the PC, only one or two comrades knew where she was. I was not one of them. I had to wait some fourteen years before I saw or spoke to her again. Rumours were rife as to what had happened to her. Had she run off with Healy's 'escape' money? Was she in some hospital or other? Some comrades even thought she had been done away with. When Healy asked me, my reply put fear into his mind. 'Maybe it's a repeat of the time when Sylvia Frankland [the secretary of the leader of the American Trotskyists] was exposed as a government agent.' This fed his fear of the state. After all, he continued to say that if the miners were defeated fascism would not be far behind.

It had been arranged that a small group of abused young women would tell close friends or family during the rally at Alexandra Palace on Sunday 30 June what had happened. Aileen's letter followed the next morning.

For a period of time Healy came in to the office as usual. His main concern was to get to the bottom of Aileen's disappearance. He was trying to monitor who was talking to whom, as had always been his practice; he was constantly breaking up conversations between comrades, no doubt running scared that his activities were being discussed. He was more eager to stop the youth from talking to each other in case they were comparing notes. The establishing of relationships had always been completely taboo.

During this time political positions were taken. Dot Gibson had the unenviable task of remaining at her post to keep close to Healy's movements and activities. At first Sheila Torrance supported the exposure of Healy and worked for it with the others, but then her position changed. She supported a proposal that Healy should sign a statement promising to 'cease his activities with the youth'. Others said they would withdraw their demand for a Control Commission of inquiry if this was done. The following letter dated 8 July 1985 was signed by G Healy.

> To Comrade Mike Banda – General Secretary
> To Comrade Sheila Torrance – Assistant General Secretary
>
> Dear Comrades
> In accordance with our agreement dated 5/7/85. I unreservedly undertake to cease immediately my personel [sic] conduct with the youth.
>
> Yours fraternally
> G Healy

A number of comrades, led by Dave Hyland, who later collaborated with Dave North, leader of the American Trotskyists, began demanding a Control Commission. The London youth committee demanded a Control Commission. Mike Banda, the General Secretary, was very prominent in opposing this, saying it would damage the party. At a meeting of the Central Committee, an American delegation led by North opposed the expulsion of Healy and said that they had come here not to take sides but to bring the two factions together. He then led his delegation out of the meeting.

It was very difficult working at the Centre at this time, made easier by comrades from the branches coming in to see us and talk to us throughout the day and night, showing their solidarity and support. Naturally this started to establish where comrades stood in the struggle to oust GH and his supporters.

London aggregates and national meetings of all members were held in the warehouse at the Centre that by now had been converted into a decent-sized meeting hall. These meetings were, to say the least, very lively. At one such aggregate meeting Comrade Slaughter outlined Healy's misdeeds, and at one point attacked Healy's personal behaviour very forcefully. Many comrades were very moved and upset at what he had to say. The Redgrave supporters of Healy heckled him, calling him 'petty bourgeois' and 'puritanical'. Comrade Slaughter then revealed that the section of his speech which they were attacking as 'bourgeois' was a quotation from Lenin.

Corin Redgrave said that what Healy did in his spare time was his affair and was to be separated from his politics. Corin went on to say that he was 'neither for nor against rape' but 'for the social revolution'. He went on to say that Aileen's letter was a provocation orchestrated by the state machine in order to smash up and destroy the WRP. (This line was later supported by Ken Livingstone.)

At a London aggregate meeting it was revealed that *News Line* photographers had been asked to take photos for the Saddam Hussein regime of Iraqi Communist Party members on a demonstration. They refused. This was an indication of Healy's unprincipled relation with bourgeois national leaders.

Ted Knight, who was an ex-Party member and former full-time worker of ours, and who was now the Leader of Lambeth Council, did not to my knowledge ever make any statement on Healy and the accusations against him. How this fitted in with the fact that he used to receive an envelope on a Friday I do not know. Maybe what was in the envelope was a note of thanks from Healy. I know he received these envelopes because I took them to him in the Lambeth Leader's office. This still happened on the Fridays when many of us received only a very small note of thanks or no note at all.

Discussion of communist relations or, more to the point, the lack of them in the WRP, was bitterly opposed by the Healyites who constantly tried to prove theoretically that Healy's actions against the youth had to be kept separate from his politics, and that we were just middle-class moralists and, of course, social democrats.

By this time Mike Banda had joined us, and at a high point of anger at one of these meetings tried to get our supporters to leave the meeting. Wayne Poulsen and I pushed Mike and the others back, telling them not to abandon the meeting to Healy's supporters.

Healy himself never once had the courage to attend any meetings or face the members. So much for the claim that Healy always led from the front! There was a lot of passion around at the first meetings. The Runcorn comrades turned up ready to smash the place down. Dave Hyland was telling comrades not to go into the meeting because the place was going to be blown up.

Whenever there was a Central Committee meeting members from all over Britain used to make their way to the Centre and hold a continuous meeting in the warehouse. Central Committee upstairs, members downstairs. I often found myself chairing the downstairs meetings and trying to answer the questions of the worried and angry members. I was often asked if I had known about the activities of Healy. When I answered no, I would be asked why not. Did I know and choose to keep quiet? My answer to that one was always an emphatic no. It was very difficult for the comrades to understand how and why I, and others at the Centre, did not know.

The demand for a Control Commission to be set up to investigate the contents of Aileen's letter was finally conceded by the Central Committee. All this time Healy was holed up in his flat leaving his supporters to fight his corner. The Control Commission elected at the previous annual conference consisted of former Liverpool dockers' leader Comrade Larry Kavanagh, experienced Party organiser Comrade Jean Kerrigan, and me. I acted as secretary to the inquiry. Our job was to establish whether the contents of Aileen's letter were true or not, and report our findings and recommendations to a national conference of all Party members.

The identities of all those who were victims of Healy's abuse have to be protected. We took verbal, hand-written and typed statements from everyone we interviewed. They are all owed a great deal of respect and recognition for their courage in coming forward to make their statements. Everyone during these interviews held on to the basic principle of the need to fight for a socialist society. After the Commission had been sitting for a couple of weeks Jean Kerrigan failed to turn up for a session. She had decided to split away from the WRP with the group led by Sheila Torrance, Healy and his supporters. They were all expelled from the WRP at the next Central Committee meeting.

I gave the following Report of the Control Commission to the Special Conference of the Workers Revolutionary Party on 26 and 27 October 1985.

THE REPORT

We have to start by saying that we were appalled at the way Comrades were pressurised into withholding their claims for the Control Commission to investigate their grievances. It is the right of every member to be able to approach their Control Commission without the interference of committees or leading members.

While we were involved mainly in investigating the contents of the letter of Comrade Aileen Jennings dated 30 June 1985, it has become very obvious that the Commission will have to investigate further because of the introduction of other aspects and complaints.

What follows will be an example of the way Healy either broke down the will to resist his advances or was able to keep the Comrades under his domination. One Comrade who was a member of the International Committee gave in her written statement a vivid example of how he operated.

'In the middle of 1975 I explained to GH that I wished to finish the personal relationship. According to his reaction he was obviously prepared for this. He feigned to be offended. Of course I am old, of course I am not young any more. But don't you see it is a political relationship. He ended up by stating, if you finish the personal relationship you finish the political one.

'I found myself in a difficult situation. I had the responsibility for my section and could not light-mindedly break the political relations towards one of the most important leaders or even make him my enemy without thinking exactly about it.

'At the end of 1975 I explained again that I wanted to finish my personal relationship. He grumbled and said: "It is a privilege to speak with me; others may not see me at all. Why do you say it is a personal relationship. It is a political relationship. If you cut off the personal relation I cut off the political relation."

'Confronted with my responsibility for the section and the fact that GH was the most important contact to the International Committee, that I felt myself completely isolated in the IC and had no real political contact with anybody, I did not see myself going into a confrontation with GH.

'After my marriage the relationship with GH became a burden to me. Each time I went to the IC I thought if he goes to bed with me I do not go to England any more. When I was called to GH I stared at him full of hatred. He complained about this: "She wants out but I do not let her out, I do not know who she is, CIA or anything. If something comes out here I will deny everything." After he had accused me of being CIA he opened his pants to undress and said lowly: "I don't care I rape her." My reaction was: "Please, if you imagine this is it, you can take my body but you will never own me," and I looked to the side.

'The affairs with GH led to a psychological instability as early as 1975 and to depressions till I arrived at the conclusion to look for a friend. When I had a kidney operation in 1976 this was connected with my psychological instability so I had to take treatment. It was a connection of political pressure and the burdening personal relationship from which I could not free myself.'

The following is an extract from a statement made by a youth comrade.

'I was regularly called in for discussions with GH in his office and at his flat. Approximately one month after I had started work at the Centre while in one of these "discussions" at the flat he cuddled and kissed me as I was leaving. I thought that this was very strange behaviour and pulled away. He immediately became angry and said: "What's wrong, am I a leper or something?" Because I didn't understand what was happening, and after all he was the leader of the party, I ignored it although it worried me.

'The next evening when I was again called in for a discussion, he told me to sit on the bed, which I did. He started telling me that he had a "political relationship" with me and that he would "train" me. He said that he had been watching me for some time and could train me to be a revolutionary leader. I was grateful that he was paying so much attention to me. He then came and sat down beside me on the bed and started patting my knee and kissing me. I pulled away again, this time in tears. He again got angry and said: "You think I am an animal, you're just an idealist who does not want to be trained". I couldn't stop crying so he sent me out of the room.'

Within minutes this comrade had gone from one who could be trained as a revolutionary leader, to one who was an idealist who didn't want to be trained. The only thing that had happened in those few minutes was that she had rejected GH's advances.

'The following day he kept calling me into the office saying: "I don't know if you can be trained; I'm not satisfied with your development, we may have to send you home."

'That night I was called into the flats again. I was terrified. This time he told me to take my clothes off. I thought he was joking and just laughed. But he started shouting: "What's so funny?" And he sent me packing out of the flats. The next day continued as the day before with me being called into the office and shouted at. He said [other comrades] would be very disappointed with my "opportunism". He then told me that he wanted me to come to the flats that afternoon.

'He said that I had to tell no one where I was going and was to tell the guard at the gate that I was going shopping. This time I was so terrified that I asked another comrade to come with me. She asked me why and I told her what he had been doing to me. We went to the flats, he opened the door for us but when he saw the other comrade with me he shouted: "What do you think I am – a dirty old man?" He then had a brief discussion with us and sent us back to work.

'That night he called me into his flat again. He was undressed wearing just a dressing gown, which was open. He told me to sit on the bed again which I did. He then started to tell me that I was an opportunist because I expected to be trained without going through the training. He said that I showed real idealism and backwardness and wasn't sure if he could continue training me. He said that I only thought of superficial considerations, young boyfriends and not the politics of the man. He said that I was an individualist and told me that to be trained I had to subordinate myself to the leadership of the party and he was the party. He kept stressing this point of subordination. [. . .]

'He then became very angry and said if I told anyone about this he would denounce me as a police provocateur and have me thrown out of the party.

'He said that if I refused to subordinate myself I would be expelled for backwardness. He said: "Do not try to raise this on the Political Committee, because I am the Political Committee and they won't believe you."

'By this time I was in a complete state. I did not want to go through with it, but I knew that he was capable of having me thrown out and that would not only have meant breaking with the party, but with [friends] as well. I knew that if I left the Centre he would say that I was backward and in political retreat. [. . .]

'I was still crying when he told me to take off my clothes. I eventually did this.'

So here was a position where subordination to the party was reduced to subordination to him. If she refused, she would be sent home, sacked or expelled as backward or in political retreat. She was in this state of mind when he told her to take her clothes off and she submitted to him. It is at this point that what can only be described as rape took place. There are many other examples of a similar nature described by other comrades.

The following is an example of how terrified Healy was of being exposed, and how he had to break up any relationships his victims were having. Six months after one female comrade started working at the Centre GH found out that she was still in touch with a boyfriend. He went mad, and said that this was proof that she was untrainable. She was sent home for two weeks. [. . .] She was told that she had flouted party discipline and that she had to go before the Party Congress to apologise for being untrainable.

We will try now to give a picture of the conditions that those who worked closest to Healy had to work under.

The special International Committee school of 1980 was closed down because GH sat down on a toilet seat that had just been cleaned and was damp. The comrade responsible for the school was charged with not providing the proper conditions for the school to operate. Comrades had travelled from all over the world for this meeting, which would have cost many thousands of pounds to organise. Some comrades, particularly from South America, would have travelled at significant personal risk to themselves.

During the three-month cadre school the comrade in charge of the school advised one of the girl students to go for a pregnancy test as she was concerned about her condition. The comrade in charge of the school was then charged with lowering the moral standing of the school and destroying three months of political work.

Another example was when the manager of the school was called down to Healy's bedroom where he complained that the sheets were damp. He left in the middle of the night to go back to London. The next day the two comrades were summoned to London to attend the Political Committee and were charged with trying to kill him – such as catching a cold, etc. The Commission was also told that during a row with a leading female comrade he proceeded to hit and kick her continuously and finished by throwing her against a wall.

Then in 1979, following a PC meeting, the same comrade was sweeping up a broken glass that GH had broken while in a rage. He grabbed the broom from her and began to smash the windows. She tried to stop him; he then proceeded to attack her with the broom and struck her across the hip and back. This blow caused her permanent injury. She has one shoulder two inches lower than the other, and the whole of that side of her body is damaged in some way or another.

This continuous physical and sexual abuse of comrades; the knowledge that many more young female comrades, not only in the British section, but also from the other international sections [were in danger], also the added knowledge that after the 'Release the Jailed Miners March', due to end on 30 June, another layer of young comrades would be taken to the school and exposed to his domination: Aileen felt at this point that she had to send in her letter.

Throughout this physical and sexual abuse the comrade stayed at her post in spite of her injuries. At one point she went into hospital for an operation, and her doctor told her that this was as a result of injuries to her back. So great was her loyalty to the party that she never told anyone the truth of how the injuries had been sustained. She said it had happened when she turned round in the car to lift a heavy package off the back seat.

Compare this loyalty to the accusations made against her after she had left the letter and 'disappeared'. That is, to accuse her of going off with the party funds and of being a police agent. In fact, all the other female comrades who were victims showed just this kind of loyalty to the party and their determination to fight for the revolution and stay within our party. They never told anyone of their personal experiences with Healy. They did not go to their parents, they did not go to the bourgeois courts which would have opened up the party to enormous provocations.

On two occasions Healy told two of the girls not to go with black men as black men carried diseases. This can only be described as a racist remark and not the remark of a communist.

We have met for the last eight days. We have interviewed nine comrades who appeared on the original list. Seven say that the accusations are true. One said that it was true but nothing happened to her. The other said that advances were made on many occasions but she always managed to put him off. There was also another statement saying it was true from a comrade who was not on the list and was from another section of the International.

The evidence gathered from those on the list as well as from many older comrades who have been in the party a long time made it obvious that stretching over the last 25 years or so, many more comrades had been subjected to this abuse. Further investigations will be necessary.

We must stress that the party owes a great debt to Comrade AJ and all [those] who have come forward to expose this degeneration and corruption which has dominated this party for so long. Their loyalty to the party gives great confidence that we will build the British section of the Fourth International.

Although the investigation is going to continue, we already have enough evidence of the anti-communist activities of Gerry Healy, involving the grave abuse of his authority and position in the movement, to say that the decision of the Central Committee on 19 October 1985 to expel Gerry Healy was correct.

That is the end of the report.

Norman Harding
Larry Kavanagh

The front page of the *News Line* on the next Monday carried the news of Gerry Healy's expulsion from the WRP.

17

AUSTRALIA

It was September 1986. At last my childhood dream of going to Australia was about to come true. Or was it? The night before I was due to leave I attended my branch of the shopworkers' union USDAW in Balham, with Dot and another comrade, Geoff Thurley. On the way back a police van pulled out of a side street right in front of me and the back of the police van struck the front of the car. The police accident team was soon on the spot. The inspector said it was very obvious that the police driver was to blame. After all the statements had been made I asked if I could leave the country to go to Australia the following day. He signed a note saying that it was the police driver's fault and that we should put the claim to their insurance. He said he hoped I had a nice holiday. The next evening, Dot and Les took me to the airport, and at 19.30 hours I was up and away. The flight was everything I expected it to be. Plenty of food, and free drink. We had scheduled stops at Paris, Dubai, Kuala Lumpur, Melbourne, and finally Sydney.

This trip of a lifetime came about because a few months earlier Paul Jennings had decided to join his family who had gone to Australia a few years before. Going in to work one day I had found a brown jiffy bag on my desk. It was from Paul; he had left it the evening before with the keys to his flat and a letter telling me that he had decided to go to Australia. He apologised for not having told me of his plans but he thought it best not to make it public. Quite right, too. He wrote from Australia to let me know that he was OK and invited me to go out to see him. My first suggestion was to go for a couple of weeks, not really believing it would happen. Paul's reply said that I'd better make it five. I discussed it with Dot, who encouraged me to go and made it possible. So here I was on the Jumbo.

The only stop where we did not get off the plane was Paris. I watched the changing landscapes and the solid looking, mountain-shaped clouds. I talked to my fellow passengers, who were from all over the globe, sipping vodka and tonic at the rear of our compartment, casually glancing through the windows. I struck up a conversation with an Arab who discovered that I was a supporter of the Palestinian cause. Things were going well until he said that the only thing wrong with Hitler was that he did not kill enough Jews. For the sake of international relations and the safety of the plane I broke off our discussion and concentrated on an Indonesian who was hoping to set up a restaurant in Sydney. At another time the lady next to me remarked that there were too many easterners amongst the cabin crew. I simply pointed out that maybe it had something to do with the fact that she was flying with Air Malaysia. For some reason she thought I was being sarcastic. So that ended another conversation.

At each stop I made a point of seeing as much of the airport as possible and collecting as many freebies as I could. At Dubai I met a young couple heading for Kuala Lumpur for their honeymoon. They sat in their seats not daring to move until the call to re-board our plane. To remind them of their short stay at Dubai I gave them one of the freebies and they thanked me for my 'generosity'. I just said: 'No problem, enjoy your honeymoon.' The last I saw of them was as they went into the arrivals lounge in Kuala Lumpur. I walked around looking at the beautiful mosaics on the walls or looking out over the city from the viewing area at the top of the building. The stop in Melbourne was a little more exciting. I had difficulty getting back on the plane as I had left my passport in my bag under the seat. I was let on to the plane to get my passport then I had to get off again to show them that I had one.

Saturday 20 September 1986. At last, Sydney, over 30 hours after leaving Heathrow. Now some roles were reversed. I was being met at the airport by Phil Sandford at whose place I was going to stay, along with his companion Carol and her daughter Lisa. On the way he let me see a view of the bridge and the Opera House. Then I was sure I had arrived. Phil lived in an old-style terrace house in Ford Street, off Parramatta Road, the first road built in Sydney Cove in 1820, running from the Cove to Rose Hill where the vegetable gardens were developed.

After a meal and plenty of talking I went to bed. The next morning I was collected by Comrade Derek Mortimer who took me down to Circle Quay, the spot picked out by Captain Philips, leader of the First Fleet. My imagination ran riot. In my mind I tried to get rid of the harbour, touring boats moored up to the quayside. Behind me would be the beach and the bush. And with a little imagination the roof of the Opera House became the sails of the First Fleet sailing into the harbour.

We went on a boat trip to see Botany Bay, Balmain (up to now only the names of Rugby League Clubs), and Manly. Another day Helen Voysey, who used to work on the *News Line* Editorial Board in London, took me to the rocks and showed me a block of old flats where an ongoing rent struggle was taking place. We met her mum and dad, Eve and Lou, who had worked in the Party's Sydney bookshop. We visited a park where her dad showed me a number of native Australian plants such as the Bonsai and Kangaroo Claw, and I saw my first ever Bird of Paradise. I spent a couple of nights at Helen's parents' lovely home. I was taken on a trip to the Blue Mountains where I was lucky enough to see the blue mist that comes up from the eucalyptus trees, with brightly coloured parrots flashing into view.

Carol and her mother took me to the replica of the once tiny Sydney Cove of the early 1880s. She gave me the evening of a lifetime: *Rigoletto* at the Sydney Opera House. During the main intermission, when I thought that it could not get any better, we went out on to the covered, fully glass-fronted promenade overlooking Sydney Harbour and had a bottle of Australian champers. I defy anyone who has experienced the music of Verdi and this especially beautiful panoramic view to say that it did not affect them emotionally. I shall never forget it.

A reception had been organised at Derek Mortimer's place for me to meet as many comrades as possible. I was presented with a wonderful book, *A Fortunate Life,* by Bill Facey, recording his life from a young child working his way round the bush to becoming an active member of the tramways' union in Fremantle. As a young man he was at Gallipoli in the 1914-1918 war. Wherever I went everyone that I met had to sign the book, which holds pride of place on my bookshelf. Bill Facey was voted Number One Australian of the Year towards the end of his life. A three-part film made for TV was shown in Britain shortly after I arrived back in London. If anyone can let me have a copy of the film I would be eternally grateful.

There was also a public meeting organised to listen to the tape made by Peter Fryer commemorating the 30th anniversary of the Hungarian Revolution. Similar meetings were organised in Melbourne (Victoria), Perth and Fremantle (Western Australia).

About the middle of my stay in Sydney I went to spend the weekend in Melbourne with former WRP member Andy Blunden who had gone home to Melbourne after 1986. I had too short a time with the comrades there. We walked along the Yarra River where I heard my first Bell Bird. For all the world it sounds like a wine glass being struck by a finger nail.

There was a trip to see *The Bag Lady* in a fringe theatre where two of the comrades were active, and a trip to see the film *Malcolm*, followed by a ride on a Melbourne tram. Of course we had to have a barbie, in a park on a terrace by the side of the Yarra River. You bought the steaks in the shop and as soon as a barbie became available the one allocated to do the grilling got to work. I have never seen steaks as large. What an experience! A couple of pints, and I was well burped.

Before I left Melbourne, Andy told me that he had bumped into a member from London, one of the drivers who used to pick up North London's papers in the early hours of the morning. He was now living in Black Rock just to the north, and Andy had his telephone number. I rang Dave at Black Rock and gave him the fright of his life. As soon as he answered the phone I said: 'The North London Papers are still here at the Centre. Get here as soon as you can and get them round the area.' There was deathly silence, then: 'Who is that?' 'It's Norman, who do you think it is?' We had a little chat, wished each other all the best, and I apologised for my opening remarks. He did sound a little shaken.

Returning to Sydney, I discovered that while I was away there had been a terrific hailstorm with hailstones so big that they put a number of people in hospital. A day later I heard that a similar storm was happening in Melbourne. Lucky me – I missed them both. I continued in Sydney by going to Taronga Park and Zoo from which you get a wonderful panoramic view of the Harbour and the surrounding area. I noticed the Kangaroo Paw and Bird of Paradise plants growing wild; I heard the cackling laugh of the kookaburra, and saw the pink wild galah (cockatoo), whose name is given to anyone regarded as a nuisance.

I made another trip to the Opera House, built on the place that had been called Bennelong Point, where a semi-Europeanised Aborigine built a funeral pyre and threw on his dead wife and child. She had become pregnant by another man while he was away being paraded around London. He claimed that he had murdered them so that the child would escape the life he had been forced to lead at the hands of the whites. I sat for an hour or more at a café table behind the Opera House imagining the First Fleet sailing through the two points into the harbour and heading for the cove. I visualised a landscape with no buildings and a huge lake with all the little coves and beaches scattered round the edge. Those with more experience of the harbours of the world than I say it is the most beautiful in the world.

Having tea one evening with Carol, Lisa and Phil I happened to mention that I would like to go to the Rugby League grand final at the Sydney Cricket Ground. That evening Lisa came in with two tickets for the game which she said was her contribution to my stay. It wasn't hard to get one of the younger members, Ray Ede, to go with me. The teams were Parramatta and Canterbury. We started off with a couple of beers in a local bar. Once in the ground a tray of beer had to be purchased. I settled down to watch the pre-match razzmatazz. Then something very strange happened. The crowd around me started to cheer. It dawned on me that the final had started. The dancers and entertainers were still making their way from the touch line. There had been no build-up to the kick-off. At Wembley all eyes would have been focused on the tunnel, waiting for the teams to come out side by side, led by the team managers, to a thunderous roar. The kick off at the SCC was not in keeping with the importance of the match. I remembered seeing the opening scene of *Carmen* when the dancing and singing was lively and the music was telling us that at any moment the man himself was to make his entrance – when the door opened and in he strolled, just as though he was walking into his local pub. A complete anti-climax. That's how I felt at the start of this match. I had seen a number of the players at Wembley a few years before when Widnes beat Wigan and I was lucky enough to be in the press box, courtesy of Paul Jennings.

Still on the rugby league scene, Jim Mulgrew, the ex-leader of the Australian Trotskyists, took me for lunch at the headquarters of the Sydney St George team, followed by a visit to the social club. Every inch of the wall space of this very large room was covered with fruit machines. Heavy gambling took place there!

I met a Scottish comrade who was in the SLL in the UK, Bill Haggerty, who became the convenor of shop stewards at the naval shipyards on Cockatoo Island, just off mainland Australia. He had become quite a well-known leader in the labour movement in Oz. After quite a bit of talking and lubricating of the throat he saw me on to the right bus home to Phil's place.

I finished my stay in New South Wales with a trip up the Sydney Tower. You had full 360 degrees of all-round vision. You were able to see all the suburbs of Sydney as well as the different bays and beaches, including Bondi. When I went to Bondi it was not as special as I had expected it to be – but I still prefer it to Blackpool.

The day of departure was spent with Helen and Eve. We had lunch, and then made our way to the station. I next saw Helen in 2003 when she, her partner and daughter had a couple of days with Pauline and me at our home in Micklefield. Before leaving London the travel agent had rung asking if I would like to have a first-class ticket instead of economy, which was a reclining seat and a sandwich trolley. First class was a cabin with shower, toilet, wash bowl and fold-up bed, observation car and three meals a day – steak with every meal if you wished. It was a special Australian tourist offer and it would cost me £20 extra – well worth it for my 3,000 mile journey to Perth, Western Australia.

I spent my time sitting at the table looking out of the window and making notes, or eating and sleeping, with an occasional visit to the observation car that doubled as a bar. We were soon into the Blue Mountains, leaving them behind as the evening and dusk fell. Steak for dinner, a glass of wine, and back to the cabin, where I settled down to read *A Fortunate Life*. I woke to the sound of bagpipes. I stuck my head out of the window and there in the light of the star-filled sky was someone dressed in all the trimmings playing *Will Ye No Come Back Again?* At breakfast (steak) the greeting was: 'Did you hear the bagpipes?' After a short chat I was back to the cabin, scared that I was going to miss a bush roo, emu or something.

First stop was Broken Hill, 'Silver City', on the most western side of New South Wales, the site of many militant working-class struggles. In the early 1900s the immigrants from the USA brought in many IWW members, who were able to get a hold in the main Australian industries.The cry of 'all aboard' snapped me out of it. I was last! The conductor asked me what I had found so interesting out there – 'it's only a station'. I said: 'The history of the place.' 'Ah, history,' he said, in a very uninterested way.

The following morning we were on the Nullarbor Plain, a vast area of limestone, the bed of a prehistoric sea that had stretched for 676 kilometres. There is not a single tree on the plain. The train passed the point between Oldea and Watson where the longest straight stretch of rail track in the world starts, and terminates between Nurina and Loongana, 478 kilometres without even the tiniest of curves! Oldea is the only place on the Nullarbor Plain where there is a natural flow of water. Still on the Nullarbor, we stopped at Cook, named after a former Australian prime minister, Sir Joseph Cook. Formerly a watering and coaling station for steam locomotives, it is now a refuelling station for diesels. It has a single street about 200 yards back from the rail line and a shed that sells memorabilia and post cards. A really remote place, and hhhhot! Under this sun the earth of the bush glows like a red-hot cinder.

On this section of the trip the train slowed down to less than walking pace. We passed a gate with no fencing to either side and a box on one of the gateposts with an arrow pointing to the horizon. It had a number and a name on it. The Indian Pacific train had slowed down so that a member of the train crew could deliver the mail. Soon we were at the highest point of the journey at a place between Chifley and Coonana, about 400 metres above sea level. Then on to Kalgoorlie, scene of the 1893 Gold Rush that started when Patrick Hannan found his first nugget. I went on a quick flip round in a coach and saw the remaining gold mines all lit up like Christmas trees. Then we were driven down Hay Street, the government-controlled red-light area, where the girls of paradise waved at us from the well-lit doors of their B-and-Bs. No time to stop; train to catch.

The hundreds of miles through the Nullarbor was not boring. Although the scenery did not change at all, except when you saw three shrubs together, this landscape is a work of art. Mile after mile of nothing, but if you start thinking about how Aboriginal people lived here for thousands of years, then it becomes really interesting. The knowledge they must have had!

I finished my book before I sat on my specs so I guess that was a bonus. We arrived in Perth dead on 07.00 hours on Sunday morning, 12 October 1986. Paul Jennings and his sister took me to stay at their mum and dad's place. Paul took me to a barbie with his workmates while his sister took my specs to be mended. It was Sunday so I don't know how she managed it. On the way to the barbie we went through my first drive-in off shop for a case or two of 'tinnies'. I discovered that the host's grandparents had lived just a few doors away from my paternal grandparents near East End Park, East Leeds, and that his great grandfather Wainwright had played cricket for Yorkshire and test cricket with W G Grace. So out came the photographs. All this came out because the eldest son, Ronnie, of the Robinson family who lived next door to my grandparents, was also a professional cricketer in Yorkshire. (The youngest son is Detective Sergeant Robinson, referred to in the chapter on CND.)

What I saw of Western Australia was beautiful. The first

At Wave Rock, Western Australia

settlement in Fremantle was founded in 1820, 38 years after Sydney Cove by fortune-seekers, not convicts. Friends and comrades took me to see many wondrous things. Landforms in Western Australia have been shaped by volcanoes, earthquakes, glaciations, inundations and erosion for millions of years. One example is Wave Rock, a granite cliff near Hyden, about 400 metres long and 30 to 40 metres high. It is curved with an overhang like a wave about to collapse. A truly amazing sight.

Paul and Tim took me to the Pinnacles in Nambung National Park, 200 kilometres north of Perth. The Pinnacles rise up to five metres high, and in the evening sunset made many long eerie shadows. You could have been standing on the moon surface. On the way, we stopped at a hotel near New Norcia for a beer and packed lunch, and at a monastery that housed the finest collection of paintings in Australia. On the way back we saw a sample of alternative Aussie hospitality: a gate, with no fence either side from the gate, a path to nowhere, and a noticeboard attached to one of the gateposts: 'NO petrol, No water, NO phone . . .' – with an

Alternative Australian hospitality

arrow pointing in the direction of the next telephone.

Bill Uren and his wife took me on a weekend car trip to the karri forest around Pemberton, three to four hours south west of Perth. The karri only grow in a restricted heavy rainfall area and are the tallest trees in the state. We also saw some double-spiked black boy bushes, as opposed to the normal single spike, which take ten years to grow an inch. We also went on a coach trip to a series of caves. The largest one was like an underground amphitheatre complete with stage. Singers were invited to try out the acoustics. We did get a volunteer and the acoustics were perfect. Going back to the coach I paused to photograph some beautiful wildflowers. The next I knew my name was being called; a 'search' party had been sent out looking for me. I made my apologies all round as I had delayed the coach by about fifteen minutes. It wasn't the time that worried the guide. She was worried that I might have fallen down a hole and discovered the Harding cave. Another memorable sight was where the Southern and Indian Oceans meet, marked by a distinct change of colour. Making our way back to Fremantle we stopped for a breather at a bay where I took a number of great sunset photographs.

Paul said no trip to Perth was complete without a cruise up the Swan River to the wineries. Reluctantly, I had to agree. It was wine,

wine, wine, all the way. There are more wineries on the banks of the Swan River than there are pubs in Otley (West Yorkshire). I'm sure that by the end of the day they were filling our glasses with Swan River water. If anyone had dared to ask for a beer they would have been thrown to the sharks. Yes, they have been reported quite regularly in the river miles up from its outlet into the Indian Ocean at Fremantle. At the Sandalford winery, we had a meal washed down with wine and then a tour to sample the different wines, fortified or otherwise. Here I noticed the difference in the taste of wine matured in oak casks, but after a while, no one in the party cared where the stuff was matured, if at all. The only difference with the return journey was that we were going in the other direction, not that anyone cared any more, dancing and singing and 'tasting' more wine. Back at the Barrack Street jetty in central Perth, the passengers were divided into three groups: those who could walk off, those who had to be helped off, and those who needed to be carried off. Paul and I really fell into a fourth group, where you are put into a cask and sent back upriver to be recycled. Fortunately his sister was waiting in her car to whisk us back to soberdom.

Water, or lack of it, is an important problem in Western Australia. On becoming premier of Western Australia just before the start of the twentieth century, John Forrest employed Irish engineer C Y O'Connor to oversee major public works, such as the railway to Adelaide, Fremantle Harbour and the water pipeline to Kalgoorlie and the surrounding goldfields and farms. Pumping stations pumped water from the dams in the hills surrounding Perth along pipes laid across 560 kilometres of hills and desert. The scheme took five years and opened in 1903. It is still in use today and supplies water through 8,000 kilometres of pipe to almost 100,000 people and 6 million sheep.

No.1 Pump Station at Mundaring Weir was impressive, especially when you visualised the distance the water had to be pumped. O'Connor was obviously a man of great foresight. His work is now revered and celebrated, but in those pioneering days, it was misunderstood and undervalued. Criticism of the pipeline by contemporaries in public and in the newspapers took its toll on a proud, deep-thinking and private man. A year before the pipeline was completed, O'Connor rode his horse into the ocean at Fremantle beach and shot himself. He left a suicide note:

> 10/3/02
>
> The position has become impossible. Anxious important work to do and three commissions of inquiry to attend to. We may not have done as well as possible in the past but we will necessarily be too hampered to do well in the imminent future. I fear that my brain is suffering and I am in great fear of what effect all this worry will have upon me. I have lost control of my thoughts. The Coolgardie scheme is all right and I could finish it if I got a chance and protection from misrepresentation but there's no hope for that now and it's better that it should be given to some entirely new man to do who will be untrammelled by prior responsibility.
>
> *PS Put the wing walls to Helena Weir at once.*

When garden sprinklers using water pumped from the many deep groundwater sources around Western Australia spray the pavements, roads and fences, the surface turns a bright orange, the predominant colour of the earth of the bush.

In some of the little towns I visited, such as York, about 25 miles east of Perth, you fully expected someone to ride down the main street and fasten his horse to the rail outside the saloon. One day I went into Perth on my own to look round. It was so hot, I decided to have a drink in a pub where about five Aboriginals were playing pool. Two were young women. At the end of the game one of them said: 'Hi fella, wanna game?' I put my camera down and picked up a cue. Before we started she said: 'Hi mate, better put your camera over the bar or some whitey might pinch it!'

Two or three years before I visited, V Redgrave did a tour of Australia and was taken to see some of the Aboriginal settlements and how they were treated by the government and authorities. John Troy asked why I thought she had not made a film about the plight of the Aboriginals as she had to support the Palestinian struggle. I told him there was money around in the Middle East countries, so there was a market for the film and V Redgrave Publications would have no trouble selling it. I wondered who would have bought a film of the same scale about the Aboriginals' struggles?

During a stroll around Fremantle, I spotted an ex SLL/WRP member from Bristol in a poster demonstration of teachers in Market Street. He seemed anxious that no one should know of his past political activities although his aspirations were the same. He told me that what drove him out was the concentration on individual recruitment to the party as against supporting basic working-class struggles. Outside the Market entrance, a young couple were selling the paper of one of the small socialist groups. They explained their aims. At the time I still believed in building the elite 'revolutionary party leadership' and that only we could do it. This is what cut off any further discussion about ending the rule of capitalism. We shook hands and I went on my way.

My stay in Australia was coming to an end. I took Paul and his parents out for a meal as a small thank you for their wonderful hospitality. Anyone who could make it came to the traditional Chinese farewell meal in one of Perth's many fine restaurants. John Troy gave me £50 and said: 'We have had a whip-round to make sure that you have some money in your pocket for your journey and when you arrive back in London.'

Saturday November 15, after a light lunch with a number of comrades, I was taken to the airport. Hugs all round and away I went.

At Kuala Lumpur it was announced that we had developed an engine problem. Passengers were allocated to various hotels and I was fortunate to be sent to the Hilton. Full-blown meals at any time in the day, tables laden with exotic fruits. I was in the pool at seven in the morning in the blazing hot sun before breakfast. Then back to the airport. I didn't get any sleep even though I had a scrumptious room. I just wanted to enjoy the hotel and its grounds.

I was met at Heathrow by Dot and one of her sons and taken back to Clapham.

18

BACK TO LEEDS

Immediately after Gerry Healy's expulsion we faced a lot of internal activity in the WRP concentrating desperately on trying to extract ourselves from the debts that we had inherited. This involved selling off assets gained from the hard work and sacrifices of our members.

The other side of the coin was that those of us who worked full time at the centre gained freedom of movement. No longer had we to think up a reason that would be acceptable to GH to have a weekend at home now and again. For one of my early new-found weekends I decided to get back to Leeds. I had known Pauline for many years. She had been married to my brother, and in the years after their separation our friendship had grown and I had got to know her children. So I rang Pauline and told her that I was coming to Leeds and asked if she would like to go out for a meal on the Saturday night. She agreed, so I said: 'Get on your best bib and tucker, and we will go to the Old George at Garforth.'

In the past Pauline and I had enjoyed going dancing on the few occasions possible. Now we would be able to do this more regularly. My parents were now dead so when I visited I had to stay in the spare room at Pauline's home in Eastwood Crescent, Swarcliffe. Whenever I came home we took the opportunity to get as many of the family together as possible. One weekend that stands out was in September 1986, just before I went to Australia. We all met in the gardens at the back of the Seacroft pub where we sampled the landlord's best bitter.

On my return from Australia in October 1986 I kept taking trips to Leeds, where my love and respect for Pauline deepened. My comrades in London made sure that I was able to get home to Leeds on a more regular basis. I was able to spend Christmas 1987 with my new family.

Those weekends were very precious for me. I felt that I was a welcome visitor. I was always very pleased to see Pauline, and her sons Malcolm, Graham and Steven and their children. I was always especially pleased to see the boys' 'little' sister, Debra.

In the past Debra used to come over in a flash from Eastwood Crescent to see her Uncle Norman from London as soon as she heard I had arrived at my mum's flat in Brayton Grange. Now I came to Leeds for the wedding of my favourite little girl Debra to Peter. The first thing I did in Leeds was to visit Pauline in hospital, where she was recovering from quite a severe heart attack. The doctors would not let her go to the wedding, even with a nurse in attendance, so the only thing to do was to have a second reception in the ward. The nurses became Pauline's attendants and helped her to dress and get ready for the reception. The hospital staff were tremendous and everyone in the ward was part of the reception.

Then, on Easter Weekend 1988, after giving Pauline her breakfast in bed in her room (oh yes, it was still separate rooms) I asked Pauline to marry me. I had to wait 24 hours for my answer, but it was a yes.

Now we had to start making plans for the wedding. The first thing was to tell the family, starting with Pauline's dear old mum, who immediately wished us all the best. Then I met my brother Keith in the Hope Inn on York Road, just up from where the old Woodpecker had been. When I told him he was very pleased and immediately got up from the table and rang Pauline to give her his congratulations. We really wanted to get the youngsters all together at one go but this was not possible, so we had to tell Debra separately when she came to see us with precious baby Leoni.

Her response was to fly across the room, still clinging to Leoni, to give her mother a big hug. We met Malcolm and Anne, Graham and Dawn, Steven and Julie, in the Manston Pub, to tell them the news. A week or two later I asked Pauline if she would like to go to Malta for two weeks before the wedding. Even though Pauline was more than a little nervous of flying, she readily agreed. So we booked a holiday at the Galaxy apartments at Sliema. When I told the lads at one of the many gatherings in the Whinmoor pub at Swarcliffe that we were going for two weeks to Malta, Malcolm announced to the whole pub that I was taking his mother on a dirty fortnight!

At this time I was still living in London at the flats in Clapham High Street. Peter, Debra and Leoni came to London with Pauline to have a few hours there before we went to Luton airport. Somehow Comrade Dot found the time to come to the flat to get some food ready.

At Luton airport the departure time kept getting pushed back. Every time this happened Pauline got more and more nervous as this was her first flying experience. But she conquered it, and stuck it out until we finally boarded the plane. The first day in Malta I made the mistake of suggesting a walk along the seafront to St Julian's Bay, which was further than we thought. But she forgave me, and at midnight on 3 June 1988, on the seafront at Sliema, I put the ring on Pauline's finger and we were officially engaged to be married.

We brought the wedding date forward to Friday 5 August 1988. It came at us quite fast. The rest of the family had got over the initial shock that this confirmed bachelor was to get married. I set off on the morning with Graham, Dawn and Ryan for the Register Office in Graham's car. Pauline thought Graham was going to take her. But her four children had other ideas: a white Rolls Royce and chauffeur had been booked and Debra went to Eastwood Crescent to help her Mum get ready. Everyone who knows Pauline will understand how she felt when she came out of the door to step into the Roller.

Natalie – Malcolm and Anne's daughter – was her bridesmaid, and her lifelong friend Olga was her matron of honour. My comrade and friend Geoff Pilling was my best man. I had known Geoff since he was a student at Leeds University, and then for the period when I was in London.

Between the actual wedding and the wedding breakfast there was an hour or two to kill, so we all stopped off at the Railway Inn at Rodley Bottom by the side of the Canal. My family mixed with

Signing the register. Best man Geoff Pilling on the left and matron of honour Olga Patterson

my friends who had come from London for the wedding. I remember feeling quite proud of the fact that my entire life was represented there. Maybe my family were relieved that my comrades from London were not wearing combat jackets and black berets, as depicted in television's 'United Socialist Republic of Tooting'. This short interlude allowed everyone to get to know each other before we moved on to the restaurant where we sat down to roast beef and Yorkshire pudding, with special arrangements for vegetarians. The big difference between this reception and all others I had attended was that it was mine and Pauline's.

Telegrams and cards brought greetings from various points of the planet, and many from my friends throughout Britain, including the regulars at the Plough, opposite Clapham Common tube station. Pauline made her first public speech when she thanked everyone for attending. My ex-nephews and niece – who had now become my stepsons and daughter – all demanded back pay for the pocket money that I owed them. They had already asked me what I would prefer their youngsters to call me. There was no competition with the alternatives I was offered. It had to be Grandad Norman. I now

All the family assembled for the wedding photo

have seven grandchildren: Kirk, Michael, Natalie, Jonathan, Ryan, Scott, and Leoni.

Following the reception, Pauline and I, along with close family, went to take Pauline's Mum her wedding meal and cake. After spending a short time with her we went back to the Griffin Hotel in Boar Lane, close to the Railway Station and Leeds City Square for a get-together with a number of other friends and the London guests before they set off home.

The next morning we went to London. Comrades John and Bob Archer picked us up from our hotel to have a second reception with our London friends and comrades in the social club at the Lambeth Town Hall. There were comrades from many organisations there: old members, new members, non-members. It was a very exciting evening. Pauline only knew one or two people, but if I was not around Dot was always close at hand. We received many wonderful gifts. A few comrades put together and bought us a JVC ghettoblaster with detachable speakers which is still in regular use. There was a big surprise for us when John and Rayleen Troy, from Fremantle, Western Australia, walked through the door. They were on their way back to Australia after visiting family in Greece.

The second reception in London

After the reception we were put into a taxi and sent off to our London hotel on Bayswater Road opposite Hyde Park. On the Sunday morning we took a walk in Hyde Park and fed the ducks. Later we met Dot and spent some time with her. Going through this routine again on the Monday morning, we sat on a bench by the side of the lake. Looking up I was amazed to see – of all people – Gerry Healy walking towards us. Pauline's camera was the handiest so I took a photograph of him as he approached. He looked at me, shouting for Corinna Lotz, who was with him. He passed by, and that was the last time I ever saw him. Amen. I gave Dot the picture.

That night, courtesy of Doria and Geoff Pilling, we went to see *Les Misérables* in the West End. Then on Tuesday morning our good friend and comrade Les Ford came to spend the day with us. He later helped us with the luggage to Euston Station where we set off for Manchester where we were to spend the night at Bob Myers' house before leaving the next day for our honeymoon in the south of France.

The first day there we walked along the front. It was hot. We came to a tower with a sign giving the temperature, over 100 degrees.

Pauline developed heat stroke and as soon as we got back to the hotel she had to lie down. The hotel was on the front, and that is all you can say about it. The electric sockets were falling off the wall, the room was miserable and the view from the window was a brick wall. The whole place was unwelcoming and unfriendly. To be unwell in a place like that must have been ten times worse for Pauline. We went out again but she lasted about fifteen minutes before I had to help her back to the dump. On the third or fourth day Pauline told me to go out and take some photographs so she would be able to see where she was supposed to have been.

In the evening I went out for a few hours, leaving Pauline with water, food, a rifle and five rounds. I was sat at a table outside a café with a family from Huddersfield at the next table. We got talking, as you do, and after a while they asked me if I was on my own. I told them no, and that my wife was poorly, back at the hotel. Oh dear, they said, hope she gets better soon. I said: 'Thank you, but it's a lousy way to spend your honeymoon.' 'Waiter, give that man a pint,' was the reply, and that wasn't the last. Nice people.

At last the day to go home arrived. I had arranged for Alan and Iris to pick us up from Manchester Airport to take us back to our home in Swarcliffe – a welcome sight, especially for Pauline. By 1988, 40 Eastwood Crescent had been home to Pauline for 22 years and the boys had lived most of their life there. Debra was born there and lived there with her mum until she was eighteen. We soon sorted out the few domestic appliances I had brought from London and Pauline got to work (and is still working) on the bad habits that I had collected during my bachelorhood.

Pauline's Mum died on 14 October 1989, after a spell in hospital and then in a nursing home in Bingley. She had spent most of her adult life in service, working in rich people's houses. As a little girl she had lived with her mum and dad, who was a farm labourer in a village near Scarborough called Hutton Bushell. Pauline had lost her father when she was just a child, so was brought up in difficult circumstances by her mother. We arranged for someone to come and clear the flat. I had to be there as Pauline could not face it. The most I could get for the life-long belongings of a 90-year-old lady, a lady who had known nothing but a struggle for existence all her life, was £15. For me this was the final act of exploitation by this lousy rotten economic system of someone who had lived a hard and honest life.

I started to develop unknown skills, such as tiling and collecting lengths of two-by-two timber and anything else that wasn't screwed down. No skip in the area was safe. With some of this timber I built a gazebo in the corner of the back garden. The amazing thing was that it stood up, defying the law of gravity. Then Graham built a greenhouse in the back garden (Crystal Palace Mark II), four metres long and two metres wide. I became a very keen gardener. I put in a fishpond with a little rustic bridge over one end. The rest of the back garden was taken up with vegetables and the front garden was dedicated to flowers. The following summer I collected four firsts and three seconds at local flower shows. I also received second prize at the Leeds Flower Show at Roundhay Park for my Coleus plant, not grown for its insignificant flower, which is nipped off to help the multi-coloured leaves develop.

Our summer holidays were mainly staying at Clare and Charlie's caravan at Whitstable, in Kent. These were very pleasant holidays. Pauline and I are very fond of Whitstable, especially the beautiful sunsets that can be viewed from the edge of the beach. Scores of yachts and boats are moored close together on one section of the beach. The tall masts stand silhouetted against the sunset sky with the long lengths of metal sail-stays stretching down the masts, each one giving a different note as the stays hit the masts in the wind. Drinking a pint in the garden of the yacht club overlooking this scene – that is Whitstable. The sunset, the twanging wires, pebbles being walked on, oysters, cockles, and not forgetting the pint, could all be put to music. No doubt they already have. Thanks Clare, Charlie, for giving Pauline and me, along with some of our friends, the chance to enjoy this.

We have also been able to have four relaxing long-stay winter holidays in Malta. We made friends with a Maltese family as well as Dorothy and Ray from Bolton (Lancashire) and Irene and Wilf from Herne Bay (Kent), with whom we are still in close contact.

On the second of our long stays Pauline won two weeks' accommodation for four at the Santa Maria, St. Paul's Bay, where we were staying. Debra and Leoni shared this with us.

Leoni was still a baby when I married Pauline. Debra and Peter lived at Garforth. Both were working, so I gladly took on the job of going there every morning, letting them get off to work and then getting Leoni up. I will never forget the times when I went upstairs to her room; as soon as she saw me she would smile and raise her arms to be picked up. I would change her, wash and dress her, and feed her. When all that was finished I would put her in her carrycot and take her home to Nanna, who was only too pleased to take over. This routine went on for quite a long time.

I treasured the memories of being with my nephews in earlier years, and especially the times that I was able to take them on holiday, just as Pauline and I now enjoyed having Leoni around, watching her grow during that early period of her young life. When she started nursery, I would take her and bring her back home for Debra to collect her after work.

About 1994 I noticed that taking a decision, no matter how tiny, would start to bring on panic attacks and these became worse. Isolation either in bed or in a corner would be the order of the day. Bursting into tears became a regular occurrence. As I became worse, Pauline recognised the need for medical advice and sent for the doctor, who prescribed medication and shortly after decided that I needed specialist advice. A psychiatrist came to see me and I told him the whole story. After a couple of consultations he said that my breakdown was tied up with the time I had spent in London, and that guilt played a strong part in it.

During this period Pauline had to help to get me through it. She had the correct attitude — not simply telling me to pull myself together. Our good friend and comrade John Davies, who lived in Leeds at the time, kept close contact with Pauline, as did Dot from London. Pauline had only to to phone John when things were bad for him to come straight over to see me. Pauline thinks of John as her rock during those twelve months when it was bad.

Events at this time had made it necessary for Debra and Leoni to come and live with Pauline and me in Eastwood Crescent, using the small bedroom. I dreaded the time for them to get up in a morning. The conditions they were living in were the ingredients for little differences between Debra and Leoni in their hurry to get ready. I was always relieved when for some reason or other they were out and we were on our own. Feeling like this about two of the people that I love most in the world added more guilt. John rang the council office and explained the overcrowding in the house and my medical situation. This was backed up by the psychiatrist and my doctor. A few days later we had a visit from a social worker who agreed the conditions were not good enough. That same day Debra and Leoni were offered a beautiful council house in Garforth. It had well-kept gardens front and back, and it was in a nice quiet cul-de-sac.

I was told that when I came out the other side of my breakdown and my chemical balance was restored I would be better than when I went into it. At the time this was hard to believe but the medics were right. Meanwhile back in Eastwood Crescent we had to consider the fact that it was getting more and more difficult to keep up with the cleaning etc. Pauline's arthritis was getting worse and mine was starting to develop, and the pair of us had heart problems, making the steps more of an obstacle. We started making enquiries about transfer to a council bungalow but, as expected, the waiting lists were enormous. Then out of the blue we received an offer of a bungalow in Micklefield, an ex-mining village on the outskirts of Leeds. We went to view it and found a bungalow with a front, back and side garden overgrown to waist height. Mounds of cinders from the coal fires were in turn overgrown. The inside was damp and cold and it needed a lot doing to it after standing empty for many months.

Nobody wanted it, so that was how we came to get the offer. We struck a verbal agreement with the housing department that if I tackled the gardens, they would give the interior a thorough overhaul and put up fences where needed. They wanted to get someone to live there to get it off their lists. The housing office did their bit and now five years later the garden is unrecognisable. We

Children 'forced to play among cars'

BY LESLEY GIBSON

Residents fear tragedy unless council acts

NEIGHBOURS on a Leeds council estate claim children are in danger of being knocked down by cars because there is nowhere for them to play in safety.

Residents of Eastwood Crescent, Swarcliffe, are calling for more provision for children both indoors and outdoors.

Norman Harding, 66, who is leading the campaign, said: "Children are playing in a yard where there are about two dozen garages because there is nowhere else.

"Cars are constantly going in and out and the children are so engrossed in their play that they don't always hear or see an approaching vehicle.

"There have been many lucky escapes and unless something is done to provide a safe play area soon, someone is going to be killed."

Mr Harding said that up to 30 youngsters play near the garages.

He added: "As well as in danger of being run down, they have also been seen climbing on the garage roofs and even cycling on them."

And, claimed Mr Harding, the youngsters were abusive towards residents who challenged them.

He said: "The elderly people daren't do anything for fear of reprisals. Some tenants are seriously considering moving because they feel they can no longer put up with the stress."

Two years ago, youngsters in the area organised a petition calling for a play area. Local councillors responded, but nothing came of their plans.

Councillor Suzi Armitage (Lab, Whinmoor) said she and her colleagues had made efforts to convert some land near the Whinmoor Hotel, Stanks Road, into a play area, but people nearby objected.

She said play facilities in several parts of the ward had been improved, but admitted there was still a problem in the Eastwood Crescent area.

Coun Armitage said: "When the estate was built in the sixties, they didn't think about cars and kids, We are sympathetic and we will do what we can to solve the problem.

"There are outreach workers talking to kids in the area and we are looking into the problem."

I found myself campaigning for a safe children's play area

are still receiving compliments from the old Mickiers who say we have made a large contribution to the appearance of the area.

The initial clearing could not have been done without the assistance of the children in Churchville. We had as many as ten youngsters beavering away taking down overgrown hedges, levelling, getting rid of rubbish, and many a good evening burning the rubbish. It has now been turned into a little park with evergreens, bushes and bedding plants all in raised beds, a fifteen-by-eight-foot shed, a summer house with double glazing and leaded windows, and a patio made of the slates that came off the roof when the council replaced it. The whole project has been based as far as possible on recycling. The children in the area show a great respect for the garden; after all, they helped to create it. The potential we saw when we first moved in is now closer to being realised.

I do what I can to help improve living conditions in the village. I helped to start the Micklefield Residents' and Tenants' Association, of which I am chairperson. Along with our secretary Pam, I am a

Speaking at a Leeds Tenants' Federation meeting, 2004

representative to the Leeds Federation. Back where I started, so to speak.

The nicest thing to happen to us since we came to Micklefield must be Debra's marriage to Colin Beeks. On the morning of the wedding the bride, bridesmaids, and the bride's mother were all in our little bungalow having their hair done. What a morning! It was like feeding time at the zoo – what a racket. Certainly no place for a mere male to be. This was a very wonderful weekend as most people stayed overnight at the hotel where the wedding took place. A good time was had by all, and Pauline and I were kept very busy getting to know our new friends and relatives.

Over the last period I have made many friends and associates through the Residents' and Tenants' Association and through being a reader mentor at the school. This activity enables me to put into perspective my politics and to understand more and more how other members of the community think about the society we live in. This comes out in casual discussion and does not need to be provoked by a sharply pointed political statement.

There is a family in Micklefield with whom I have a close relation because of my work at the local school. The mother is an active Christian who encourages her children to be the same. I feel that I am closer to these people when it comes to our aspirations than I am to those atheists who only turn their attention to opposing religion. When the time comes for the present capitalist system to enter a process of rapid change, it will involve countless millions of people. Being an evolutionist will not be a precondition to participate in what will be the most important change in social relations since humans started to live together in groups.

The problems in this world are not caused by religion, but have their origin in the very nature of society. Religion goes through changes, reflecting changes developing in social relations and culture, which happen in accordance with developments in the productive forces; throughout history these have established the relationship between humanity and nature.

It is very important to understand the development of life that has taken place throughout history. This will help us understand the developments taking place at this very moment. Failure to try to understand current tasks from this historical standpoint is surely one of the sources of political sectarianism and its twin, opportunism.

Let me give an example. At the moment of writing US and British forces are waging war on Iraq. The 'experts' of both left and right are trying to understand the situation by examining which political faction is for or against Saddam, who will help the west to get control of the oil, etc. But a far deeper perspective is needed.

The Iraqi and Kurdish peoples living in the land of the Tigris and Euphrates, where civilisation was born, are suffering genocide at the hands of a new barbarism. This genocide is not simply the product of this or that dictator, to be stopped by this or that faction, but the product of the global capital system in the throes of its structural crisis. The capitalist system, through its leading personifications in US business and politics, supported, maintained and armed the regime of Saddam Hussein, which in turn butchered and tortured countless thousands of men, women and children. Now they proceed to butcher thousands by their own hands, because this latest phase of US capital's need for world domination requires the direct control of Iraq and the Middle East. The plight of the Iraqi and Kurdish people sends this signal to all the peoples of the world. These people needed, as a life-and-death matter, the overthrow of Saddam's rule. But that was *their* task and no one else's. Only the establishment of a socialist, democratic Iraq and Kurdistan can offer them a future. The US juggernaut is rolling over them precisely in order to establish a world order which can prevent the peoples of the world from achieving socialism and preserving their future. Thus the Iraqi and Kurdish peoples are paying a terrible price for the fact that the re-founding of an internationalist working-class socialist movement still lags behind in the pressing task of organising against and confronting globalised capital.

19

SUMMING UP

Millions of youth are at the moment taking up the fight against capital. If some get a chance to read this book and by so doing recognise the danger of putting too much trust in self-appointed leaders, it will give me a great deal of pleasure. My life has shown me the dangers of putting too much trust in organisations which claim to be the only leadership that will free the masses from the very real and imminent risks of starvation, poverty and war.

We have to move on from this kind of 'vanguardism'. These organisations claim to be the leadership that will lead the working class to power. 'Join us and build this leadership so that we will be ready for the time when the masses need us,' they say. In fact these organisations are riddled with the twin fatal diseases of working-class leadership: opportunism and sectarianism.

The Workers Revolutionary Party had both of these in our attitude towards the nationalist leaders in the Middle East. During the1984-1985 miners' strike, we members were not allowed to work with the rank-and-file support groups while Healy snuggled up to the union bureaucracy, opportunistically. The opportunist Healy sang the praises of Saddam Hussein, while the sectarian Healy betrayed Iraqi trade unionists to the same regime. Likewise we had an opportunist relationship with Ken Livingstone during the struggle against Margaret Thatcher's closure of the Greater London Council. Our opportunist/sectarian vacillations, along with the Party's brutal and anti-democratic internal regime, destroyed layer after layer of devoted communist members, especially youth, over many years.

Since we challenged the WRP leadership in 1985, many comrades have been struggling to understand what it was really all about. Was it a simple case of the king is dead, long live the king? Was it just a job of replacing a bad leadership with a more understanding one? Or did we have to examine where the leadership and our policies came from? Over the following years I have struggled with these questions. The principle of building an elite leadership 'for' (rather than 'of') the working class – and the corruption and abuse for which that concept provided fertile ground – was the primary cause of the downfall of the WRP. To have said anything like this to G Healy would have brought a tirade of abuse and the accusation of being a social democrat and a reactionary or, more probably, an agent.

No doubt some people think that to suggest a re-examination of old methods is selling out to the ruling class and liquidating ourselves into the quagmire. But this is wrong. In fact it is the prerequisite for pulling ourselves out of the quagmire and getting back on to solid land.

One of the earliest problems for human beings was to secure heat and light. Fire brought about the hearth that humans sat round for heat and security. Then came the fire torch that enabled people to venture further into their cave or into the surrounding area at night. Fire remained the only form of heat and illumination for a very long time. As society and social relations changed so did the methods of heat and light: candles for home and workplace, then gas lamps. These were not adequate for the factory, and soon came the use of electricity. The fight for heat and illumination was not 'betrayed' because there were changes in the methods of achieving them.

There have been great changes in society the world over, especially over the past 50 years. For what has still to be done, it is essential that we study the implications of these changes. The freeing of the world from starvation, disease and war demands it.

It is only through this that we can win back the moral force of the word communism.

INDEX